IMAGES
of America

TROY AND THE GREAT FLOOD OF 1913

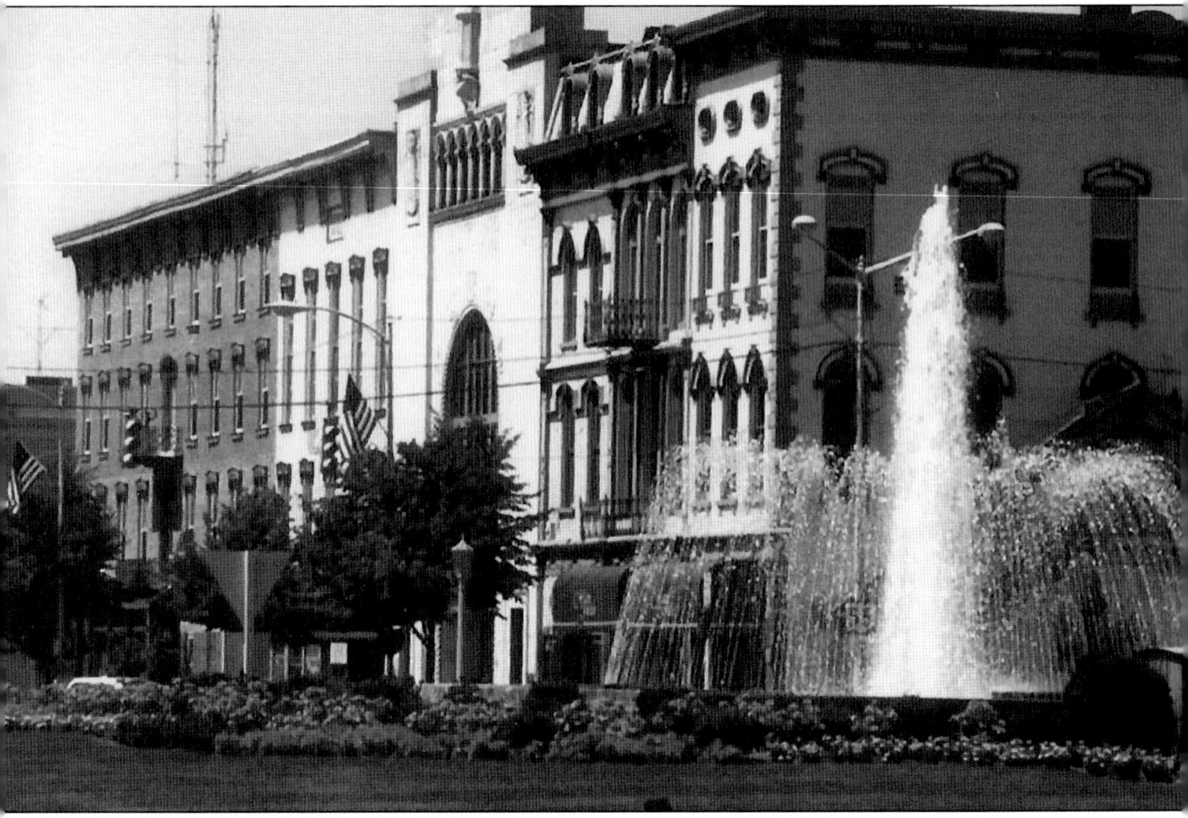

A century after the 1913 flood, the Troy Public Square remains an important element of Troy life. Buildings that in the early 20th century housed city government, businesses, entertainment sites, or places of worship have the same or similar uses today. Automobiles have replaced buggies and trains, but travelers still see the same structures where Market and Main Streets meet. Today, as then, it is where politicians speak, veterans march, and bands play. A beautiful fountain spraying sparkling water is now the centerpiece of the square. This photograph taken by Troy Historical Alliance founder Wesley Jones captures the square's historical charm. (Courtesy of Wesley Jones.)

On the Cover: When the terror-filled days of being confined to homes and shelters finally ended, Trojans walked the high bank Cincinnati, Hamilton & Dayton Railroad tracks to look at a destroyed Troy. Though saddened by what they saw, they rejoiced that they had survived and would live to rebuild the city. (Courtesy of Marilyn McConahy for the Neva Pearson family.)

IMAGES
of America

Troy and the Great Flood of 1913

Troy Historical Society

ARCADIA
PUBLISHING

ISBN 978-0-7385-9059-2

Published by Arcadia Publishing
Charleston, South Carolina

Printed in the United States of America

Library of Congress Control Number: 2012949912

For all general information, please contact Arcadia Publishing:
Telephone 843-853-2070
Fax 843-853-0044
E-mail sales@arcadiapublishing.com
For customer service and orders:
Toll-Free 1-888-313-2665

Visit us on the Internet at www.arcadiapublishing.com

In remembrance of individuals who experienced the flood at Troy, Ohio, in March 1913. May we never forget their courage, kindness, and love for one another.

CONTENTS

ACKNOWLEDGMENTS

The Troy Historical Society wishes to thank the many members and friends who helped or gave support to this project. We are grateful to local historian and author Scott D. Trostel for sharing his research, Tom Leffel for loaning us his rare books, Mike Fox for his historical photographs, and our oral history chairman Michael Robinson for rerecording audiotapes of flood survivor interviews.

We extend our appreciation to Barbara Besecker, the assistant archivist for the Troy-Miami County Public Library, for finding and scanning historical photographs, and Judy Hemmert, the Troy Historical Society trustee-at-large, for helping obtain historical photographs, particularly those of the First United Church of Christ.

We remember the 1976 Oral History Committee, whose members interviewed and recorded stories of the 1913 flood survivors: past president Lois Shilling Davies, Olive Ryan, and Barbara Shepherd. Writings left to us by historian, writer, and past society president Thomas B. Wheeler have also been invaluable in the creation of this book.

For nearly half a century, we have partnered with the Troy-Miami County Public Library to collect and preserve stories of the past. The library's preservation work has made this book possible. Some photographs used in this work are from the Troy Historical Society collections of the Barton Studio and the Rogers Studio. Unless otherwise noted, all images in the book are courtesy of the Troy Historical Society.

INTRODUCTION

Looking back 100 years to 1913 from our modern perspective and the relative safety of the flood control system of the Miami Conservancy District, it would be easy to think that the 1913 flood was devastating because the people of the day did not know now to respond or deal with floods, because that particular flood was the only serious one in Troy's history, or that there was not a large federal relief program available at the time. We would be incorrect to arrive at such conclusions.

We do not often hear of other floods in Troy, but rest assured, few events in history happen without precedent, and the Great Flood of 1913 is not an exception because there have been floods since 1913, e.g., the 1937 flood was a catastrophe, and there were floods prior to 1913 that were also destructive. The purpose of this brief introduction is to lay groundwork for understanding and context in order to better comprehend the devastating nature of the 1913 flood in the Miami Valley and, specifically, Troy.

Weather statistics indicate that the Miami Valley receives, on average, approximately 38 to 40 inches of precipitation every year, and this has been fairly constant for most of the last 200 years. According to former Miami Conservancy engineer Arthur E. Morgan, in *The Miami Conservancy District*, throughout the valley's recorded history, the "too wet" years and the "too dry" years seem to balance each other nicely; i.e., we do not have an inordinate amount of wet years over dry years, or vice versa. But, from time to time, we do see a year or two in which one extreme or the other seems to reign.

During the five days in late March 1913 just prior to and during the flood, the Miami Valley, including Troy, received about 10 inches of rain, or close to 25 percent or the average rainfall for the year. An additional problem was the fact the valley was just entering its thawing season and the ground was partially frozen but already saturated; therefore, there was no place for the excess water to go except directly into the rivers and streams, which quickly swelled, overran their banks, and caused the devastating flooding along the rivers and in the lowlands. The man-made river and stream of the day, known as the Miami-Erie Canal and its race, also were quickly inundated with water and became conduits of destruction.

As one researches the facts and history of the flood, it is clear that it was not so much that the people had not seen a flood prior to this; rather, it was the immensity and the speed with which the deluge came that caused so much damage, loss of life, and heartache.

Previous to 1913, there were 10 floods in the region that are greatly considered to have been very destructive floods. There were other years in which local areas experienced flooding, but the following 10 are considered to be comparable floods that were felt throughout the valley: March 1805 (according to Arthur Morgan, this flood was probably not exceeded in size *until* 1913); 1814; January 1828; February 1832; January 1847; September 1866; September 1866 (considered the greatest flood in the valley up to the time, excepting the one in 1805); February 1883 (three days and almost as high as 1866); 1884 (almost as high as 1883); March 1897; and March 1898 (along with 1897, one of the highest water levels excluding 1805 and 1866). According to the Miami Conservancy District's data, the worst floods in the Miami Valley, in order of size and volume, took place in 1805, 1866, 1897, 1898, and 1883. All of these were dwarfed by the Great Flood of 1913.

As one can see, about every 10–15 years there was substantial flooding in the Miami Valley; and the 1913 deluge, following 1898, was just about "on time." Therefore, it should be understood that the people were familiar with the regularity of flooding in the valley. Other factors also contributed to the cataclysm.

The Lake Erie–Ohio River watershed, which is the geographical dividing line of the flow of waters north or south in the Miami Valley, runs along the north side of Grand Lake St. Mary's; then, at the eastern edge of the lake in Auglaize County, the watershed follows a direct southern line to a point just west of Minster, at which point it turns east on a line north of the town, roughly along State Route 119, and enters Shelby County. From this point, it follows SR 119 until it intersects at the northeastern edge of Lake Loramie and then commences in a northeasterly direction following Loramie Creek on its north bank until it leaves Shelby County.

All precipitation north of this divide flows northward into streams and rivers of that area and ultimately into Lake Erie. Conversely, everything south of the watershed flows into the streams and rivers in a southerly flow until it reaches the Ohio River. Therefore, all the rains that fell in March 1913 not only fell on the land but, as mentioned above, ran off into the streams and rivers and then south, gaining more volume as the water flowed south. The southern reaches not only contended with their own rain but also with the rain and runoff from the area to the north.

In examining the Great Flood of 1913 and analyzing the data, Morgan, in *The Miami Valley and the 1913 Flood: Technical Reports, Part I*, makes an astounding statement, which helps us to grasp the immense power of that particular flood: "Simply by the condensing of the 9.7 inches of rain which fell during 5 days on the comparatively small area of 3670 square miles of the Miami River watershed above Hamilton, enough energy was released to supply 2,500,000 horsepower 24 hours a day continuously for a hundred years."

Quite frankly, given the size and power of the 1913 flood, there was not much that could have been done, besides complete evacuation, which would have lessened the loss.

We trust that by having this better understanding of the situation in 1913, you will appreciate the harsh realities of those days as you read some of the stories and view the images contained in this volume.

One

Troy's Last Beautiful Day

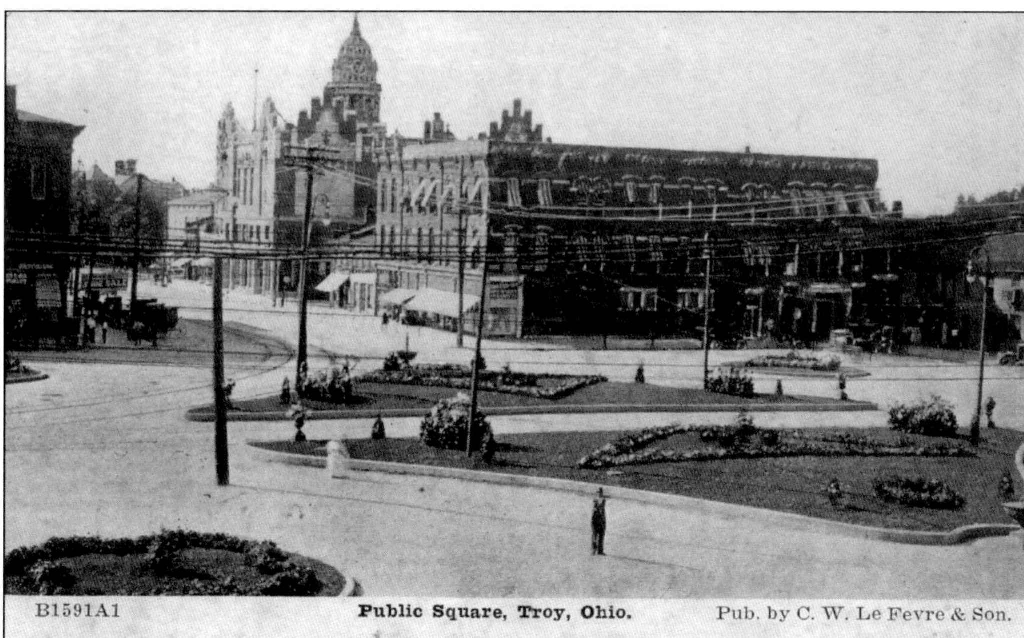

Saturday, March 22, 1913—the day before Easter—was a beautiful day in Troy. In fact, the weather was unusually lovely for the end of March. Many residents were busy preparing for holiday celebrations, both for religious services and dinners with family and friends. Although they may have heard about severe weather in other parts of the country, they had no idea that a flood would soon strike them.

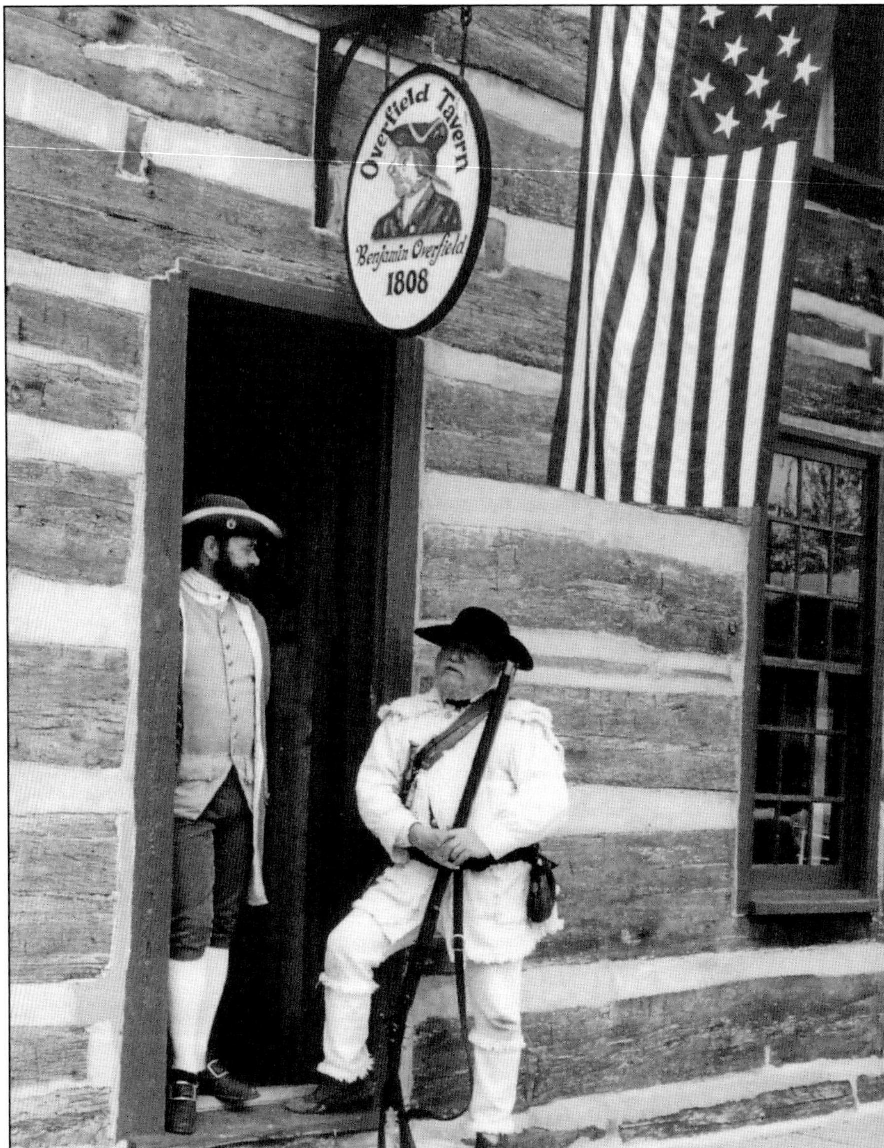

Troy was about 100 years old at the time of the flood. It was founded in 1807 and incorporated in 1814. Located in almost the geographic center of Miami County, Ohio, along the banks of the Great Miami River, it had been the county seat since the county's founding in 1807. About that time, in 1809, Andrew Wallace, who made the first survey of Troy, laid out the Troy Public Square. He also taught in the town's first school and was Miami County's first treasurer. His son, David Wallace, served as the governor of Indiana, and his grandson, Lew Wallace, wrote the classic book *Ben-Hur*. The Overfield Tavern, the oldest building in Troy, was used as the Miami County Courthouse between 1808 and 1811. It is situated near the Great Miami River, but came through the flood with little damage. Now a museum, the tavern is seen here still as it was in its early years. The building's log exterior is now covered. Pictured around 1996 are reenactors John Wysocki (left), of the George Rogers Clark Heritage Association of Springfield, Ohio, and Terry Purke, a Troy historian. (Photograph by Susan Sims-Hillbrand, courtesy of Overfield Tavern Museum.)

Troy has always been known for its architecture. The Miami County Courthouse on West Main Street is a Troy landmark and people passing by often pause to admire its beauty. Designed by architect Joseph Yost of Columbus, Ohio, it was completed and opened for business in January 1888. Floodwaters flowed nearby, but the building was not badly damaged.

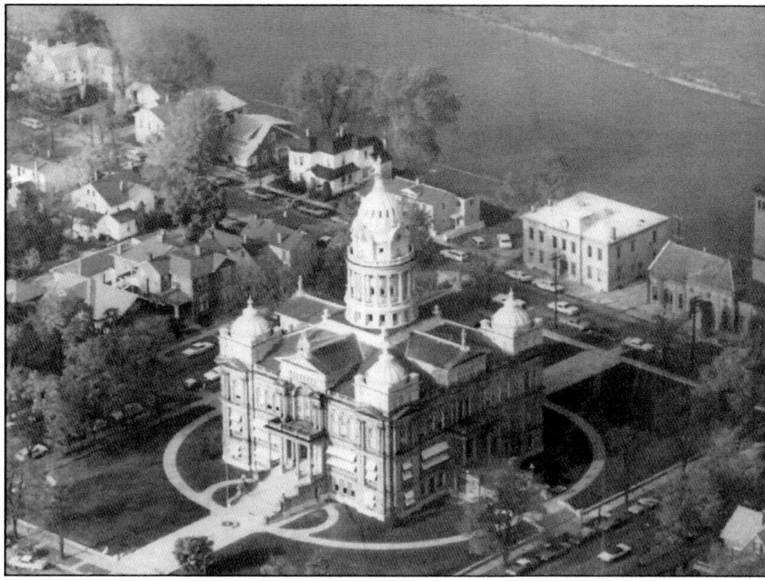

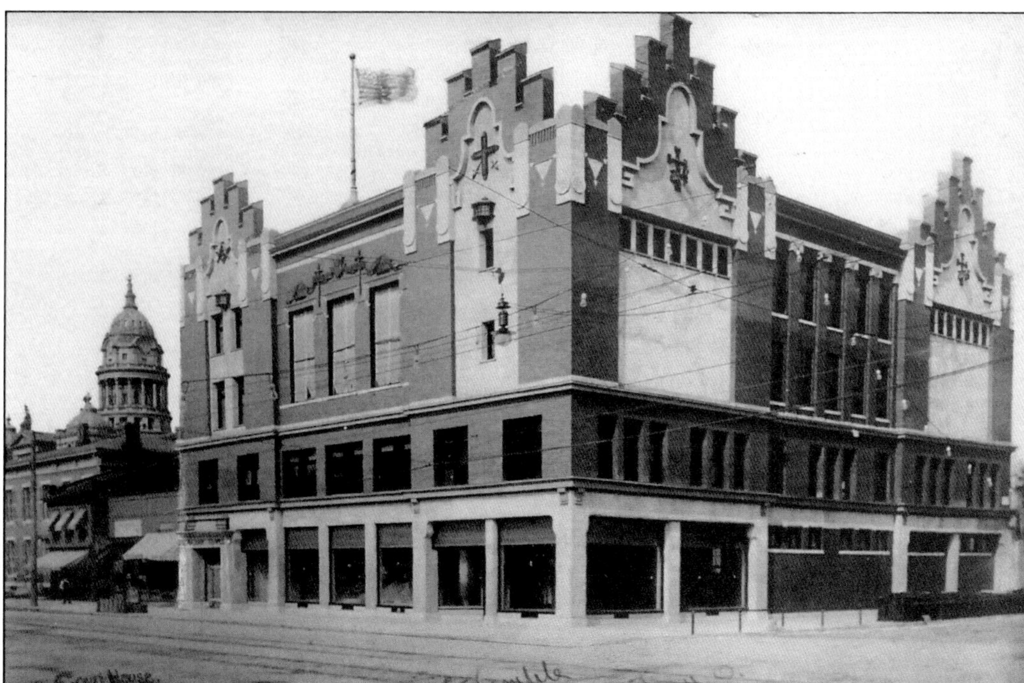

Another architecturally important building on West Main Street is the Troy Masonic Temple, built between 1906 and 1908. The structure features six stained-glass windows, marble floors, and dark wood panels. H.A. Cosley operated a hardware store on the building's first floor. This postcard shows the hardware store and three of the stained-glass windows (the large front windows on third floor).

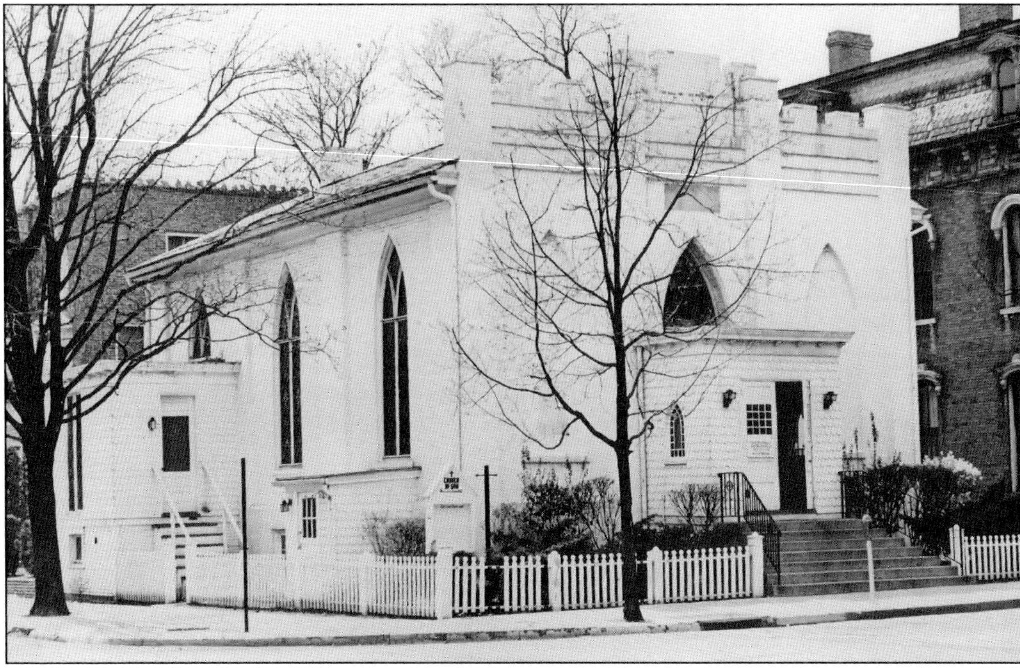

Gen. William Henry Harrison, who went on to be president, opened the Miami and Erie Canal on July 5, 1837, with a speech at the old Trinity Episcopal Church on the corner of Franklin and Walnut Streets. In the 1800s, church members helped runaway slaves escape to freedom. A tunnel runs below the church sanctuary, and some believe it was an Underground Railroad site.

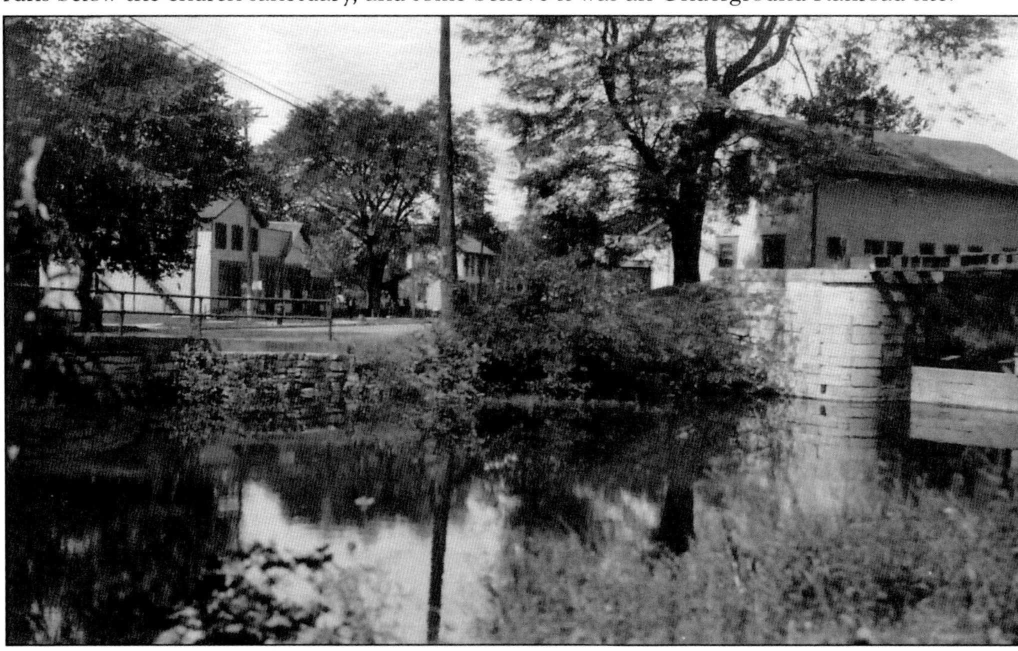

At the time of the flood, the Miami and Erie Canal and the canal race still ran through Troy, but the canal was no longer used for business purposes. Although this photograph shows a tranquil scene, the canal was considered dirty. After the canal was filled-in, the Hobart Brothers Company later built its West Main Street building over Lock 12.

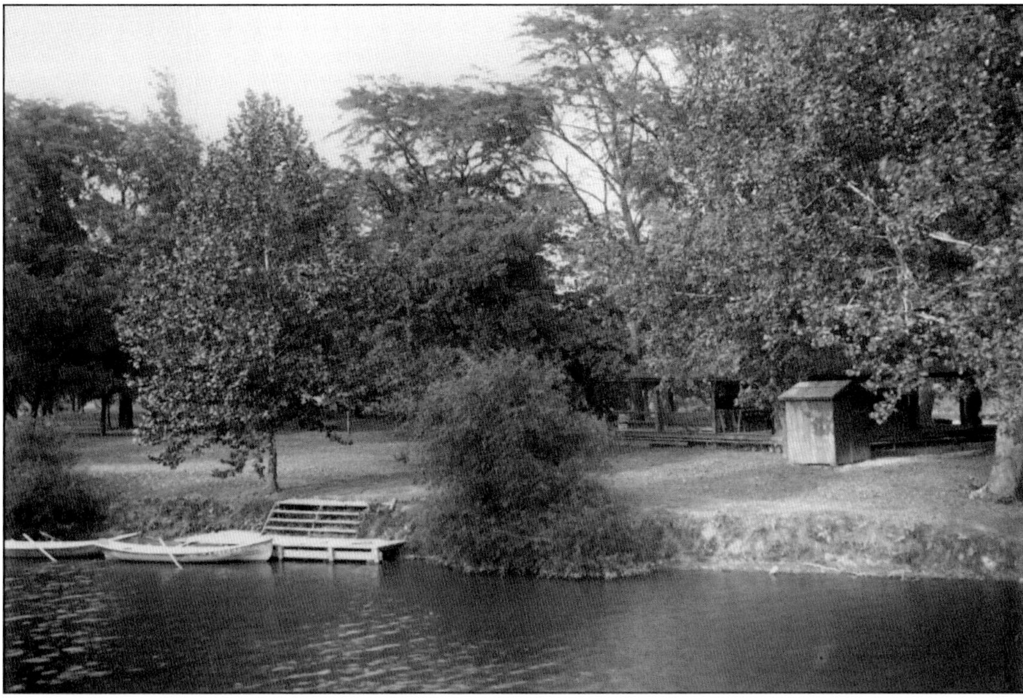

The Great Miami River has always played an important role in Troy life. It has been used for transportation, manufacturing, recreation, and to sustain life. In the early 1900s, a recreational boat outing club was set up on an island in the Great Miami River. Here, local residents practiced their boating skills. (Courtesy of the Museum of Troy History.)

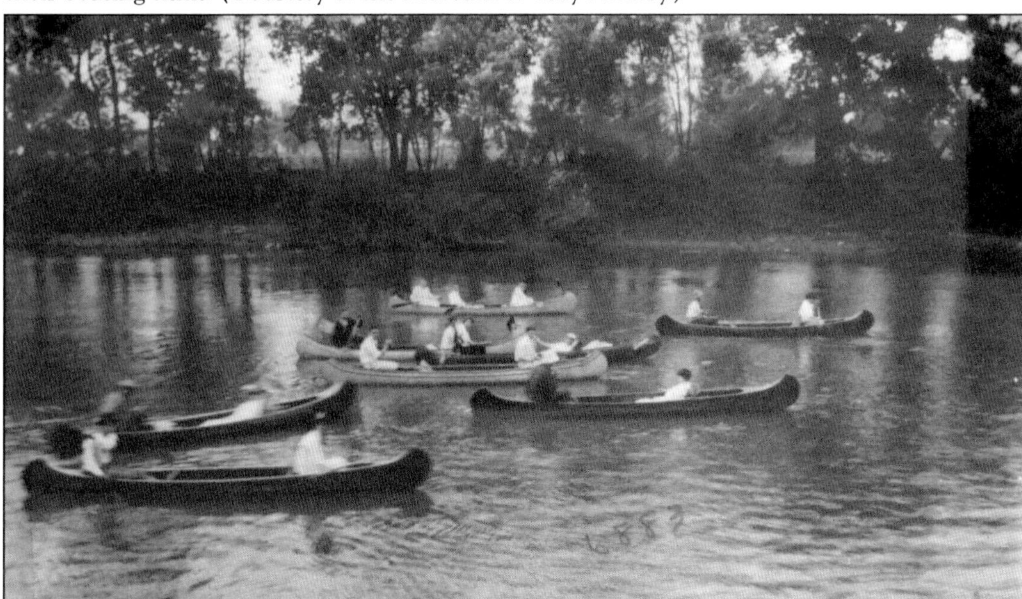

This early-1900s photograph shows people canoeing on the Great Miami River. In those days, even when they were out on the water, men and women stayed fashionable. Ladies wore long dresses, men wore white, buttoned shirts, and both wore leather shoes. Clothing was often made at home or by a local tailor or seamstress. (Courtesy of the Museum of Troy History.)

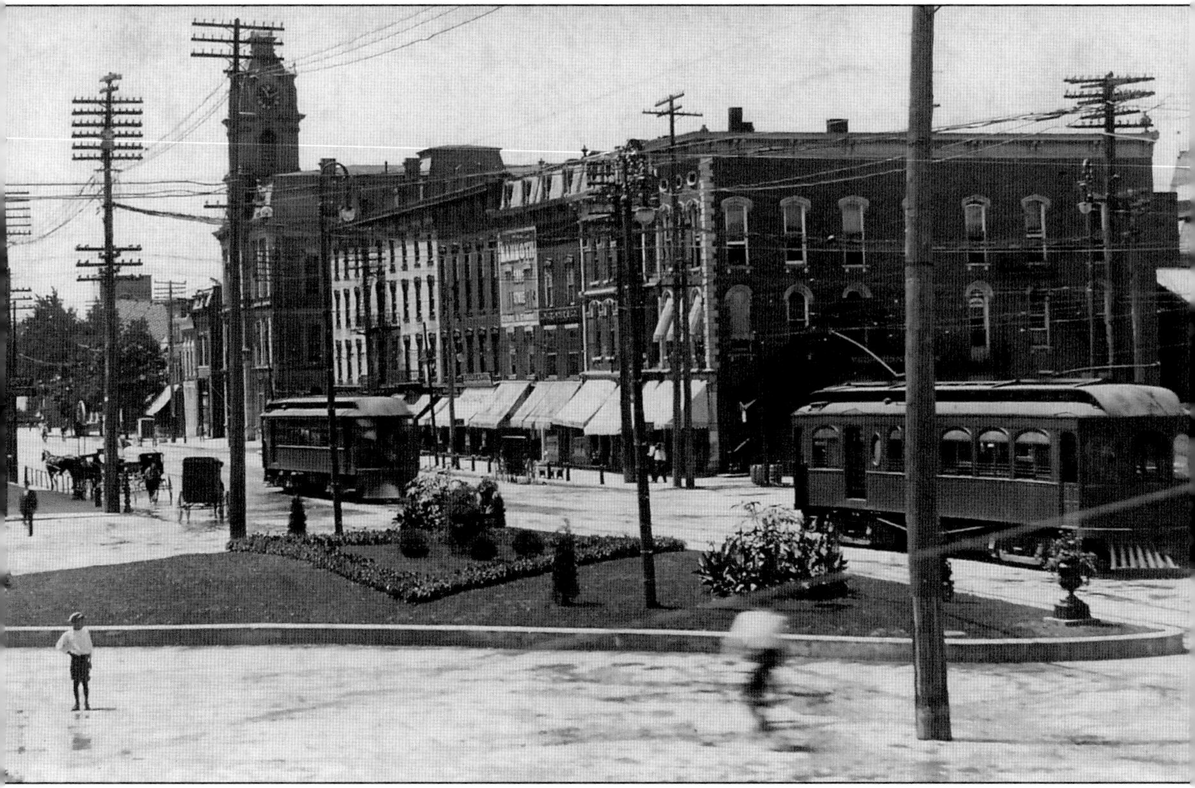

Two railroad lines and two interurban railway lines ran through Troy in 1913. The Big Four Railroad and the Cincinnati, Hamilton & Dayton Railroad weaved into town, while the interurban Dayton & Troy Electric Railway ran north and south and the Springfield, Troy & Piqua Electric Railway went east and west. Troy was a noisy place because of its many train whistles, engine sounds, and factory whistles.

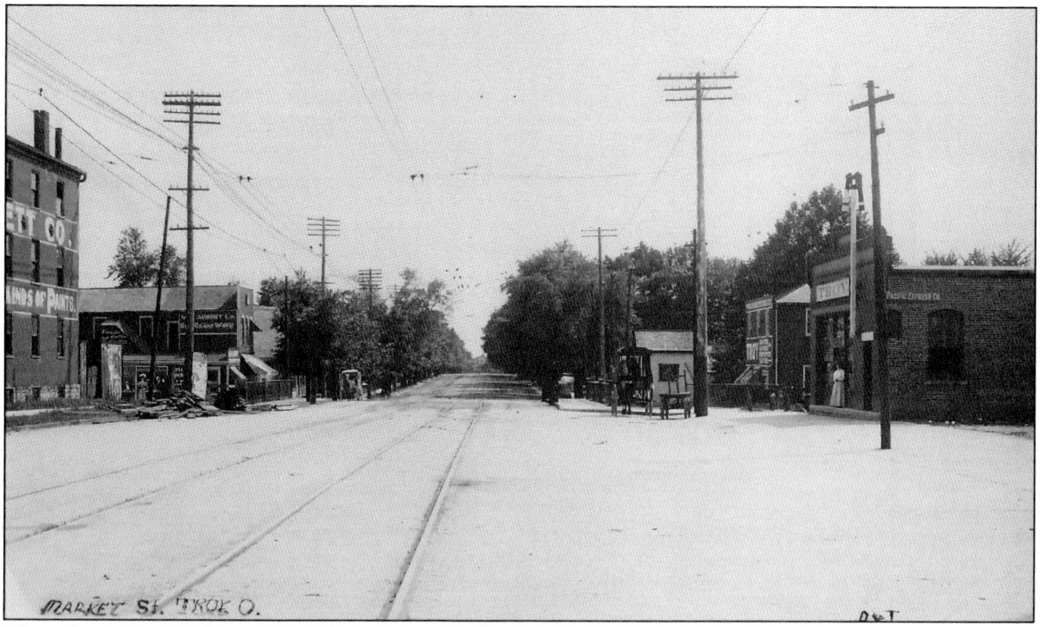

This photograph of South Market Street shows the interurban railroad tracks with the Interurban Union Station on the right side of the picture. Years ago, former South Market Street resident Hortense Cairns Mumford recalled, "The interurban ran directly in front of our house from Dayton. Two double tracks went down the center of Market Street. Sometimes the cars would pass each other—thus the dual tracks."

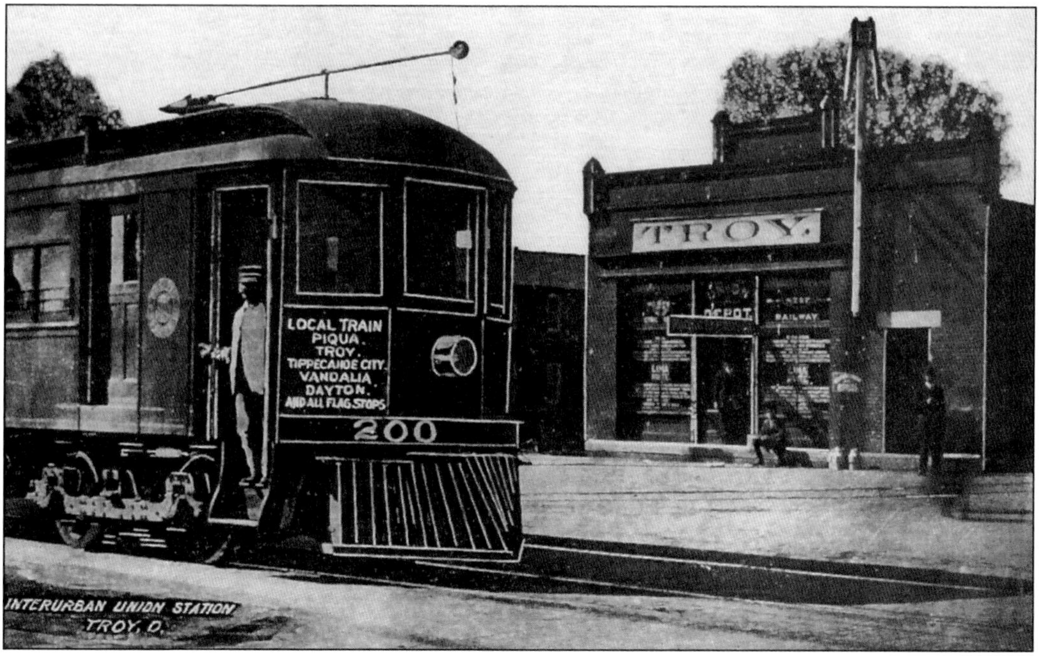

This is a close-up view of the Interurban Union Station. The interurban lines were part of what was known as the Lima Route. The name of the Dayton & Troy Electric Railway was painted on the window on the left side of the front door and the name Springfield, Troy & Piqua Electric Railway was on the window on the right side of the front door.

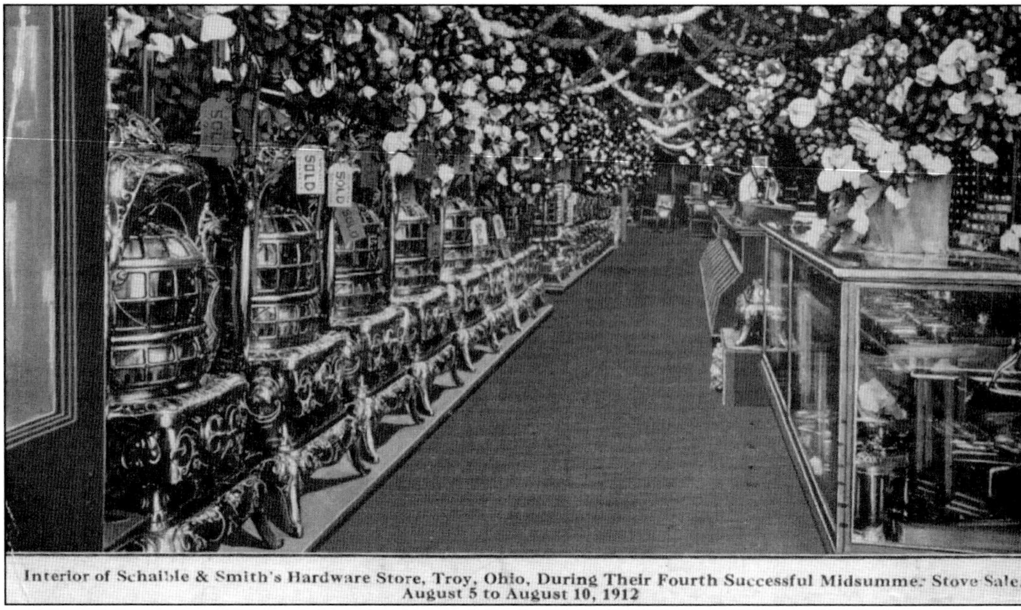

Troy was a small, busy manufacturing center. Companies specialized in transportation equipment, food machines, patent medicines, and distilled beverages. Neighborhood grocery stores were scattered throughout the town, while stores selling more general merchandise—such as hardware, fine china, clothing, and books—were located in or near downtown Troy. This advertisement postcard shows the interior of Schaible & Smith's hardware store in 1912.

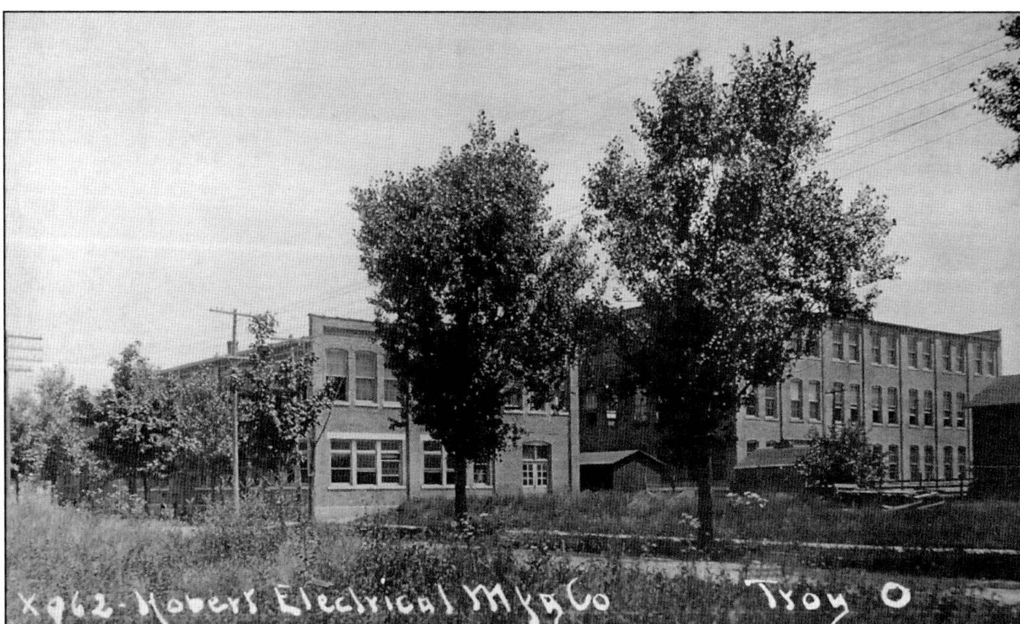

The Hobart Electric Manufacturing Company reincorporated as the Hobart Manufacturing Company days before the flood. The Hobart Manufacturing Company eventually became the Hobart Corporation and is currently owned by Illinois Tool Works as part of its Food Equipment Group. This is the last major Troy company from the 1913 flood era that is still in business

Two

A Rainy Easter and Rising Waters

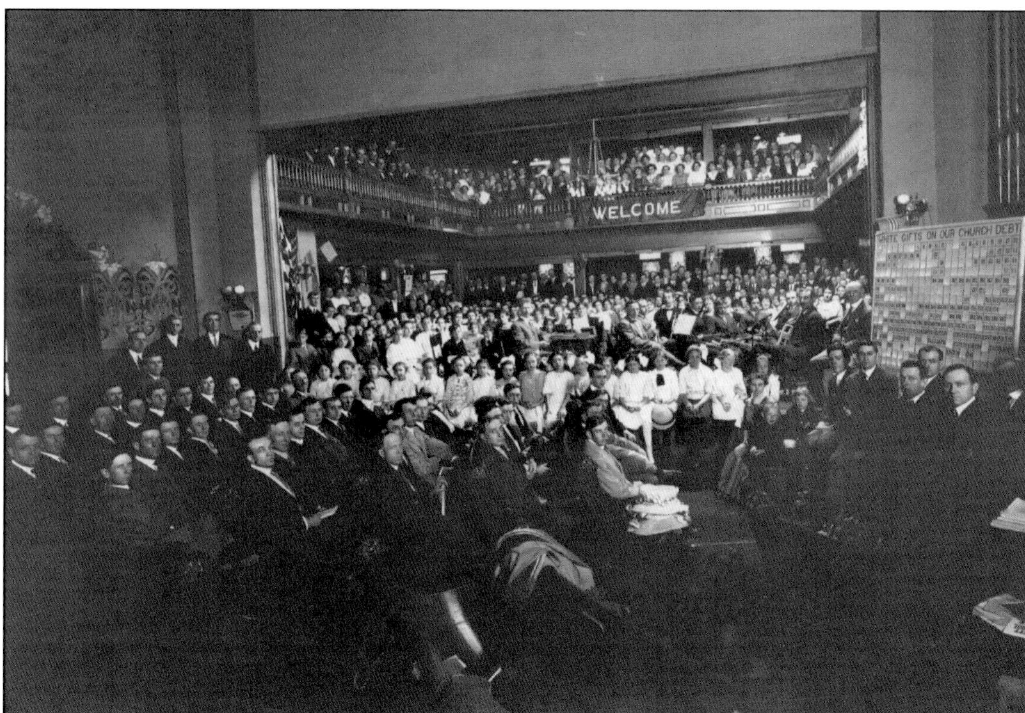

On Easter Sunday, March 23, 1913, townspeople woke up to strong winds, thunder, lightning, and rain. Churches were filled with worshippers who had arrived for services wearing raincoats over their often new and sometimes delicate Easter clothing. This photograph shows Troy's First Christian Church (now the First United Church of Christ) in the early 20th century. (Courtesy of First United Church of Christ.)

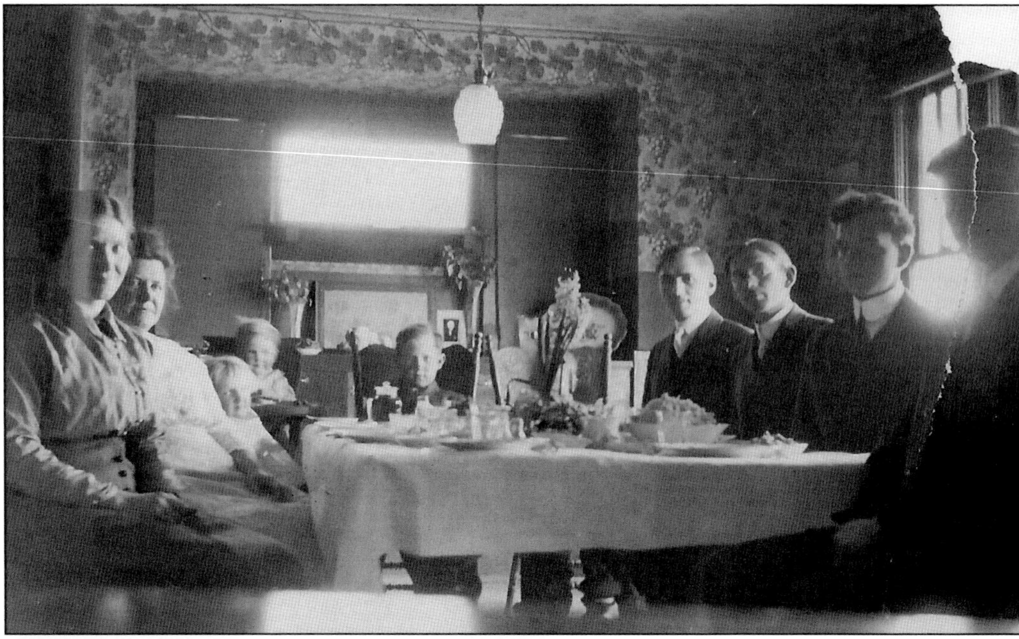

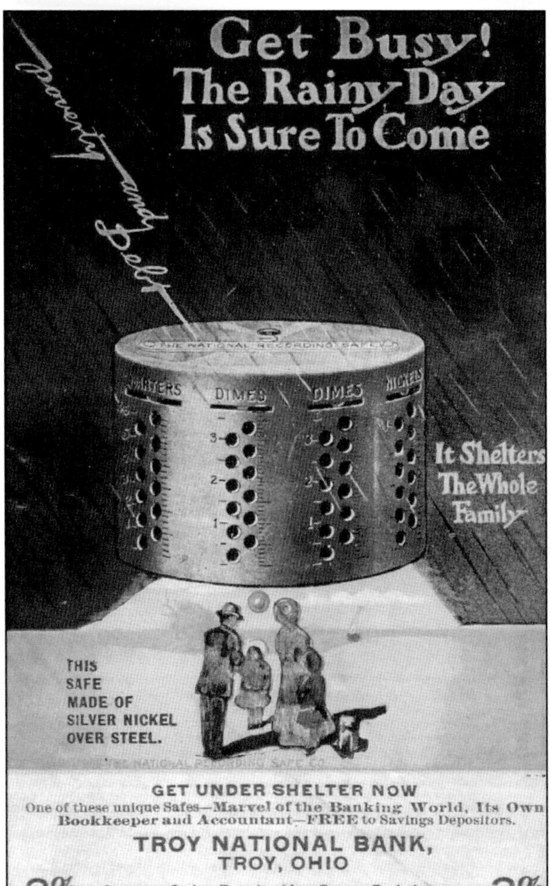

On Sunday afternoon, families and friends throughout Troy gathered for an Easter meal. While some meal items came from neighborhood grocers, much of what was eaten had been raised in family gardens. Fruits and vegetables grown at home were canned in late summer or early fall for later use. Chickens were raised for eggs, and cows were kept for milk. Residents were very self-sufficient. This 1915 Easter photograph shows what such a gathering might have looked like at the time.

In the early 20th century, government assistance programs and insurance payments were not available to cover disaster losses; people took care of themselves with help from family, friends, and neighbors. A 1909 ad for the Troy National Bank advertises a unique money safe with the slogan, "Get Busy! The Rainy Day Is Sure to Come."

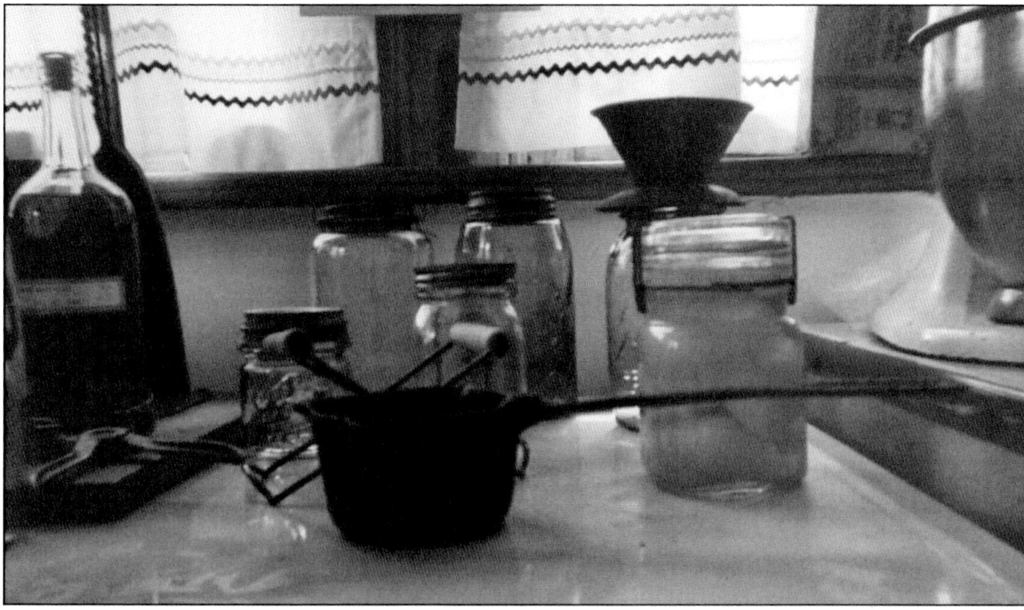

Preserved food—canned fruits and vegetables—were stored on shelves or in cabinets in home pantries and cellars. This photograph taken in the kitchen of the Museum of Troy History shows a display of glass canning jars. The museum is housed in the 1847 home of John Kitchen on East Water Street. (Courtesy of Judy Deeter.)

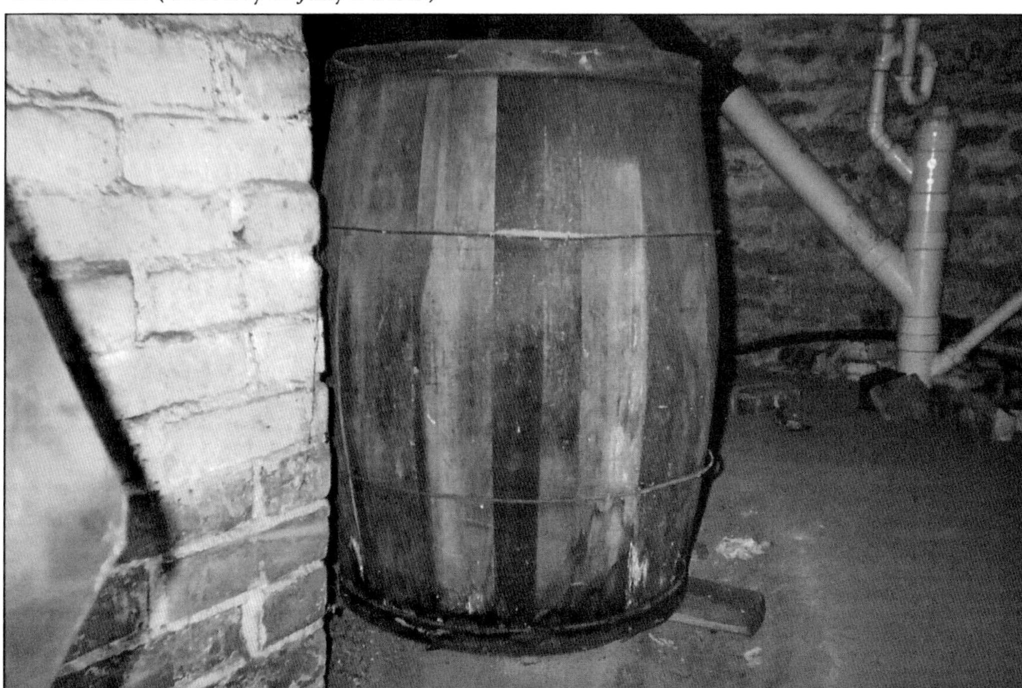

Many older homes in Troy have cellars with floors and walls usually made of brick or stone, stairways that are often steep and narrow, and poor lighting because the windows—if there are any—are small. During heavy rains or floods, water often seeped into the cellar. (Courtesy of Judy Deeter.)

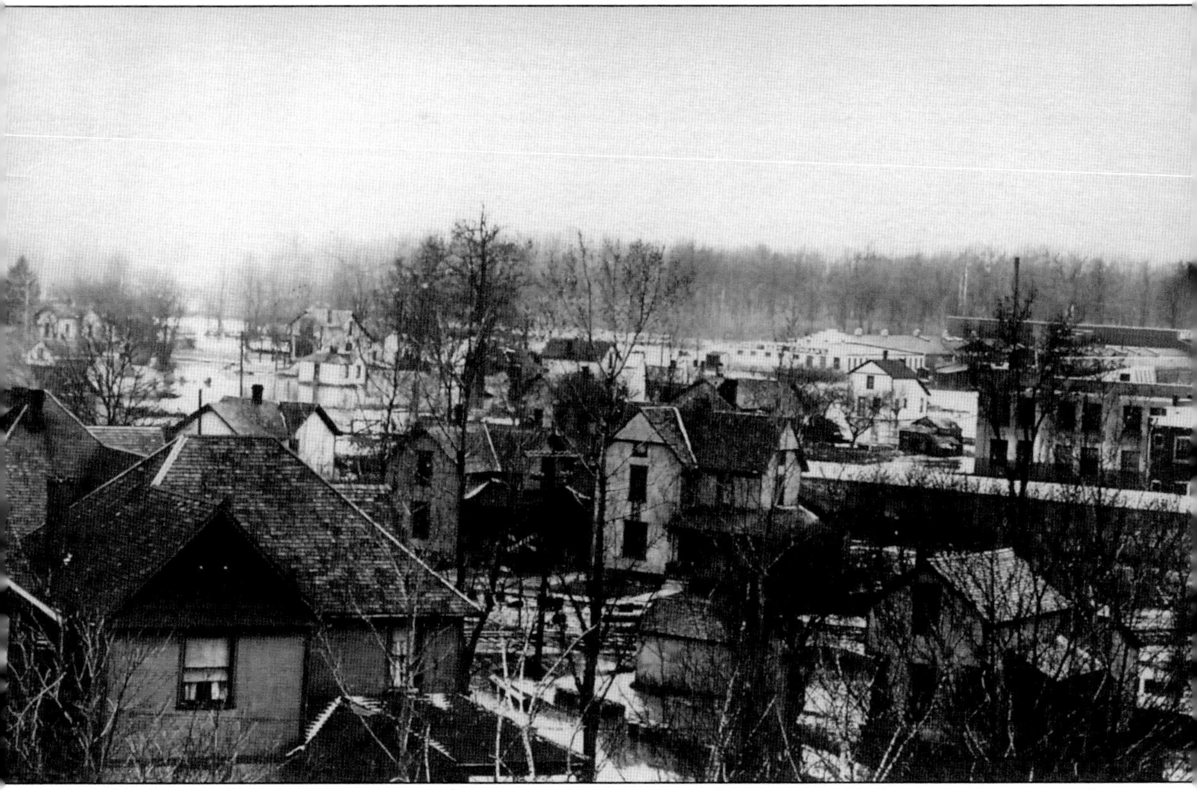

By Easter Sunday evening, residents were beginning to be concerned about the amount of rain that had fallen. In a story about the flood, Lois Davies writes, "Usually on Sunday evenings, those west side teenagers, Clayton Jenkins, Wilbur Fish, George Sipes, and Arthur and Esta Barnes would gather at one of their homes for popcorn and apples. But, that Sunday, Mr. Barnes was alarmed. The gutters were overflowing at Simpson and Pennsylvania where their home stood . . . Mr. Barnes told the boys they could not go anywhere until they helped get his chickens up into the hayloft. They waded in ankle-deep water to the barn and twenty minutes later, waded back in water up to their waists." The Hobart Manufacturing Company later built its Ridge Avenue headquarters where the Barnes home once stood. This photograph of flooded Troy was taken from the old Kyle School on South Plum Street.

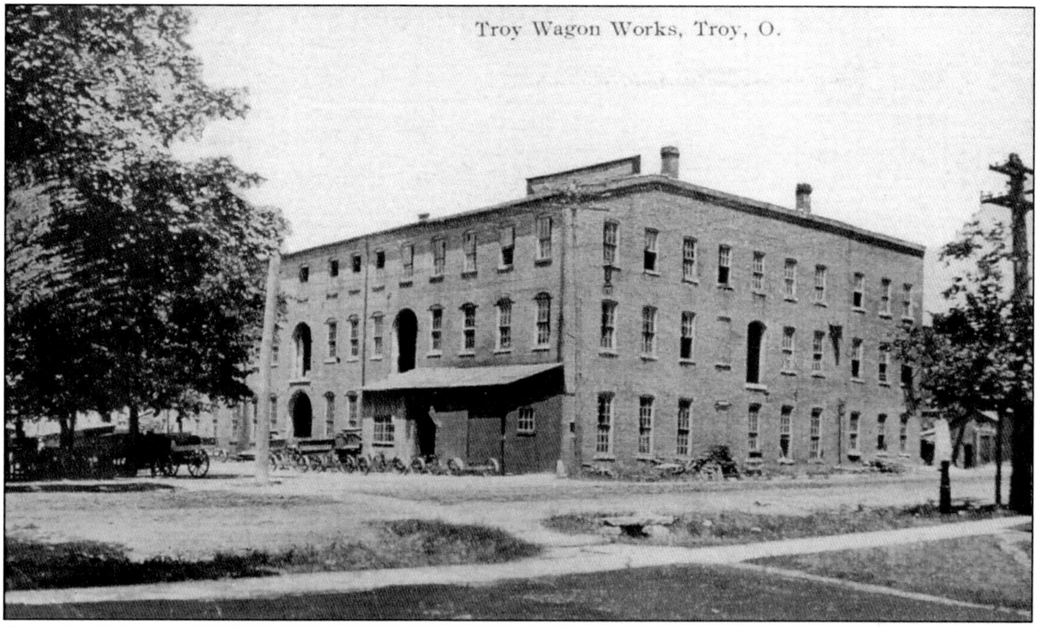

On Monday evening, Troy Wagon Works president Charles Geiger was worried about the company records. He asked his employee John Eccard to help him move the records to a higher floor in the building. Eccard went home around 11:00 p.m. When Geiger later opened the building door to leave, muddy water and boards from a nearby lumberyard greeted him. He took the boards, made a raft, and floated home.

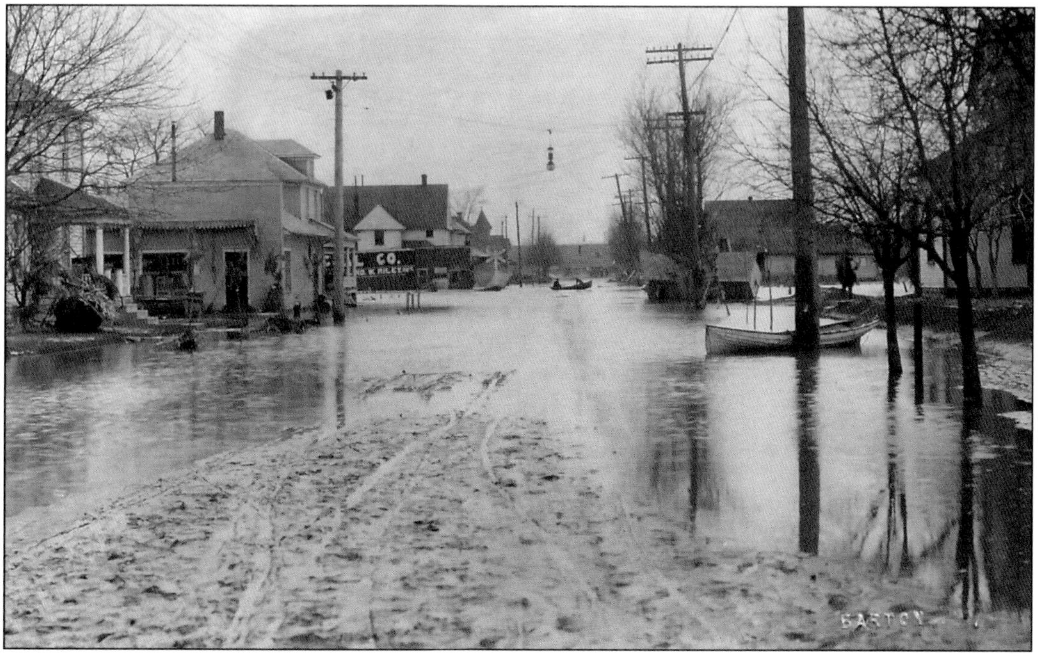

John Eccard walked through water-covered streets to get to his home near Garfield Avenue and May Street. His house, which sat high on the property, was fine. He went to his barn to check on his brand new Ford and his daughter's pony. Water had reached the bottom of the car door. He took the pony to his house, where it lived upstairs for several days.

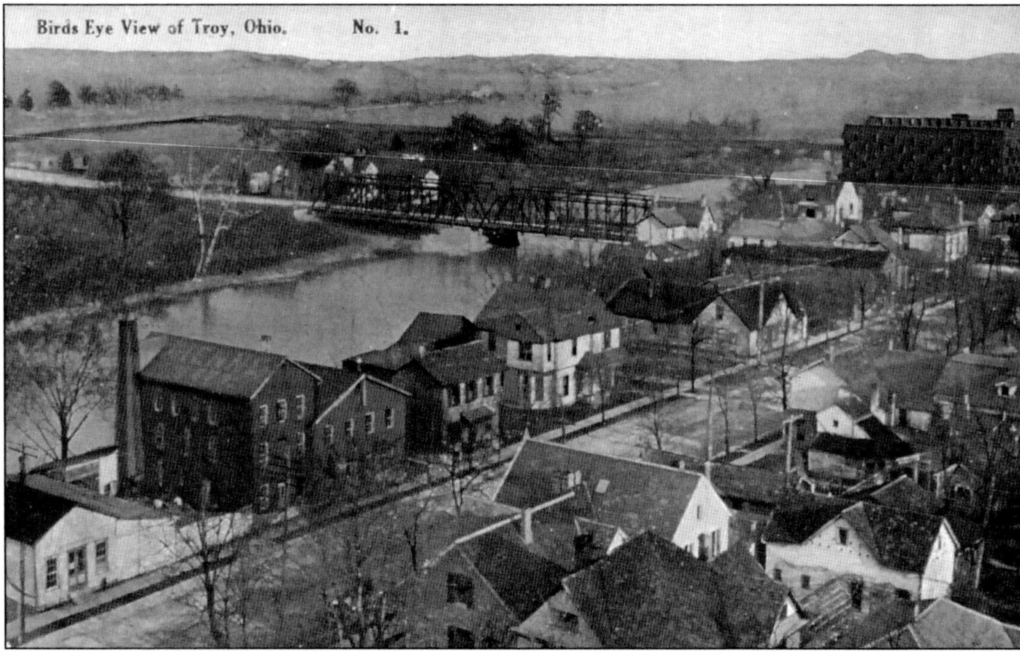

By 6:00 p.m. Sunday, the Miami and Erie Canal had overflowed and the Great Miami River was rising. Residents on the north side of the river were advised to leave their homes. Warnings were particularly given to a small, predominately African American community known as Nineveh at the southeast corner of North Market Street and Staunton Road.

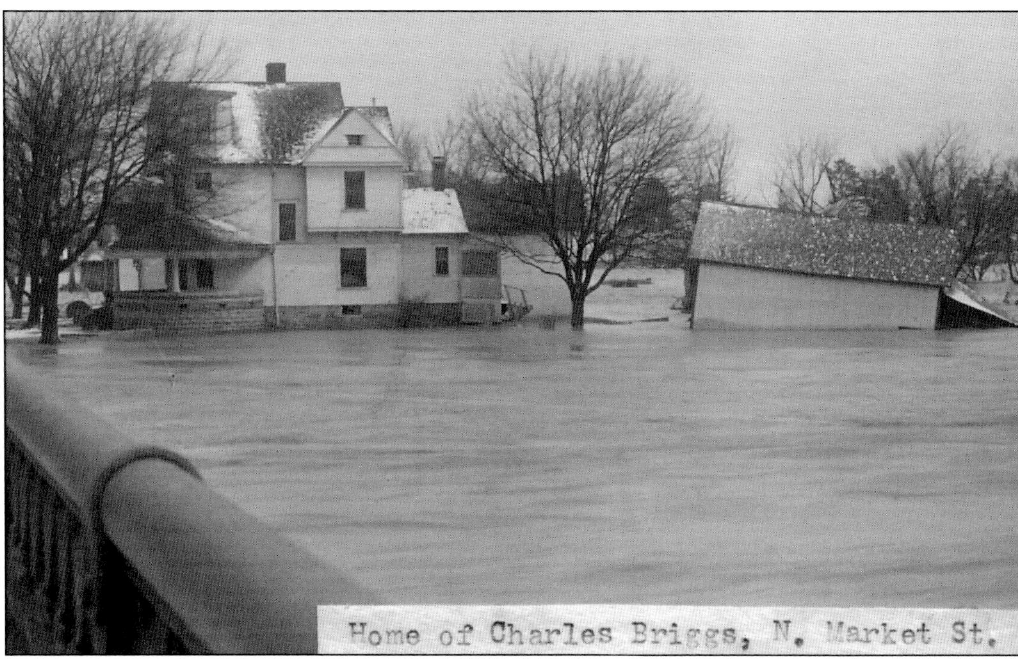

The Charles Briggs family lived on North Market Street near the river. Because of high water at their home, they had to leave the residence using ladders. Their barn, which housed two automobiles, was lifted from its foundation and partially fell over the embankment. The house was later moved to the west side of North Market Street.

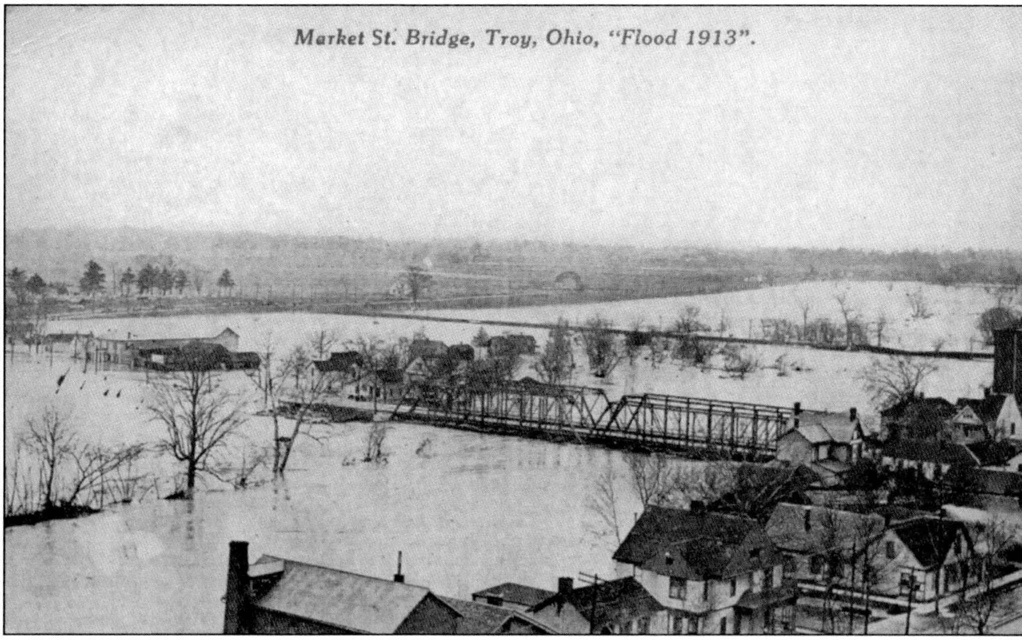

Because Nineveh was so close to the Great Miami River, it flooded nearly every spring. Some residents heeded the warning and went to safety, but others did not. Horses from the Cortez Smith Livery Stable were brought to Troy. Robert Smallenbarger recalled that as horses neared the Market Street Bridge, crossing water flowed so fast that the last horses had to swim across it.

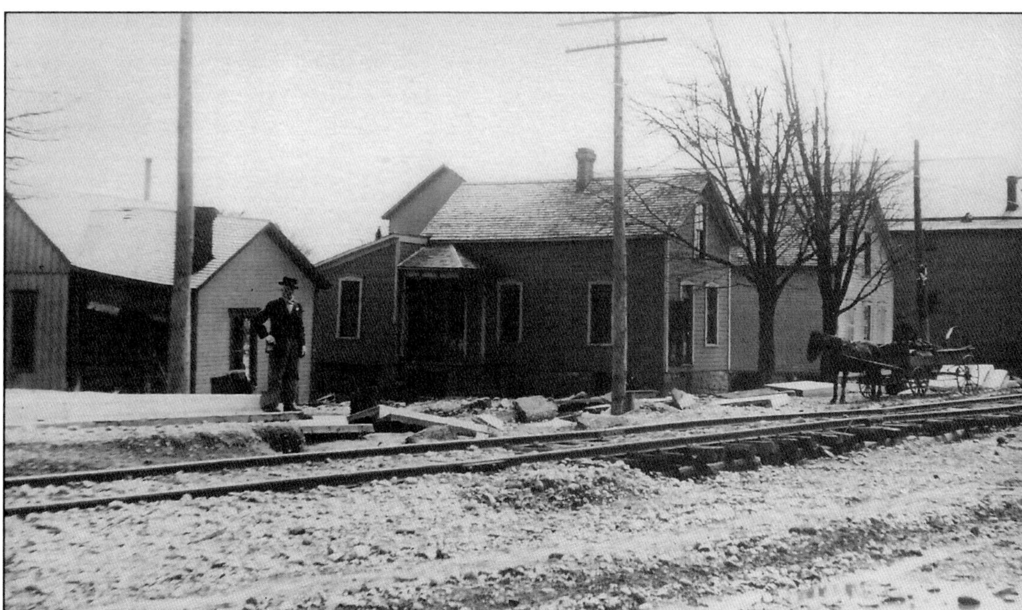

In an untitled, undated manuscript archived at the Local History Library, Robert Smallenbarger writes, "The fate of the Nineveh people concerned me greatly. It had only been several years before this that I had passed the Cincinnati Post (newspaper) to their doors and I knew and liked these people greatly. I recall the Steward family and Mrs. Jones, the faith healer, quite vividly." This photograph shows houses on the east side of Nineveh.

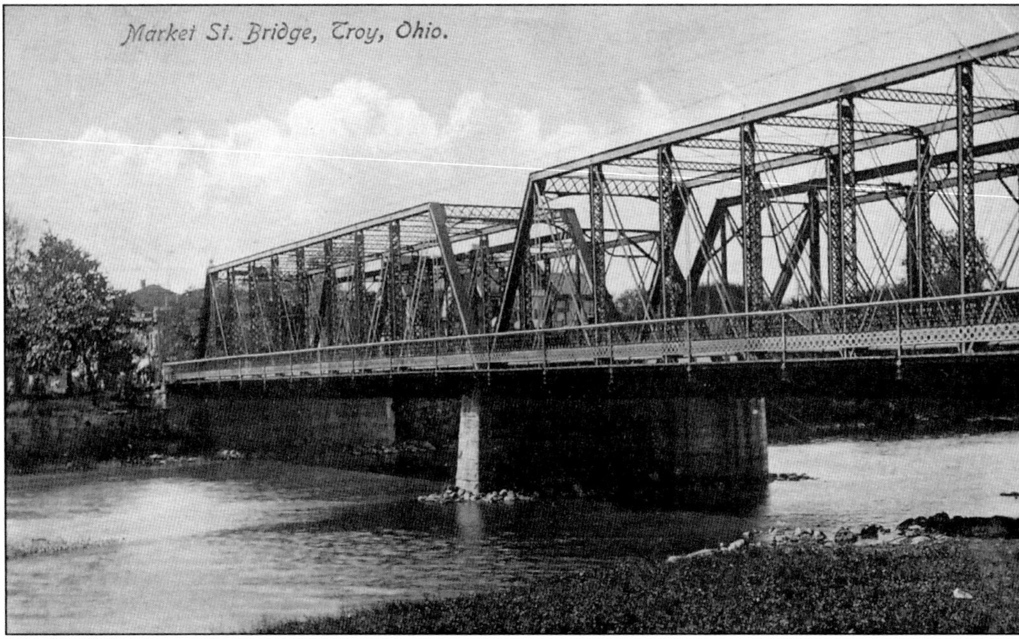

Water came down upon Nineveh on Monday evening. Wilbur "Wib" Chaffee, 22, and his friends Howard Reichard and George Torlina stood on the Market Street Bridge nearby and listened to the pitiful cries of residents clinging to trees to save their lives. Chaffee recalled, "They were really screaming and shouting for help. We couldn't stand it."

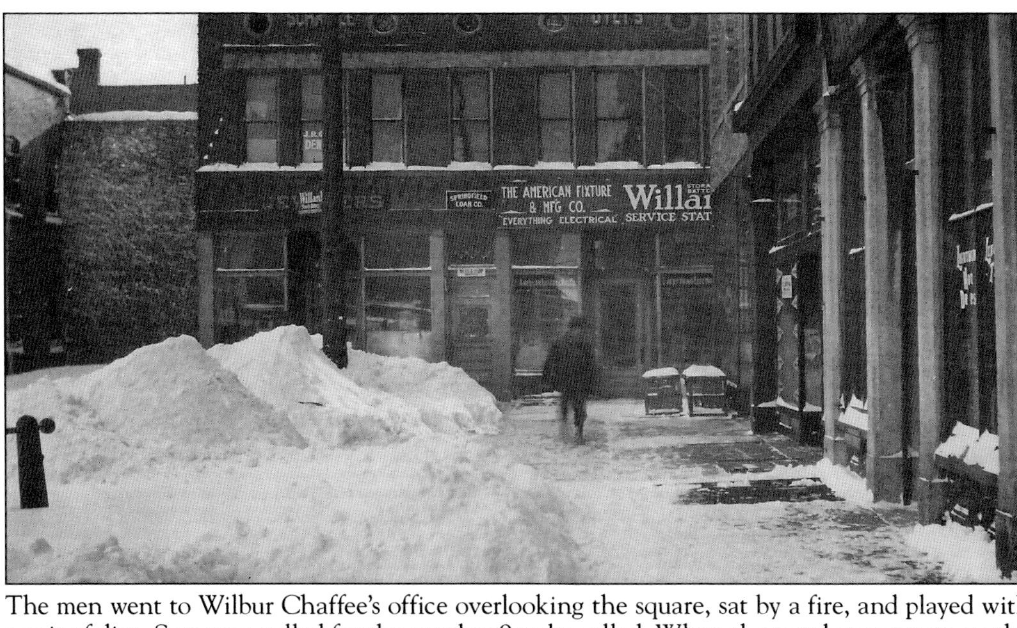

The men went to Wilbur Chaffee's office overlooking the square, sat by a fire, and played with a pair of dice. Someone called for the number 9 to be rolled. When the number came up on the dice, the fire bell rang nine times, meaning there was an emergency. At first, everyone laughed at the coincidence, but then they left the building to see what was happening.

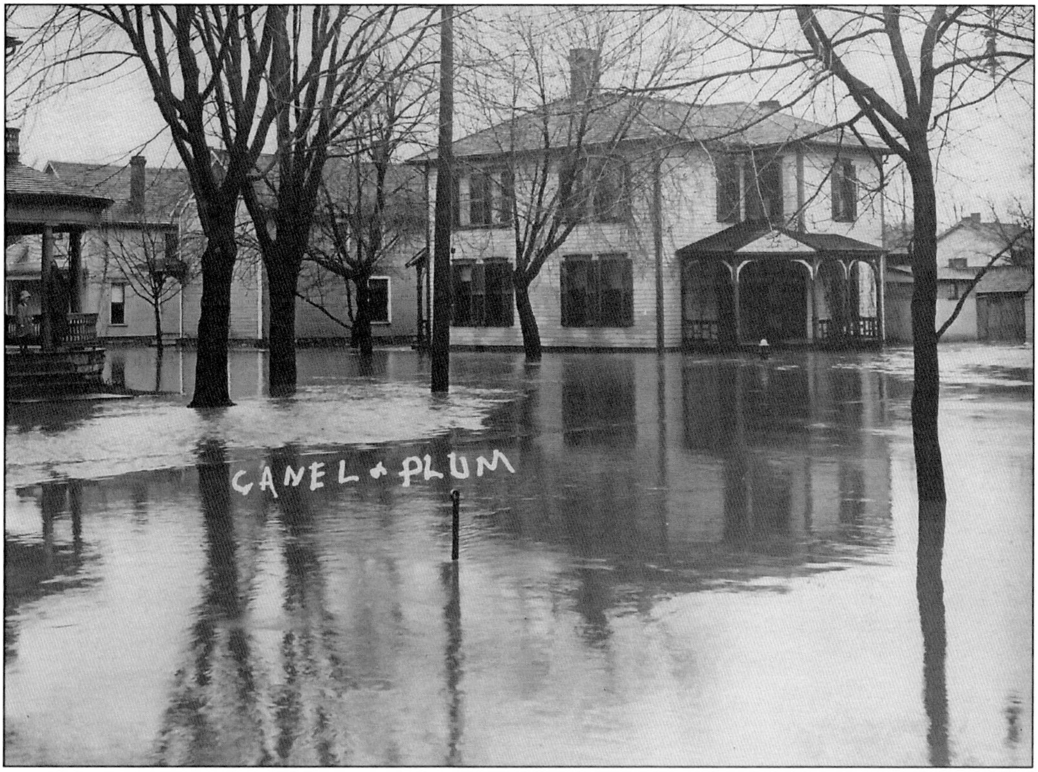

In her memoirs, Margaret Zeigenfelder Brown recalls, "That night we were all awakened by the tolling of the fire bell and seeing lights turned on in all the surrounding homes [we] realized that there was something even more serious than a fire that caused the bell to toll ceaselessly . . . The rains continued to pour down relentlessly!" This photograph is of Plum and Canal Streets.

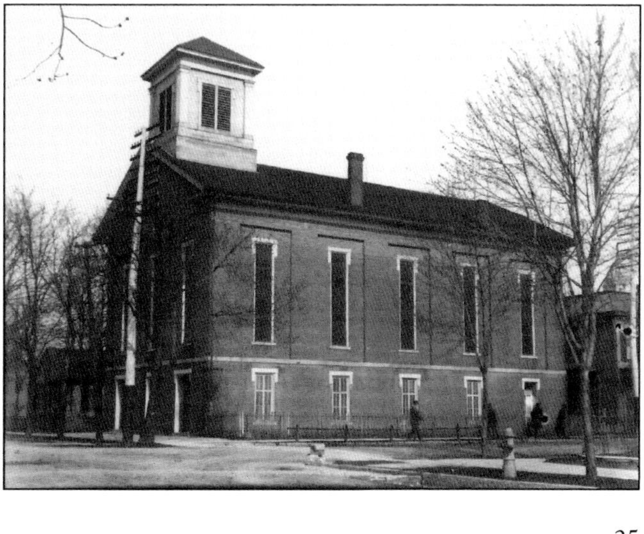

Church bells rang, and the whistle at the electric power plant blew. Men with lanterns monitored and walked the river and canal banks, watching the water level. Other men rode horses through Troy's soggy streets, warning residents to get themselves and their valuables up high. Though many were anxious, everybody got busy. The old First Baptist Church at Franklin and Cherry Streets is pictured here.

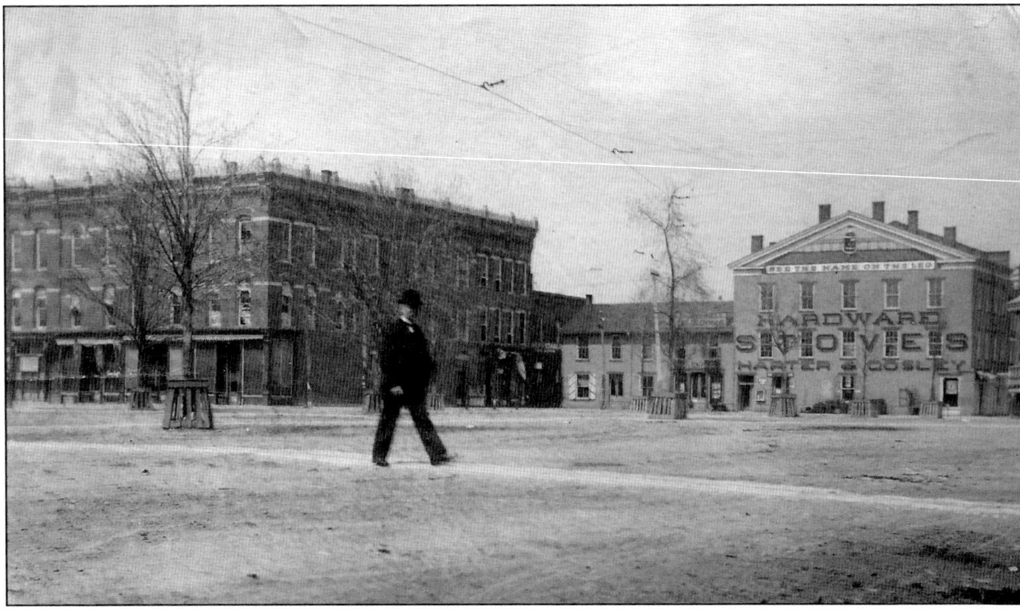

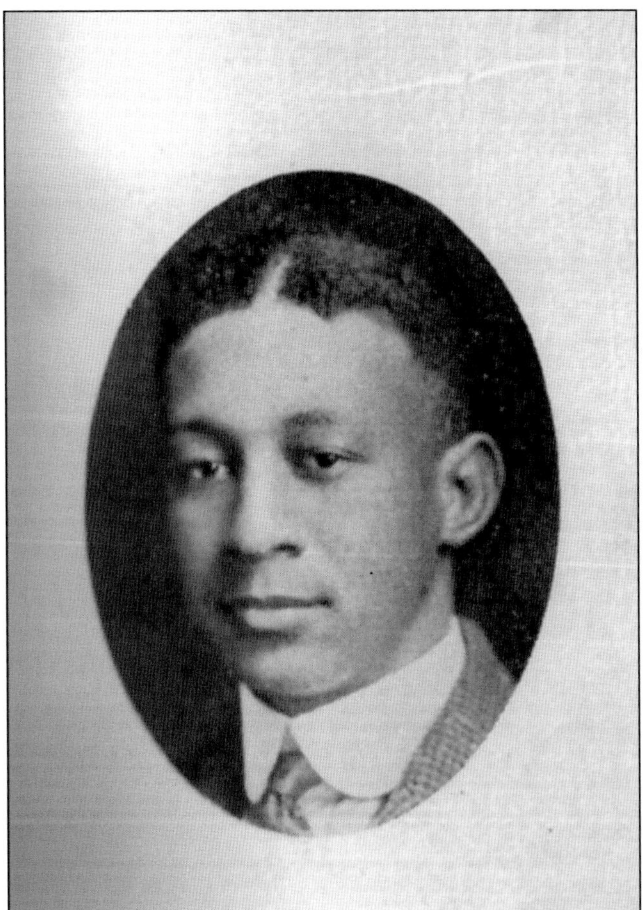

Perlema Sewell (left) once shared his memories about when the flood struck. He was 16 and lived at 101 Ash Street. Early that evening, he attended a play written by amateur playwright Rose Wilson at the Odd Fellows Hall on the Public Square. There was a terrible rainstorm, and people had trouble getting home. They joked that finally Wilson had a winning play and it brought the flood. That night, Sewell's father woke the family and warned them that high water was coming. As Perlema reached his home's main floor, he heard cellar cupboards rattling and food cans falling. He yelled, "Let's get the buckets! Let's get the buckets! I'll go down and dip it and bring the water out of the basement." His father then asked him where he was going to throw the water. The building with "Hardware / Stoves / Harter & Cosley" on it (above) was the Odd Fellows Hall.

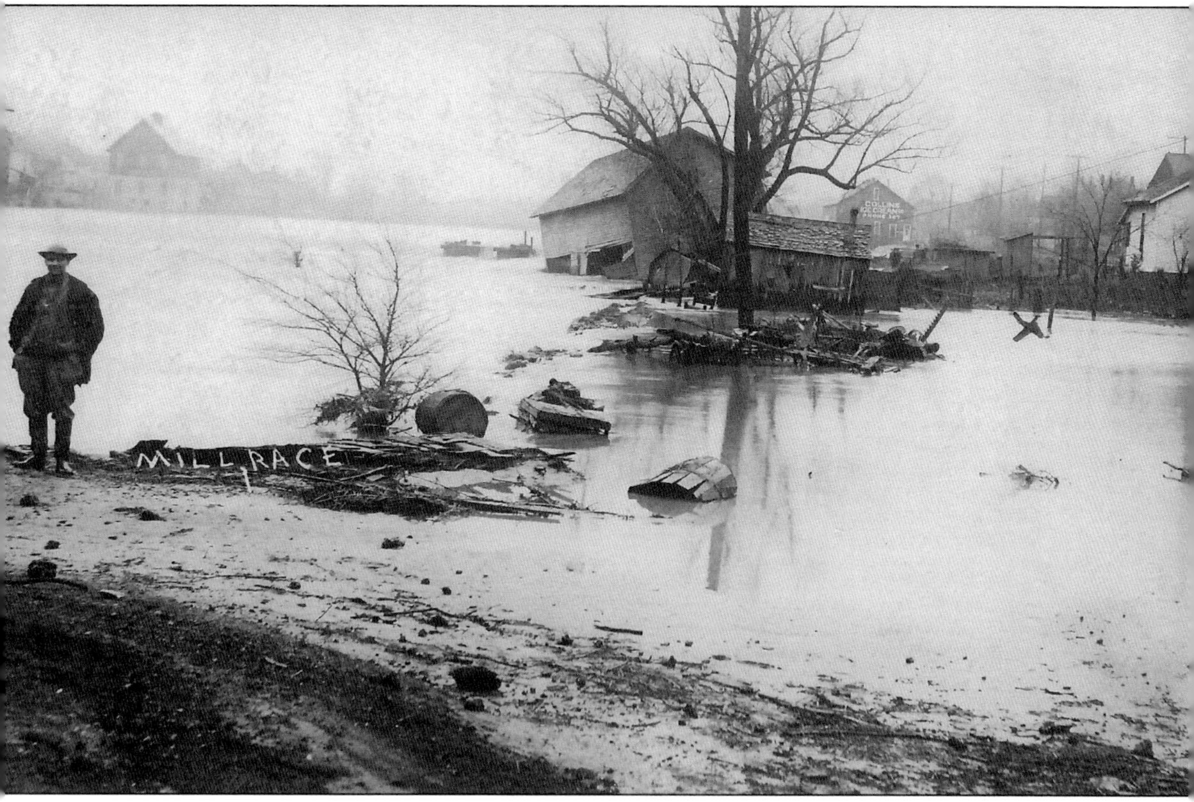

Steve English and his family lived south of Troy on Dye Mill Road near the millpond. English was in charge of opening and closing gates at the pond to control its water level. As water levels rose, two neighbors came to the English house asking that the pond gates be opened because the pond water level was high. English told them that the gates were open; he could do nothing more. The next day, with water levels still high, it was decided that if the center support of a nearby bridge were removed, more water would flow and water levels would go down. English's 18-year-old son, Ned, was tied to the center of the bridge and chopped at the center support. As he hit the support timber, they heard the bridge crack. Ned was quickly pulled off the bridge. Eventually, the span gave way.

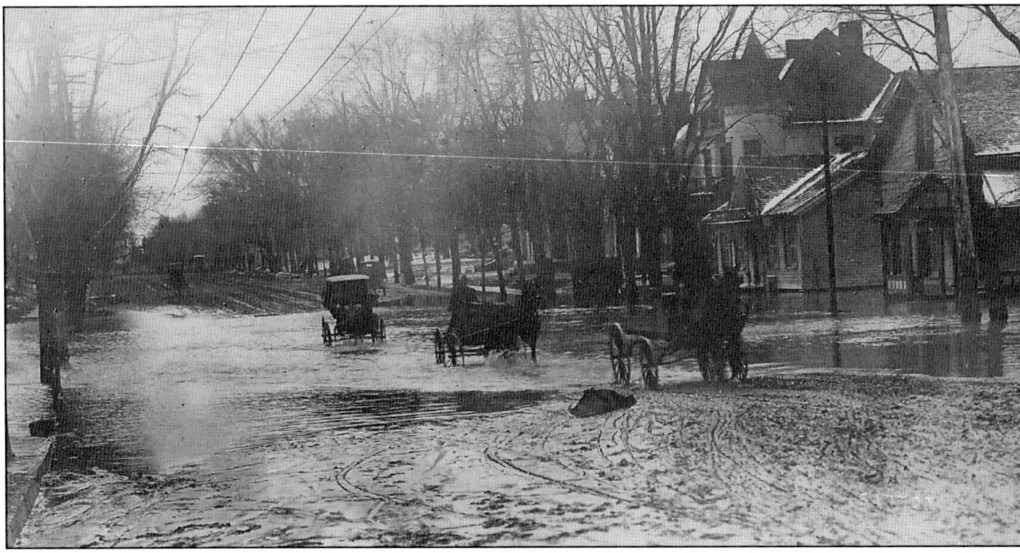

Residents living in higher parts of Troy, especially those living along the ridge on the west side or in areas not flooded, brought loved ones and strangers from flood areas into their homes. Many families took between 15 and 30 people into their houses. People from flooded homes spent lonely days with family members and sometimes their animals on the upper levels of their residences.

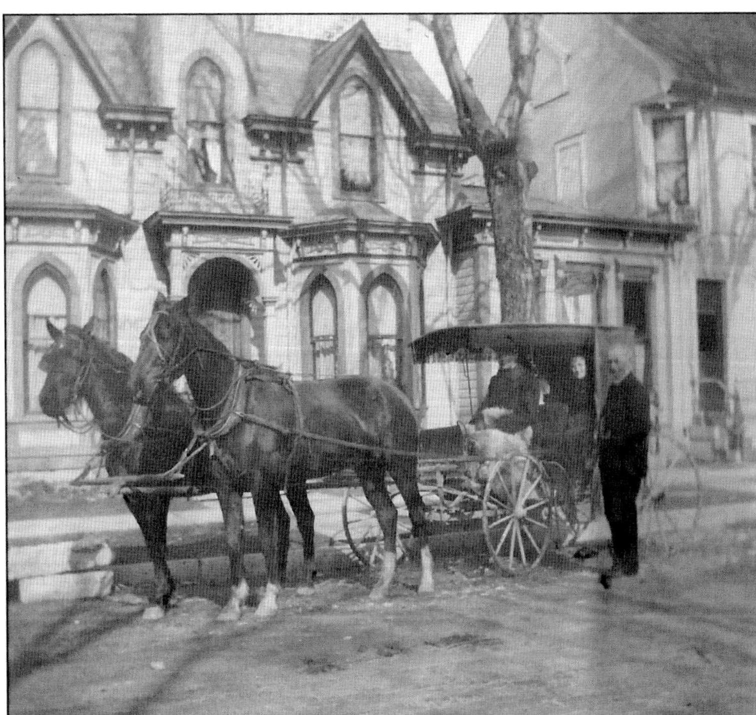

Margaret Zeigenfelder Brown writes, "As dawn was breaking, Rob took us all to generous neighbors who lived at the corner, whose house was built higher from the ground than ours. They began a funny procession of evacuation from our house and our neighbors. Rob had on hip boots to wade through the waters now surrounding our house." Brown spent some of her time during the flood at the Rossiter home, seen here.

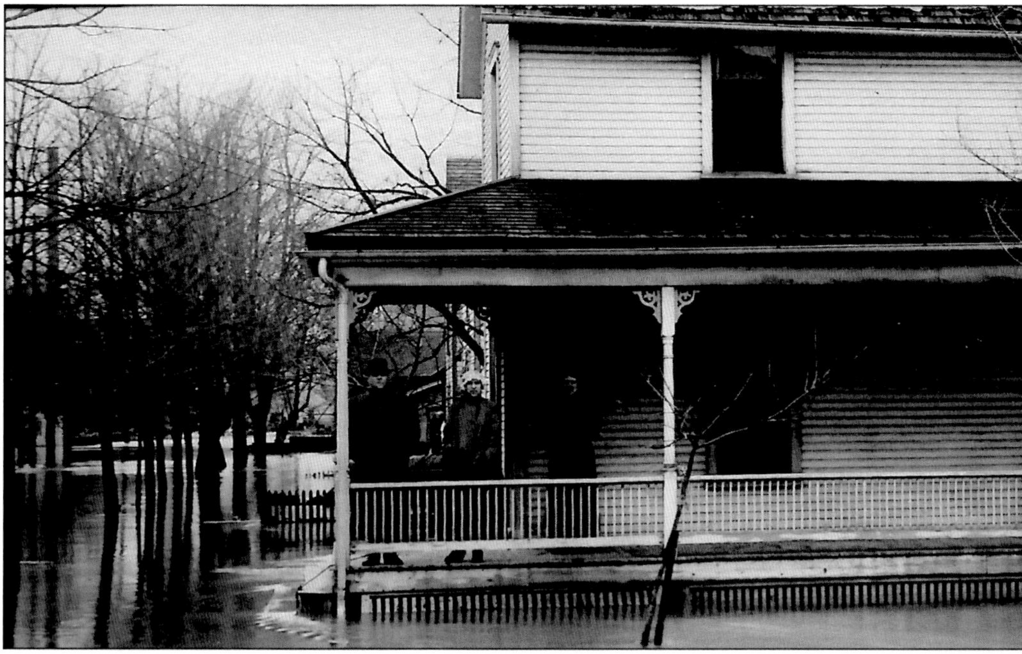

People talked to their neighbors from porches and windows and called the telephone operators for information. An article on the front page of the April 1, 1913, *Troy Record* reads: "One of the greatest troubles experienced by telephone companies at times such as this is the manner in which some of its patrons insist on 'visiting' on the lines. One would think every person in the community would realize the great amount of important messages with which every exchange district is flooded."

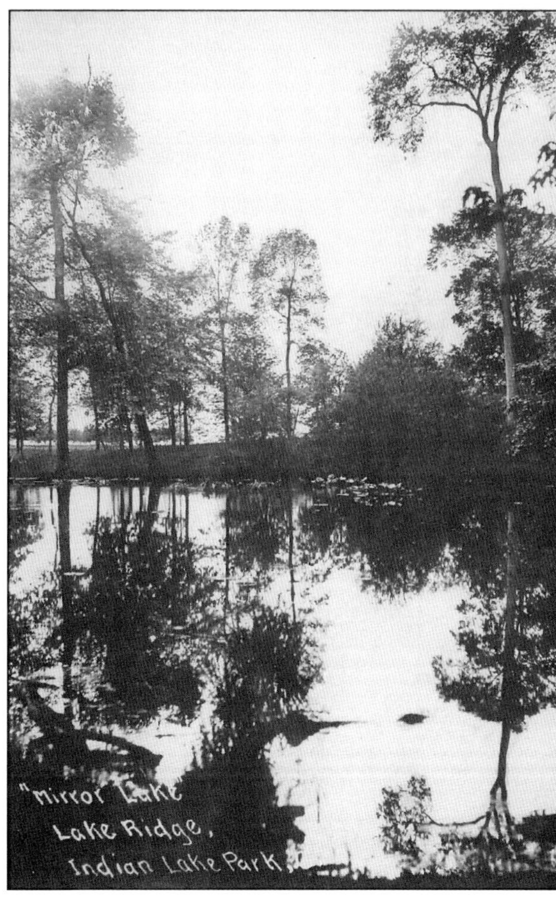

Several rumors gave the townspeople fear. Perhaps the scariest was that the Lewistown Reservoir at Indian Lake in Logan County had broken. Ruth Sharits Weaver remembers, "They did have a report out once that the reservoir had broken up north and we'd all be drown by morning. My sister and I decided we'd go up and stay on the bridge. My mother said, 'You'll go to bed like you always do.'" There had been a small break in the reservoir, but it was repaired.

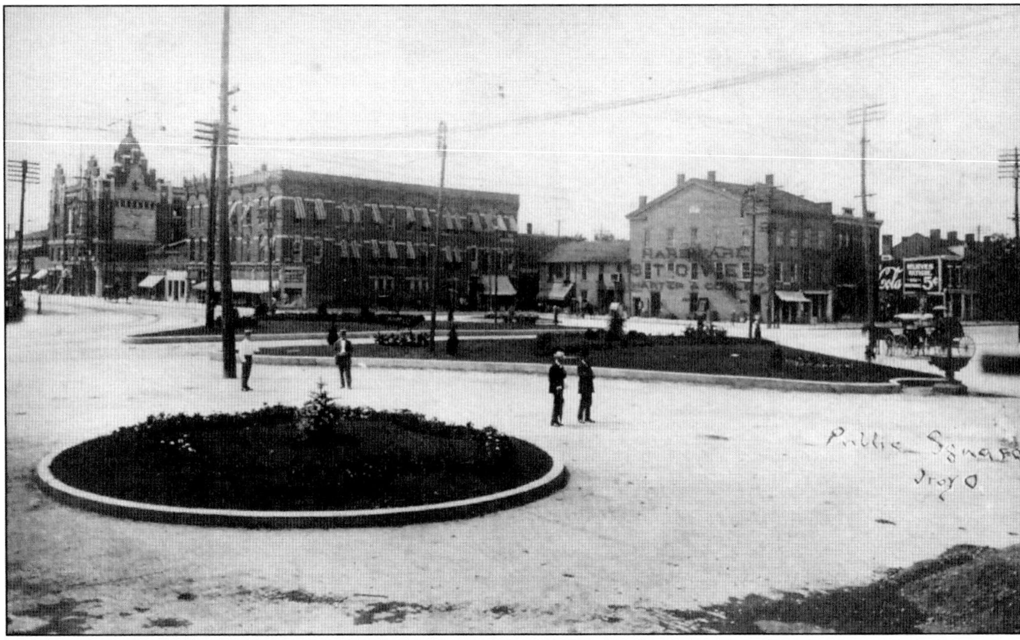

Though downtown Troy is near the Great Miami River, it did not flood. Flooded areas began to the east at about Walnut Street, to the south at about Canal Street, and to the west near Jackson Street. Buildings along Market Street—including the City Building, the Lollis Hotel (now the Morris House), where people traveling through Troy were stranded, and the Interurban Railway office—had little or no water in them.

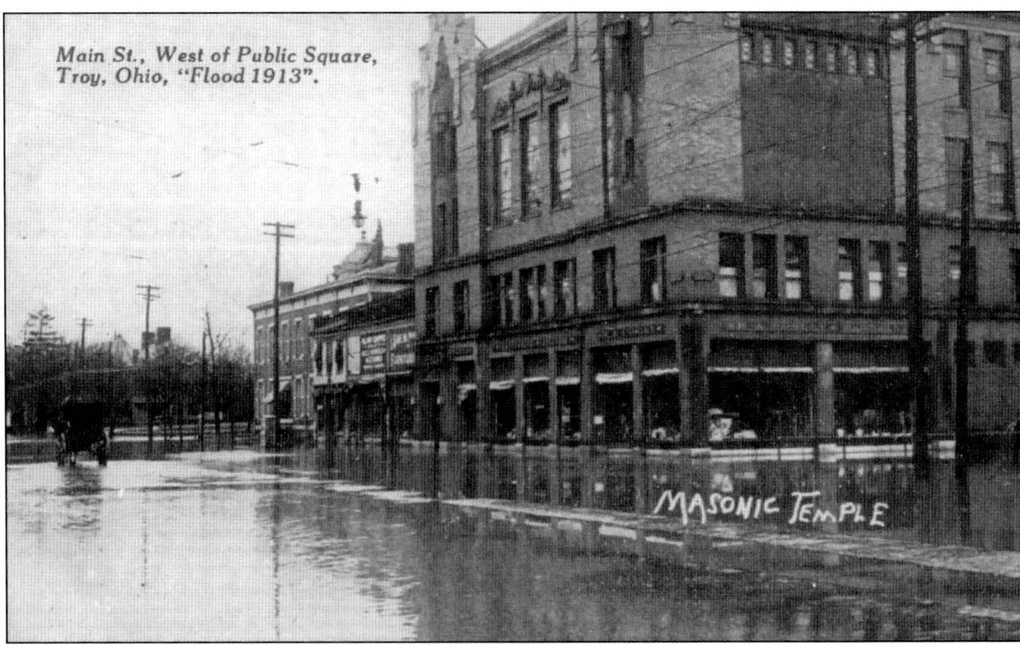

There was water on West Main Street near the Masonic temple, the Miami County Jail, and the Miami County Courthouse, but it was caused by a backed-up sewer system rather than floodwaters. Mary Miller Fish, who lived at 518 West Main Street, remembered that the street was mostly dry in front of her home but she could see rescue boats on the canal from behind her house.

Three

Taking Risks to Rescue Others

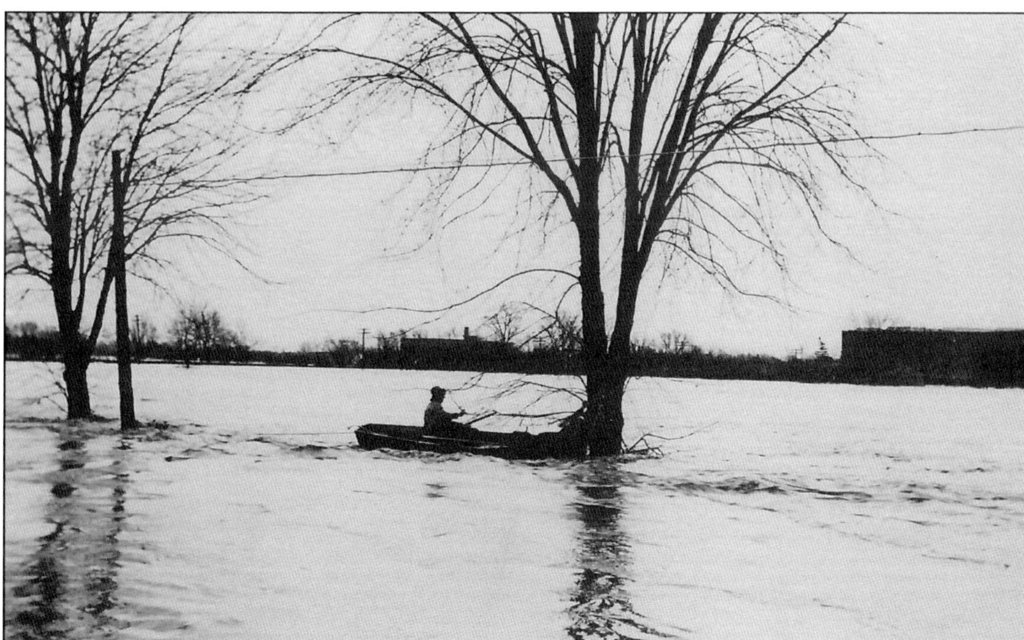

Ordinary people became heroes and heroines during the flood, some risking their lives to save people and animals. Others cared for the injured and sick, organized relief work, and prepared food for the hungry. Over the past century, the names and deeds of most of these brave people have been forgotten and few stories about them remain. This photograph shows a rescue boat near Nineveh.

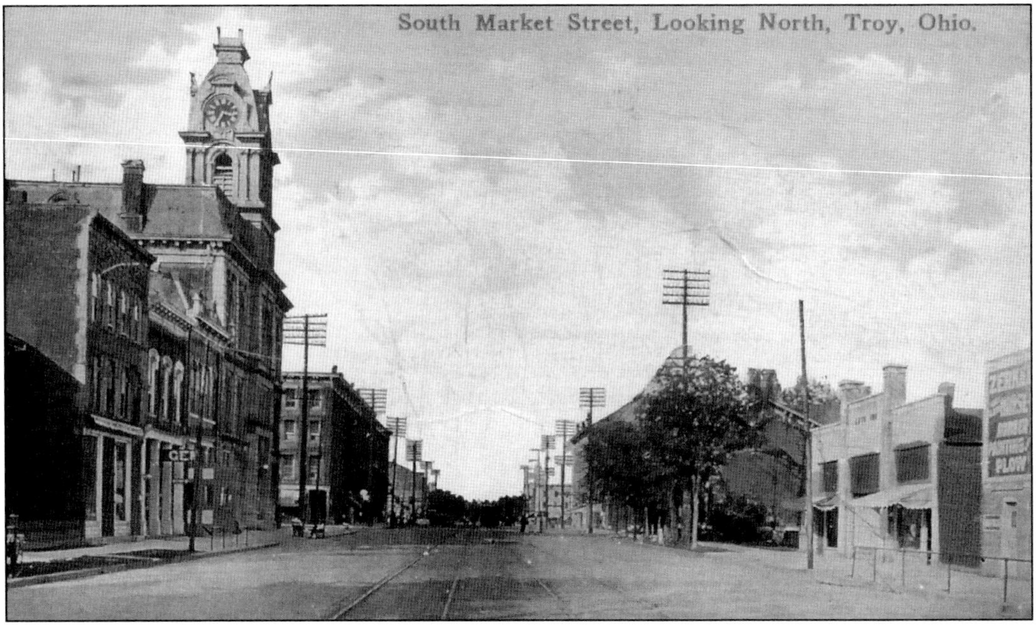

Early on Tuesday morning, Wilbur Chaffee, Howard Reichard, and George Torlina left Chaffee's downtown office and walked to Troy's city hall. There, they found Walter Thomas worried about his brother on Grant Street. Chaffee and Reichard said that if they could get a boat, they would check on his brother. The city hall building with its clock tower is on the left in this postcard.

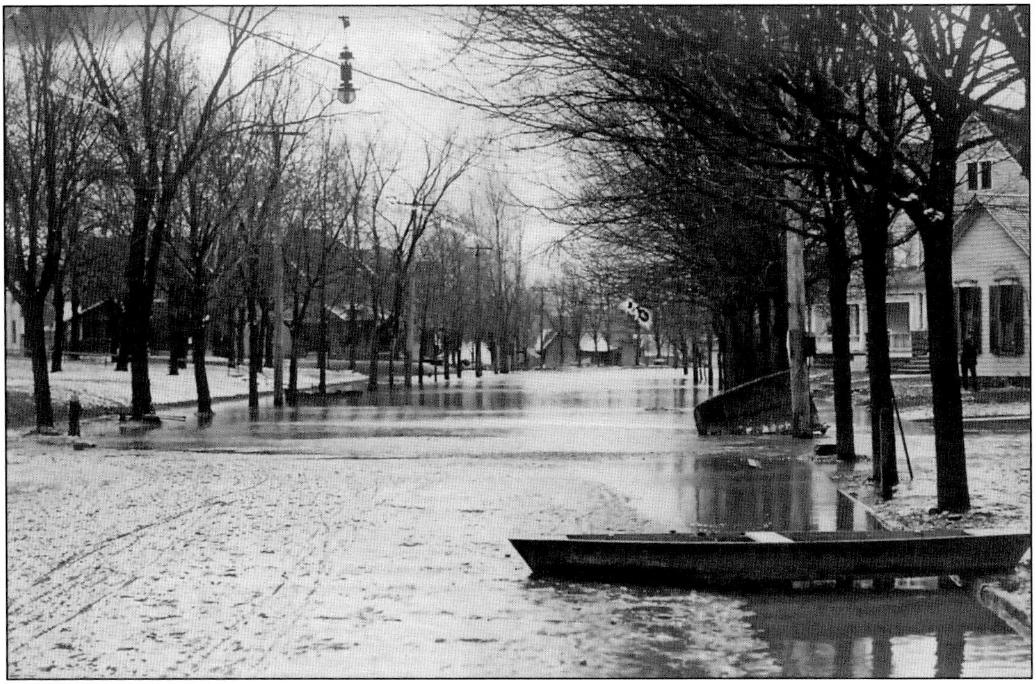

The boat was not in good condition. It had no struts, no seats, and no oarlocks. In the heavy rain of the dark night, the men soon got lost. From somewhere, they heard a man calling for help, and they found Bob Mott clinging to a telephone pole. He had been hanging on to the pole for hours and got into the boat.

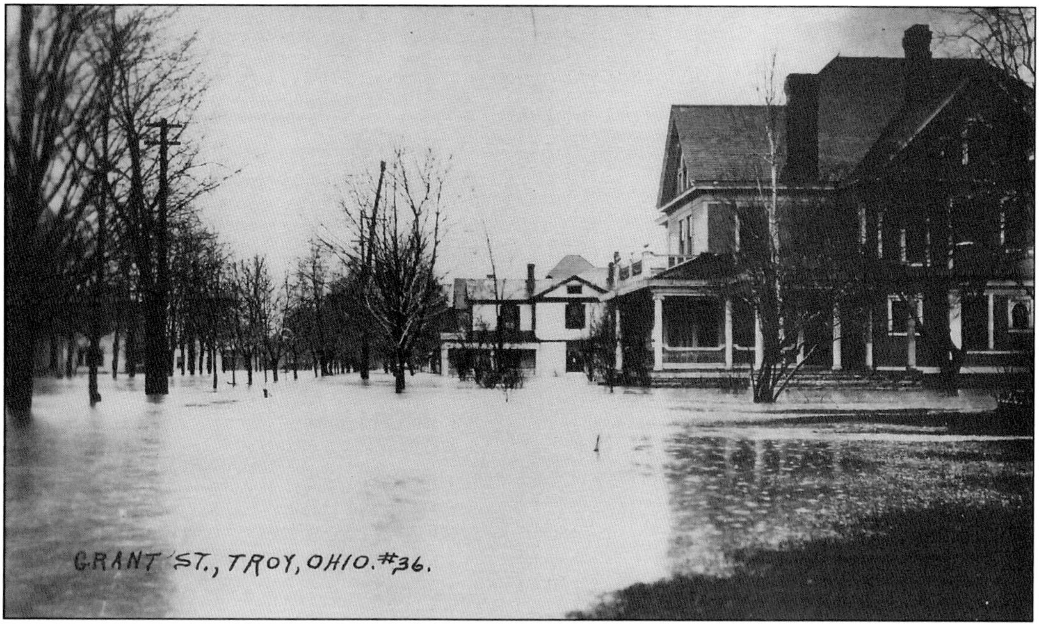

Bob Mott had been trying to help his neighbor, Mary Frances Van Tuyl, who was disabled and separated from her husband and whose cottage house was flooded. Along with Wilbur Chaffee, Howard Reichard, and George Torlina, Mott went to the Van Tuyl house and found Van Tuyl sitting in a wheelchair on top of her bed. Her son was holding it in place so she would not roll off the bed. She did not want to leave her home without the wheelchair, but it was too big to get through the door. It took a lot of persuasion to get her out of the house. Van Tuyl, her son, and Mott were all taken to an apartment owned by L.A. Thomas, the man whose safety they had come to confirm. Thomas's property, seen here, was damaged during the flood, but he and his wife survived.

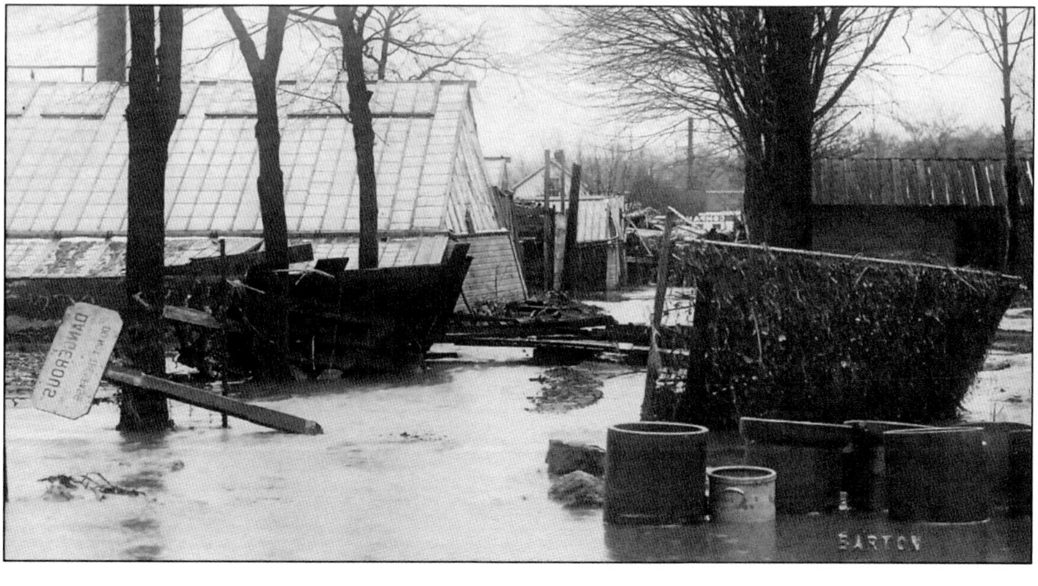

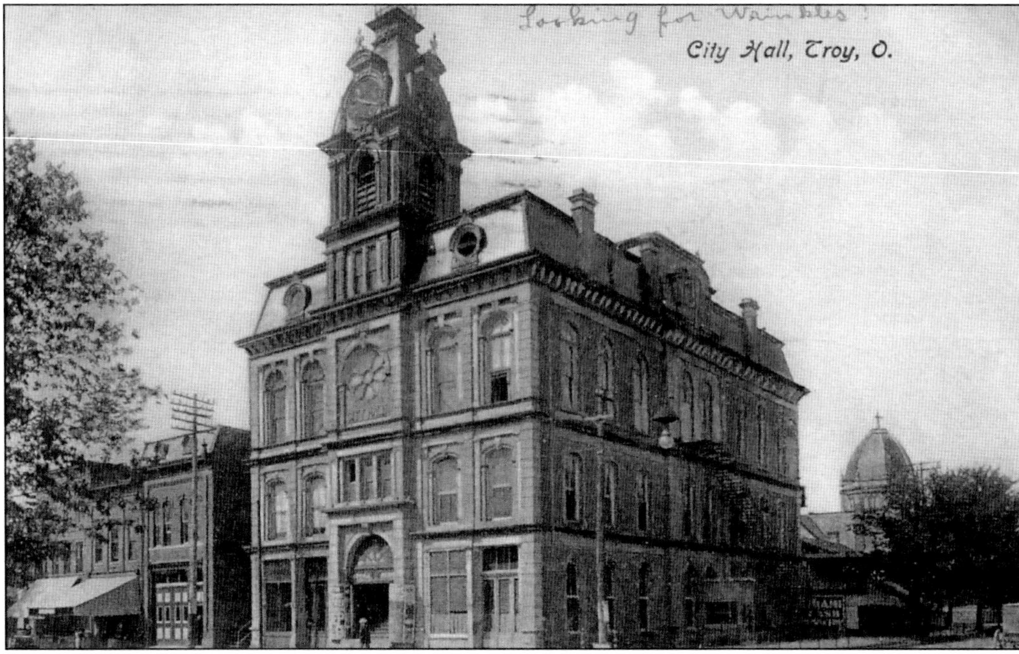

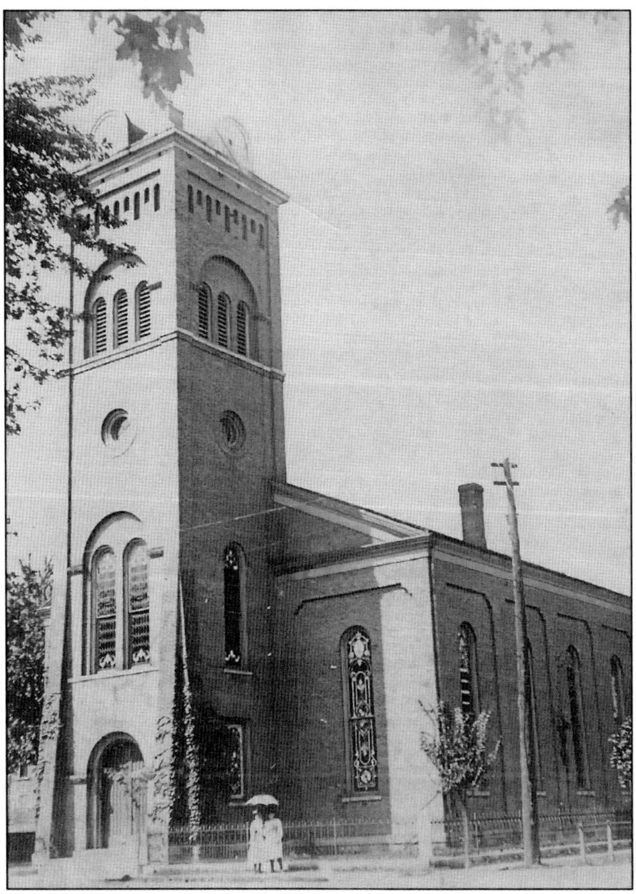

Organized relief work began on Tuesday morning. Headquarters were set up in what was known as the market house, at city hall. The market house, thought to have been a place where local farmers brought their produce to sell, became a food distribution center during the crisis. The Altrurian Club, a women's club that promoted cultural awareness, organized the food for distribution.

A second site of food collection and distribution was the First Presbyterian Church. An article in the April 3, 1913, edition of the *Troy Record* states, "The Presbyterian Church and the market house were used for preparing food that was brought in by citizens and in the homes women were busy cooking and baking food for those deprived of their homes."

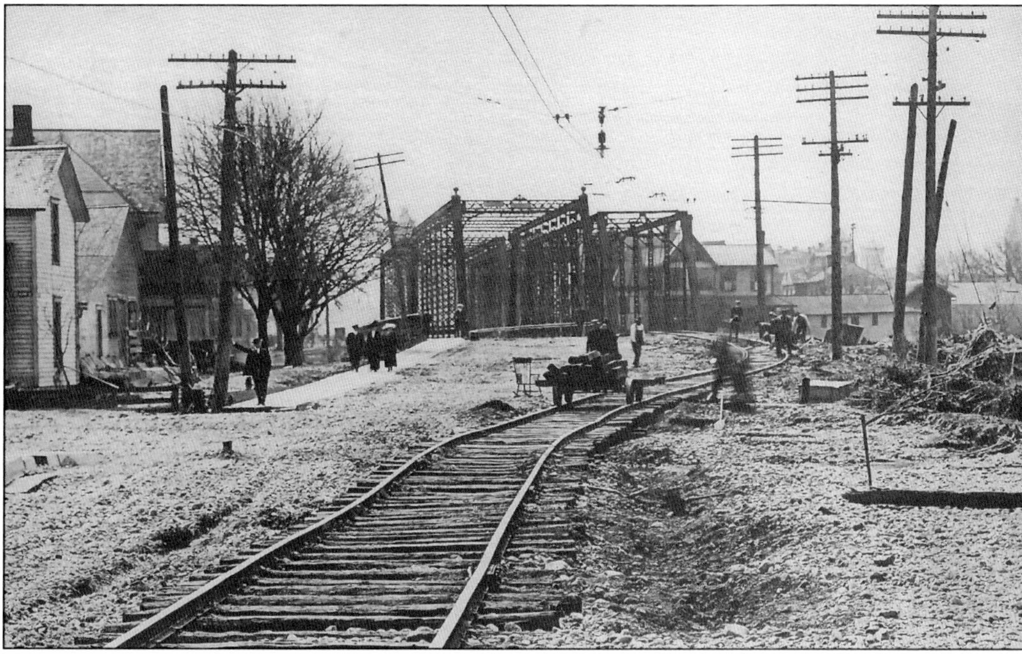

Area farmers supplied food to their flooded neighbors in town. An article remembering the flood in the March 24, 1947, *Troy Daily News* reads, "Quantities of foodstuffs including whole hams, eggs, chickens, and potatoes were brought by them to the western ridge and to a point near Rose Hill Cemetery. At the latter point supplies were picked up by men operating a handcar and brought into town over railroad tracks which were barely above water." A railroad handcar is seen here.

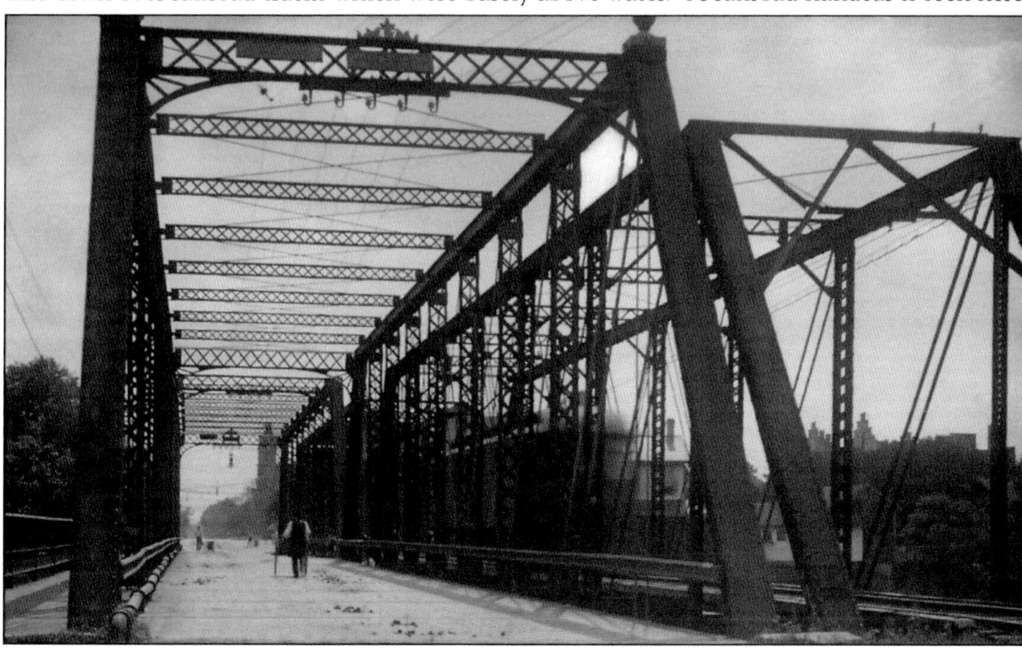

In the early 20th century, the Market Street Bridge was a double bridge, with one side used as a road for ordinary traffic—horses, wagons, and automobiles—and the other side for the two interurban railways servicing the town.

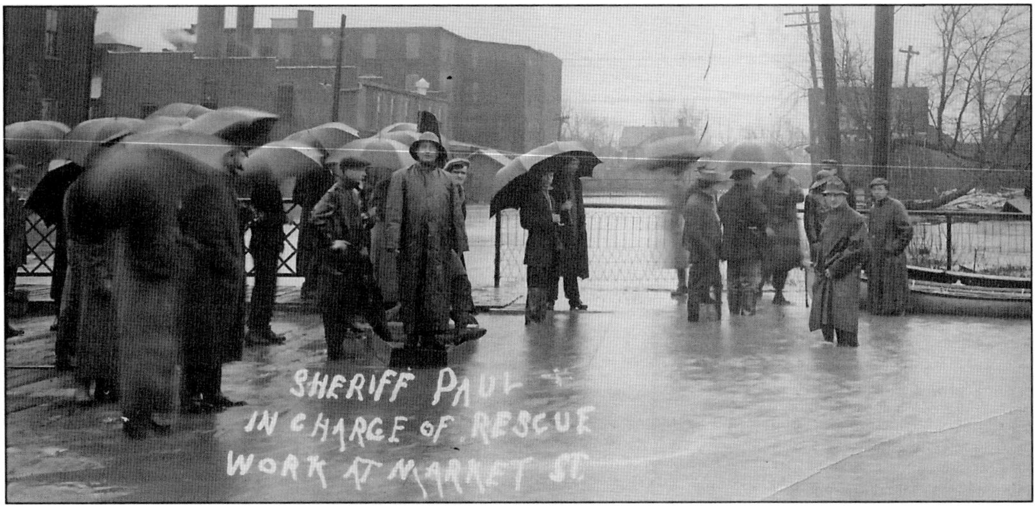

Boat rescue operations were under the direction of Miami County sheriff Louis Paul. Paul was elected to his second term of office in November 1912. Other officials involved in the flood were John McClain, mayor of Troy; J. Wilby Davis, safety director; Gilbert Hatfield, service director; John Headley, police chief; and Rollo Sharp, fire chief.

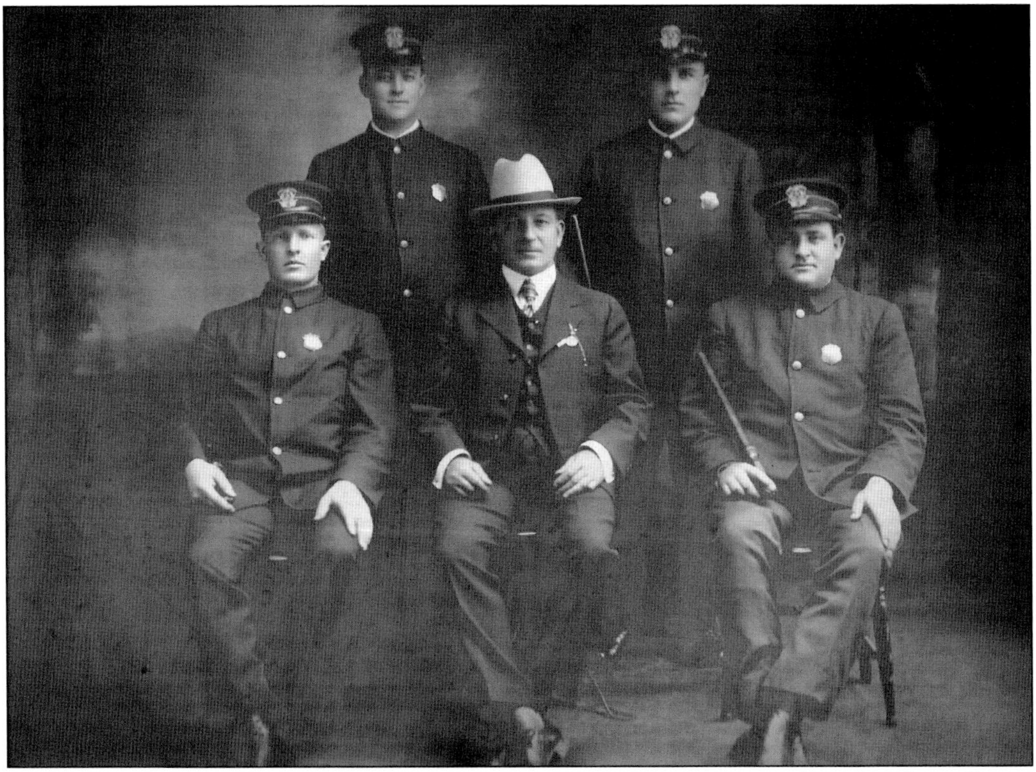

Troy chief of police Louis Paul (center, in hat) poses for a c. 1916 photograph with police officers, some of whom may have been on flood rescue teams in 1913. It is believed that Paul sent out teams of men in boats to work assigned sections of town in 1913, when he was Miami County sheriff. According to the March 25, 1963, *Troy Daily News*, "Sheriff Louis Paul and his men traveled in boats rescuing all they could."

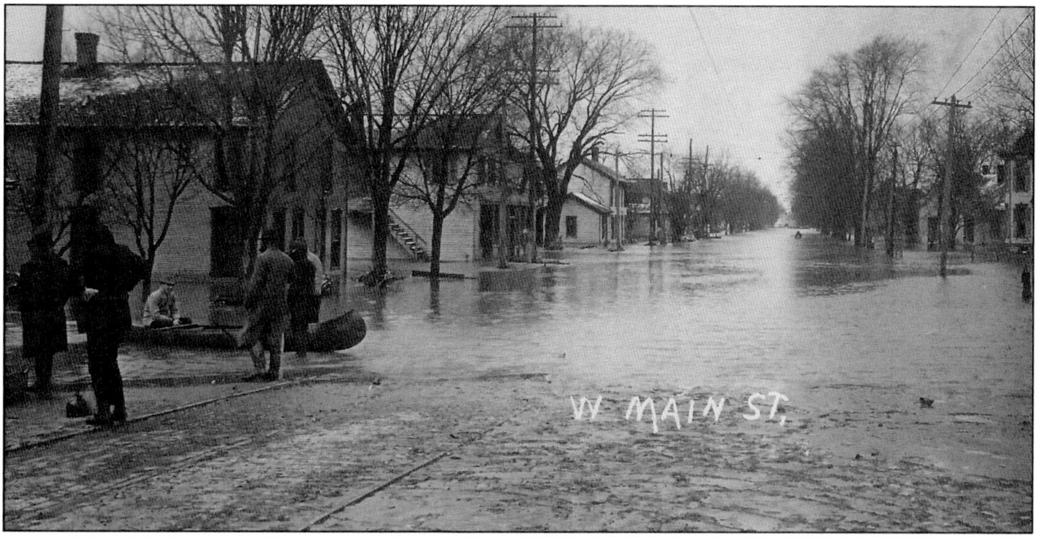

One of the first tasks of the boat rescue team was to find boats and canoes. At first, the men had only a few. People from outside of Troy came to help, including Rev. Charles H. Ashman and two other young men from Pleasant Hill. The April 3, 1913, *Miami Union* reports, "These men in a pouring rain were busy all day saving homeless and suffering people."

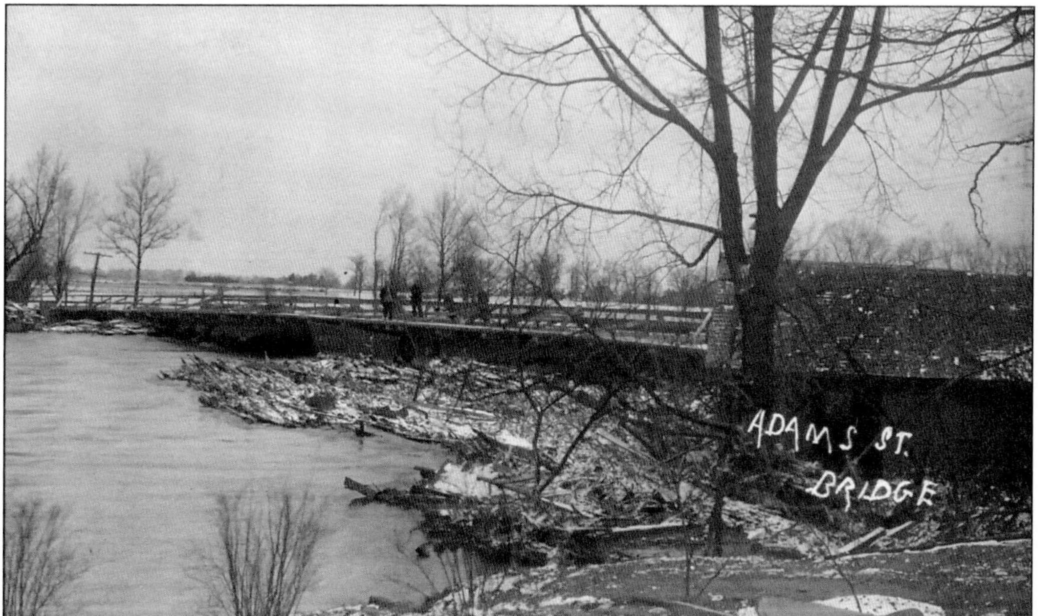

A boathouse north of the Adams Street Bridge broke loose from its foundation and crashed into the bridge. Rescuers John Sharits and Otto Sedan removed part of the building's roof and pulled out six boats and oars for rescue use.

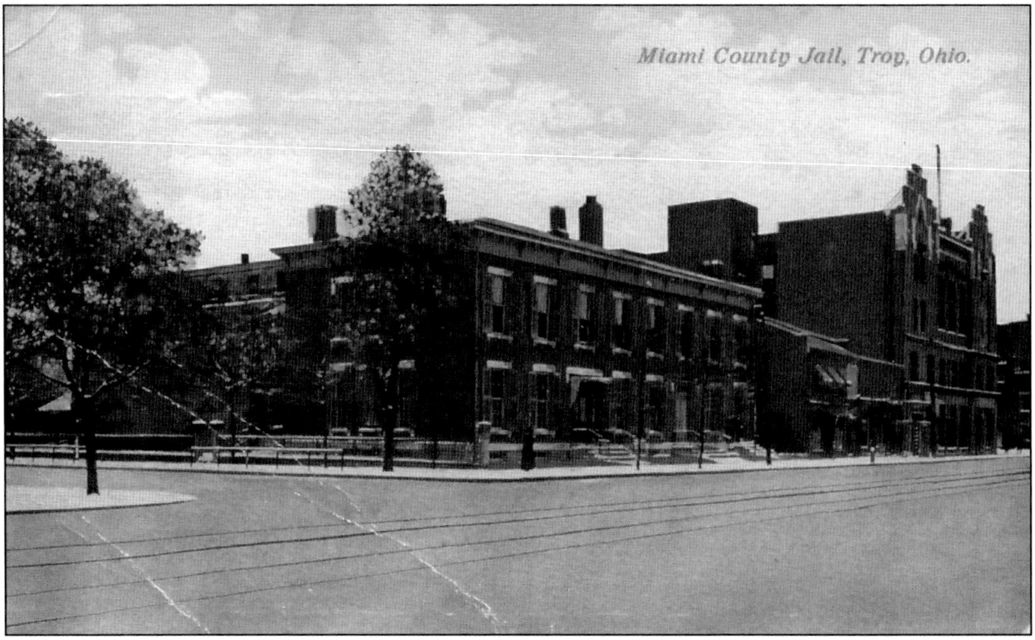

Men were released from both the Miami County Jail and the Troy City Jail to help with the rescue effort. The April 4, 1913, *Troy Record* includes an article about a young man at the city jail who pleaded with officials to help rescue people. The newspaper refers to him as "Sailor Jack" and tells about the lives he saved.

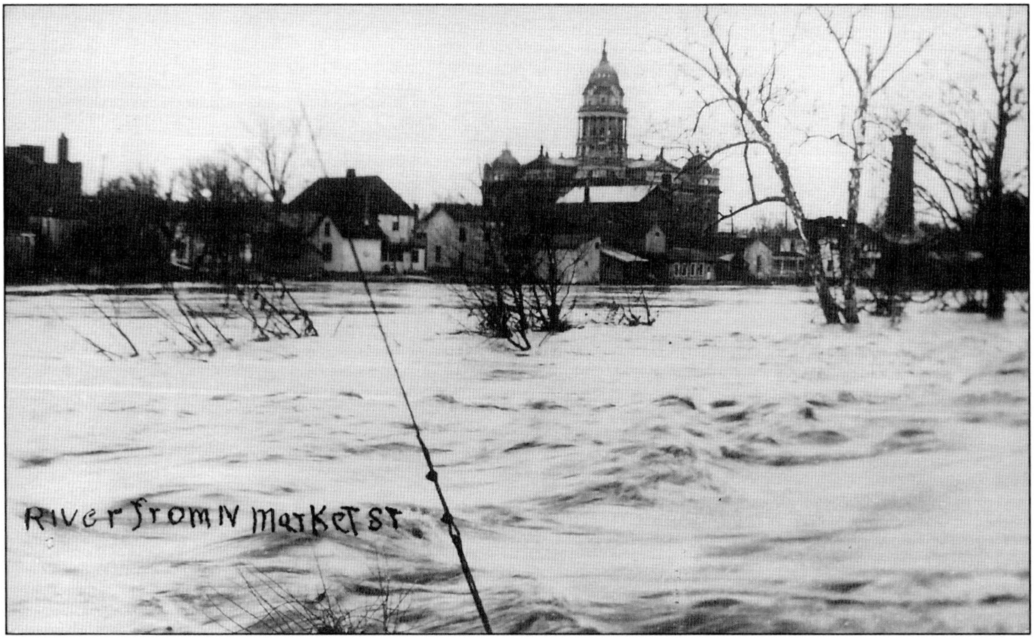

The story of "Sailor Jack" is similar to that of Otto "Slim" Sedan, who also was passing through Troy and at the city jail for unknown reasons. Sedan did not leave Troy after the flood; in fact, he eventually married a Troy lady and was known as a flood hero. Details of Sedan's rescues were published in the *Troy Daily News* on March 24, 1947. The Great Miami River is seen here during the flood.

Alfred Bretland, a former English seaman, is credited with rescuing 385 people and their pets. An article about Bretland in the March 24, 1947, edition of the *Troy Daily News* reads, "Some women had to be dragged from their roofs. Some men were passed up cold although waving greenbacks as an inducement to him. These, he explained were in perfectly safe houses, although surrounded by water." (Courtesy of Judy Hemmert.)

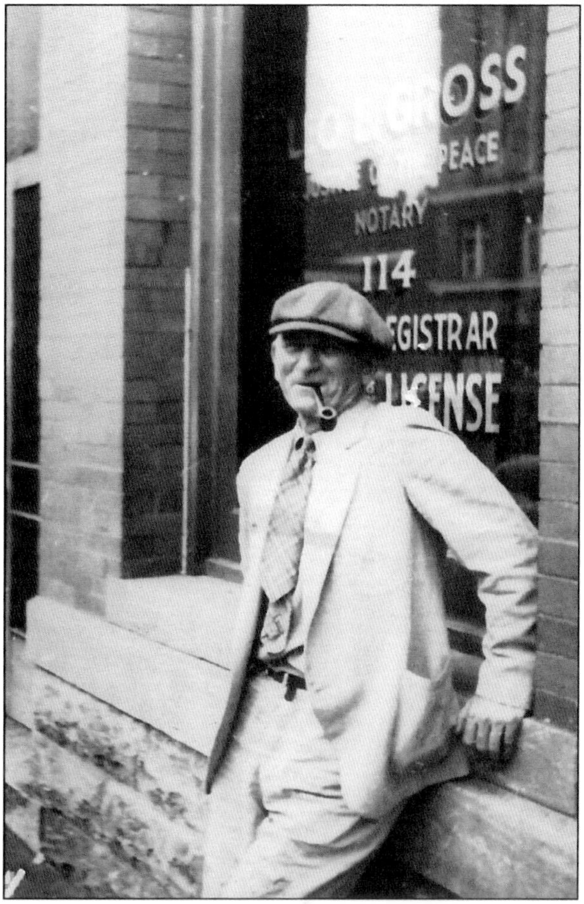

The March 29, 1913, *Troy Record* reports, "Three boats full of people, including Mrs. Harry Johnson and her sister had a thrilling ride. They were cut loose from houses on West Market Street and allowed to drift with current. They landed on South Mulberry Street, near the residence of T.J. Enyeart."

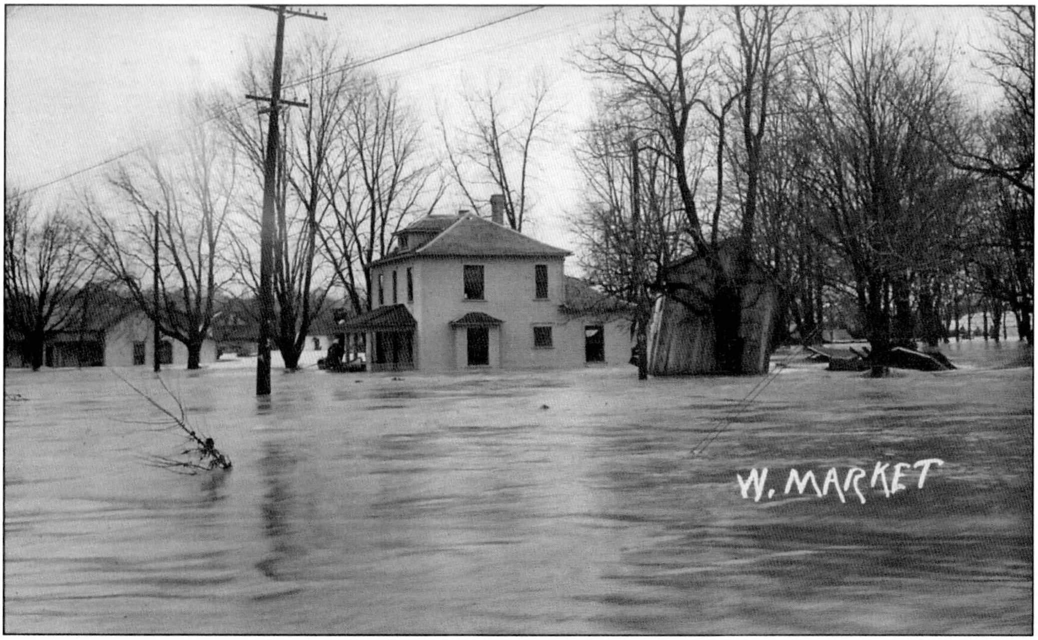

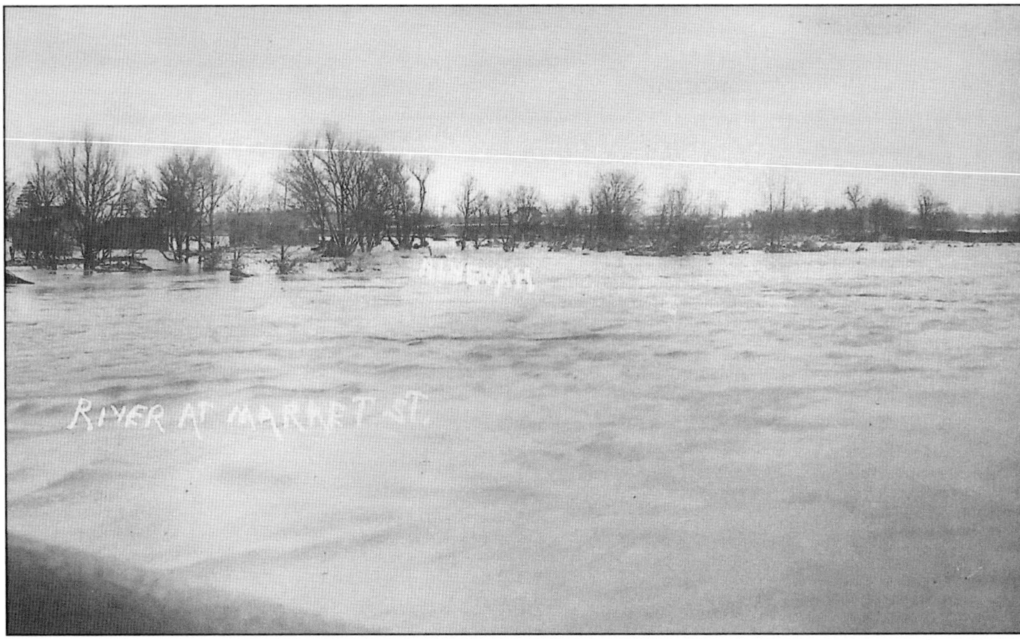

From Monday until Wednesday, cries for help were heard coming from the predominately African American community of Nineveh, where four people clung to a tree as water swept through the area. The four were pool hall owner Reuben Jones (also known as Edward Jones), Olive Bolden, Lydia White, and 13-year-old Josephine Stewart. Swift water currents near Nineveh made attempts to save them difficult.

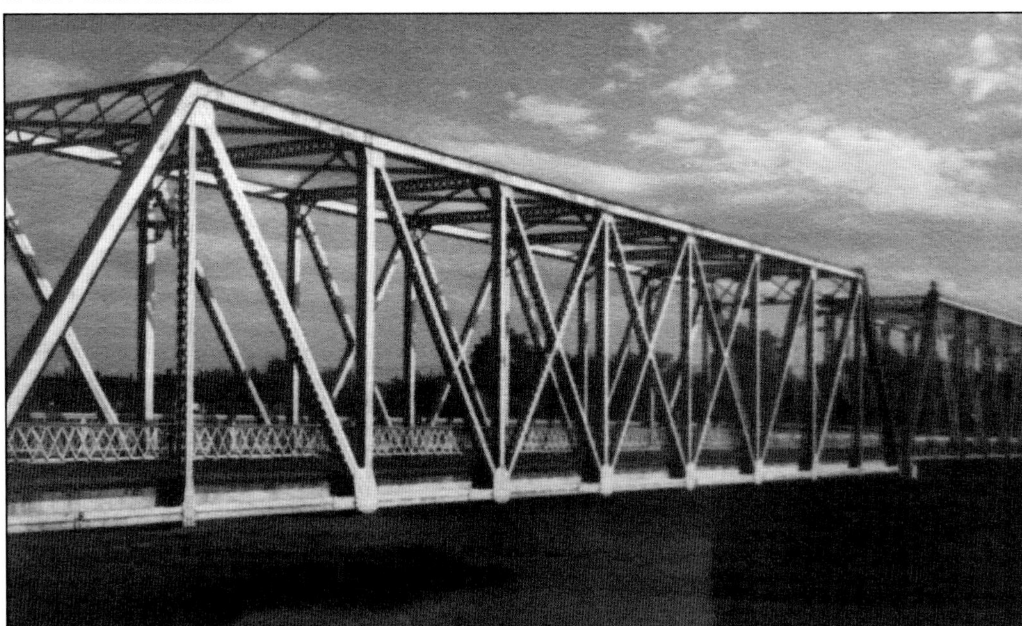

The first person to try rescuing them was Harrison Dorsey, an employee of the Hayner Distillery. He thought the current would take his boat to the tree and he could get them. Instead, the current carried his boat toward a bridge. Men on the bridge pulled him to safety just before the boat collided with the bridge.

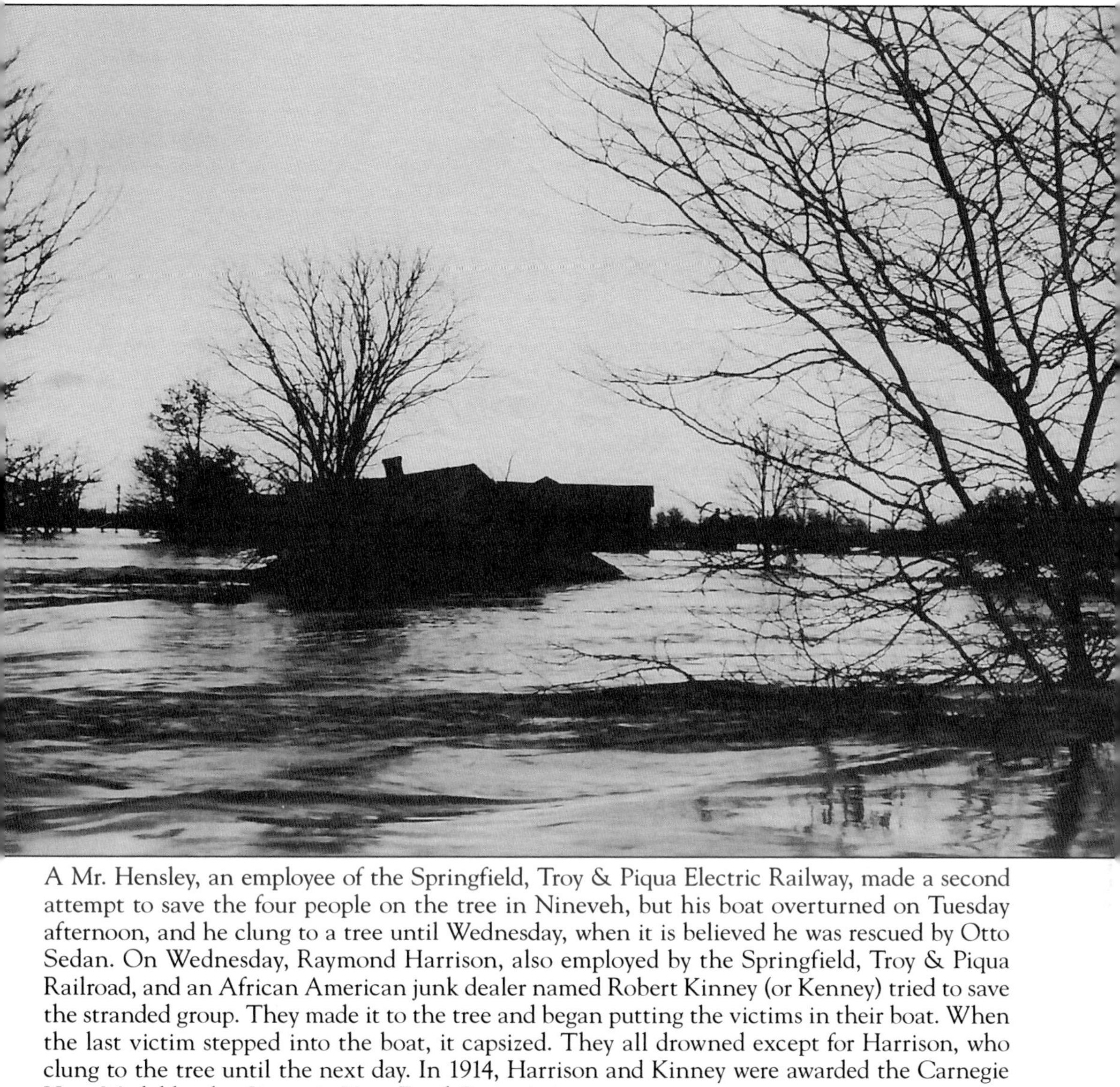

A Mr. Hensley, an employee of the Springfield, Troy & Piqua Electric Railway, made a second attempt to save the four people on the tree in Nineveh, but his boat overturned on Tuesday afternoon, and he clung to a tree until Wednesday, when it is believed he was rescued by Otto Sedan. On Wednesday, Raymond Harrison, also employed by the Springfield, Troy & Piqua Railroad, and an African American junk dealer named Robert Kinney (or Kenney) tried to save the stranded group. They made it to the tree and began putting the victims in their boat. When the last victim stepped into the boat, it capsized. They all drowned except for Harrison, who clung to the tree until the next day. In 1914, Harrison and Kinney were awarded the Carnegie Hero Medal by the Carnegie Hero Fund Commission.

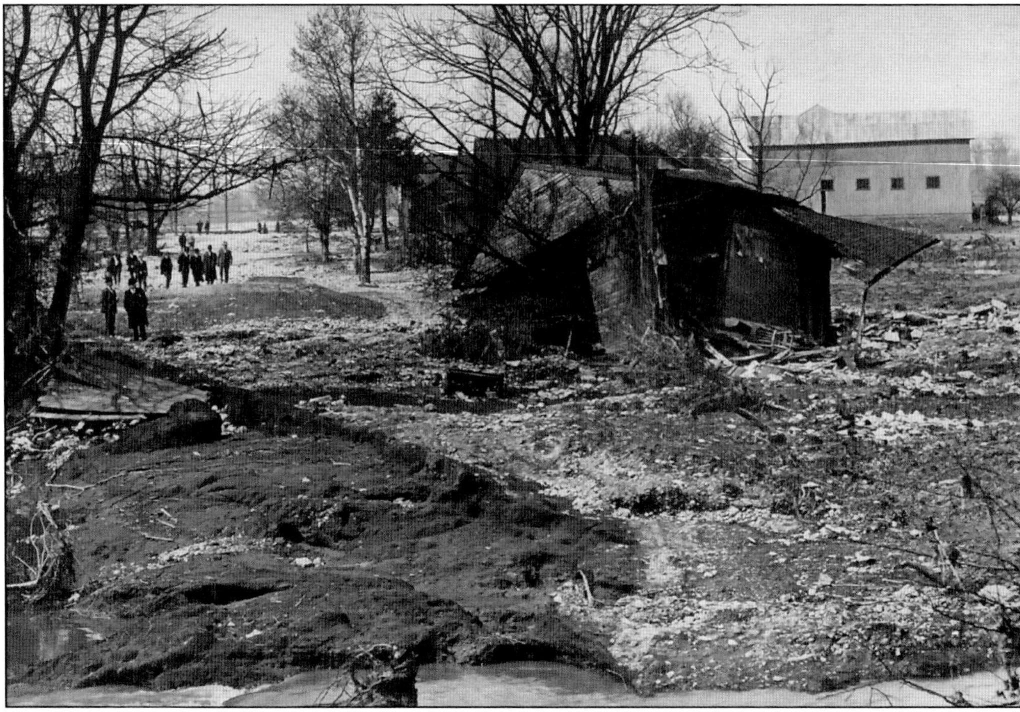

These Nineveh buildings were wrecked by floodwater. The Stewart family and their friend Solomon Liggens were trapped in the Stewart home for three days without food or heat. They put bed slats across the door to keep it from breaking open. Before a rescue boat could arrive, 87-year-old Annie Stewart died of exposure.

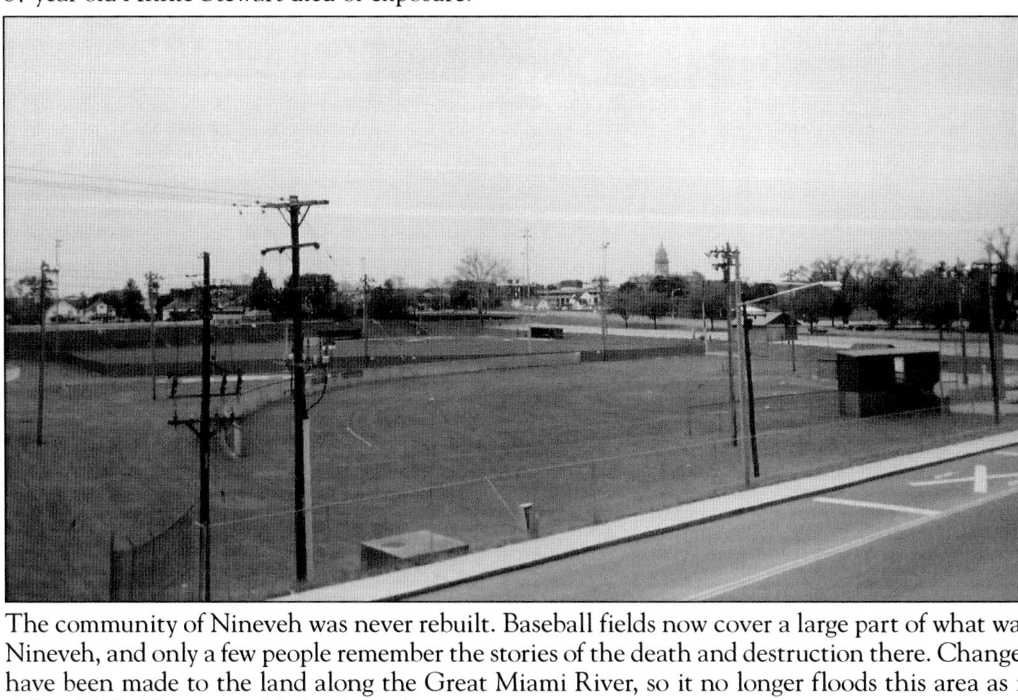

The community of Nineveh was never rebuilt. Baseball fields now cover a large part of what was Nineveh, and only a few people remember the stories of the death and destruction there. Changes have been made to the land along the Great Miami River, so it no longer floods this area as it did in 1913. (Courtesy of Judy Deeter.)

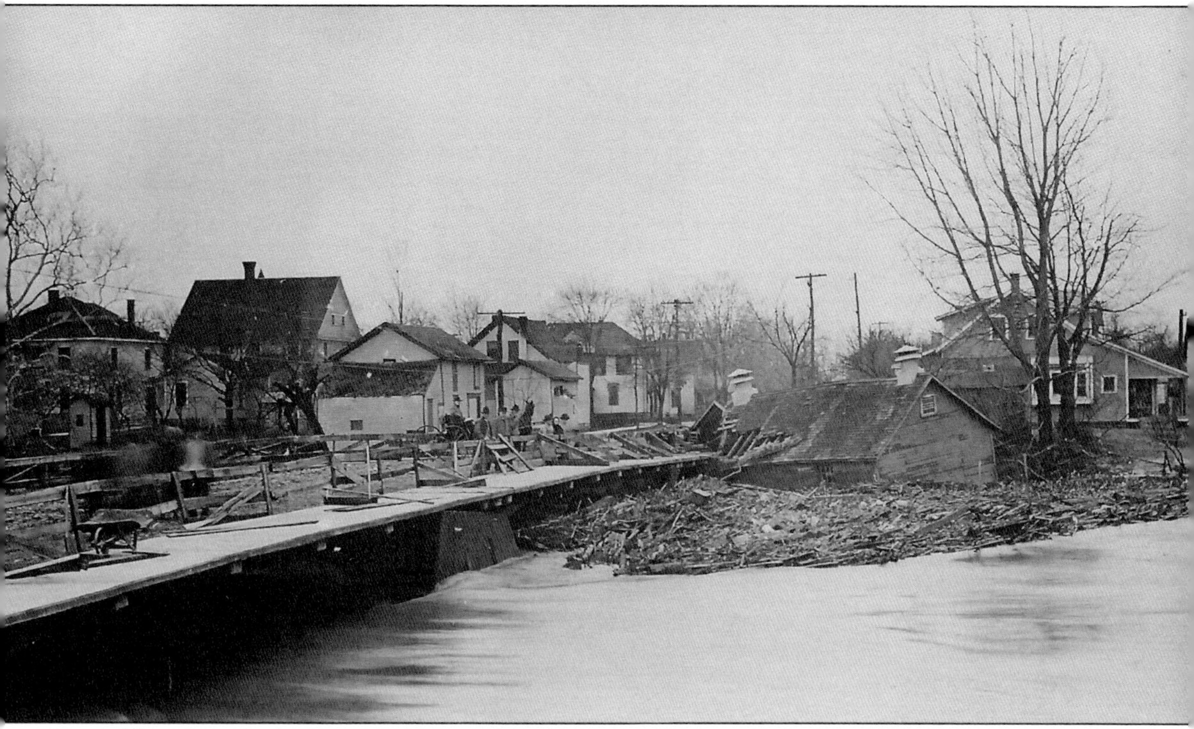

Several buildings broke loose from their foundations and came through Troy. This photograph shows a building struck on the Adams Street Bridge. John Katz of Lockington, Ohio, had to ride a rooftop downstream from northern Miami County. The rooftop caught on a tree at Eldean, north of Troy. Katz could not reach land there so he pushed away from the tree and rode on to Troy, landing near the Cincinnati, Hamilton & Dayton Railroad Bridge and receiving care at the Troy Eagles Hall.

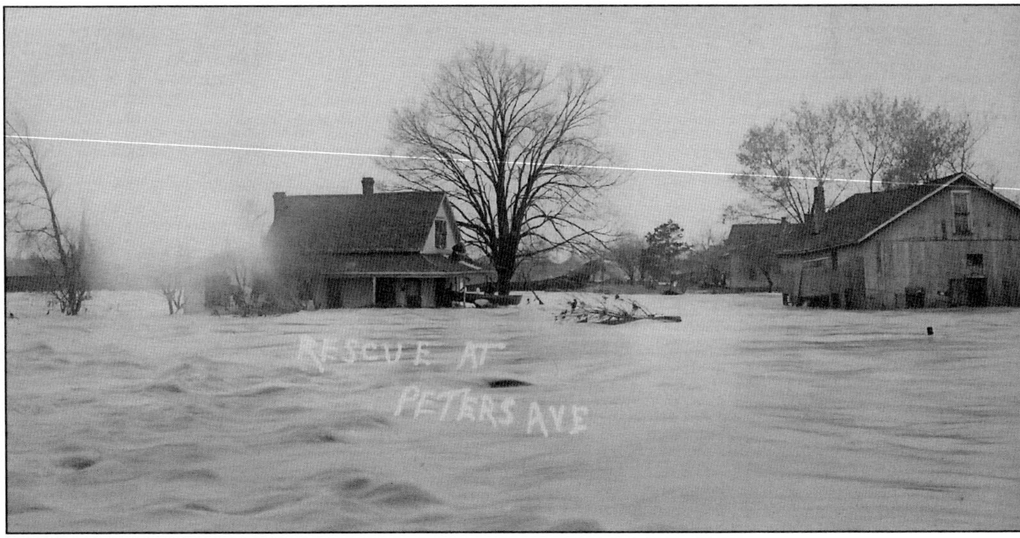

Flood survivors remembered the rescue at the Ed Bowman home near West Market Street and Peters Avenue. Neighbors could see a light in the house, but they did not know how to bring the stranded people to safety. Both Bowman family members and friends are believed to have been inside the house. This photograph shows the rescue in progress.

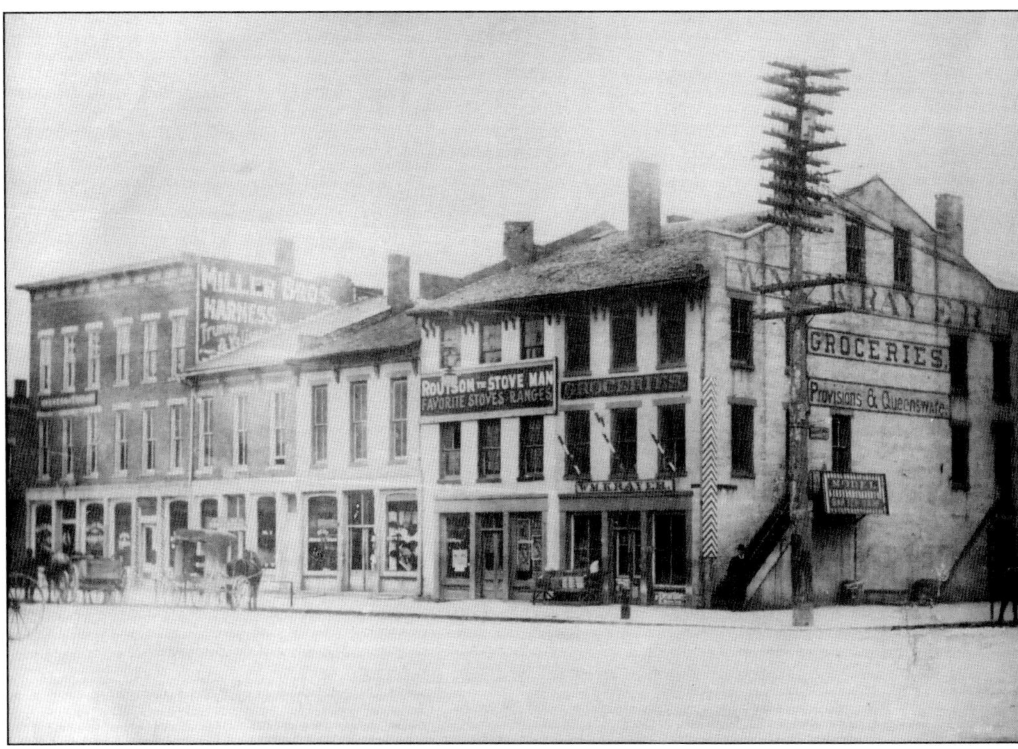

Eventually, rescuers got a long, coil rope from the Miller Brothers, a Troy harness dealer and manufacturer. The rope is believed to have been 500 to 600 feet long. Only about 300 feet was needed for the rescue, but the Miller Brothers did not want the rope cut; they hoped to sell it after the rescue operation was complete. The Miller Brothers store is seen here at left.

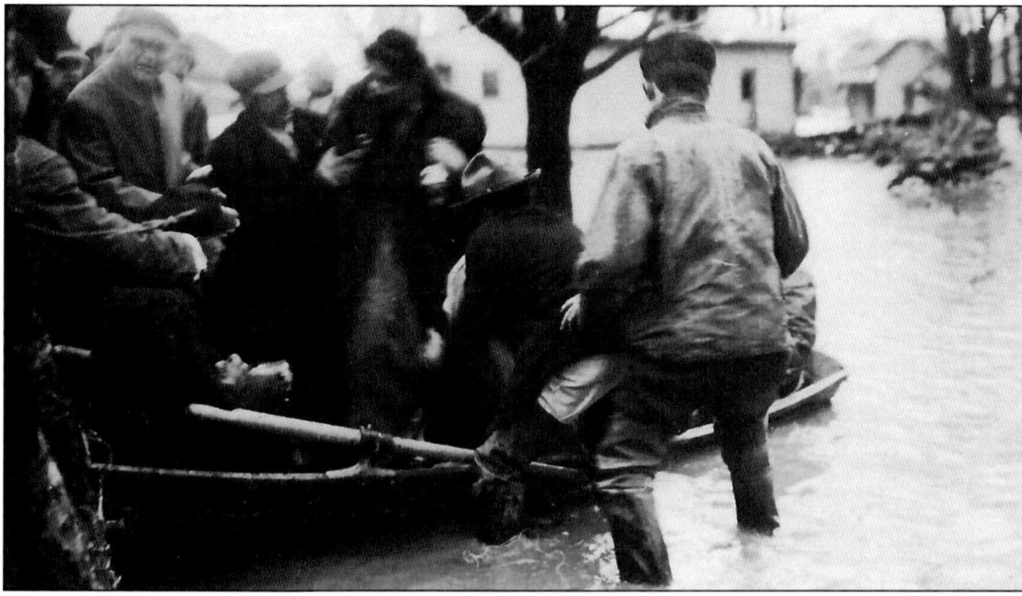

The Miller Brothers' rope was tied to a timber in a house on West Market Street. Rescuers let their boat drift to the Bowman house, victims got into the boat from a second-story window, and the rope pulled them to safety at the house on West Market Street. This photograph shows an unidentified woman being rescued from the Bowman home.

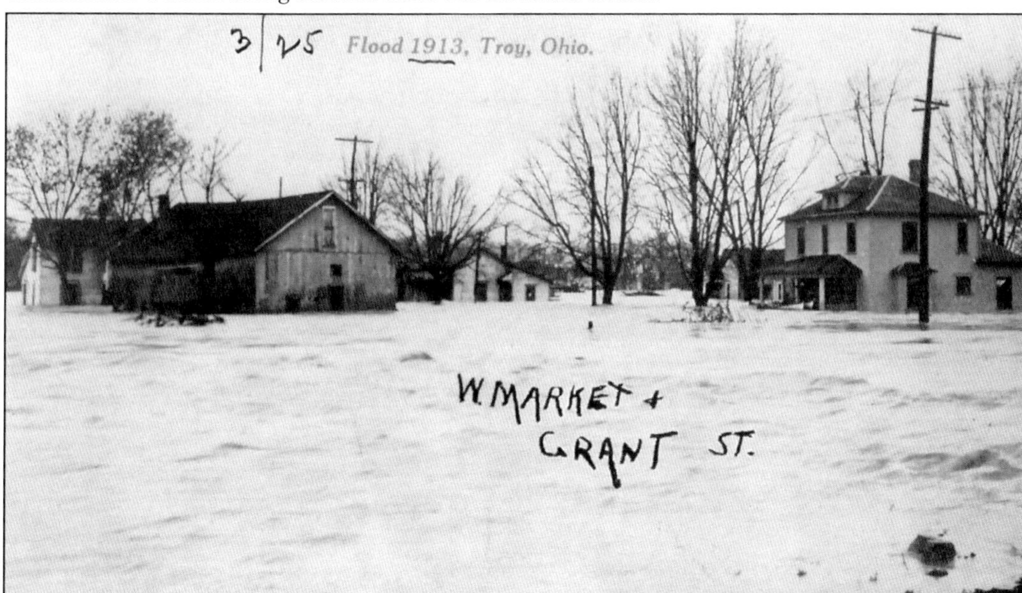

Near the Bowman home, the Big Four Railroad had built a high-rail embankment—believed to have been south of what is now the intersection of West Market Street, Grant Street, and Peters Avenue. The embankment acted as a dam, keeping floodwater high in Troy. There had also been erosion problems at a nearby open trench known as the McKaig Ditch. Officials decided to use dynamite to make a hole in the embankment so water could flow south, bringing the water level down. Troy public safety director J. Wilby Davis likely gave the order to use dynamite. Elmer Thomson, a local undertaker, is thought to have set it off.

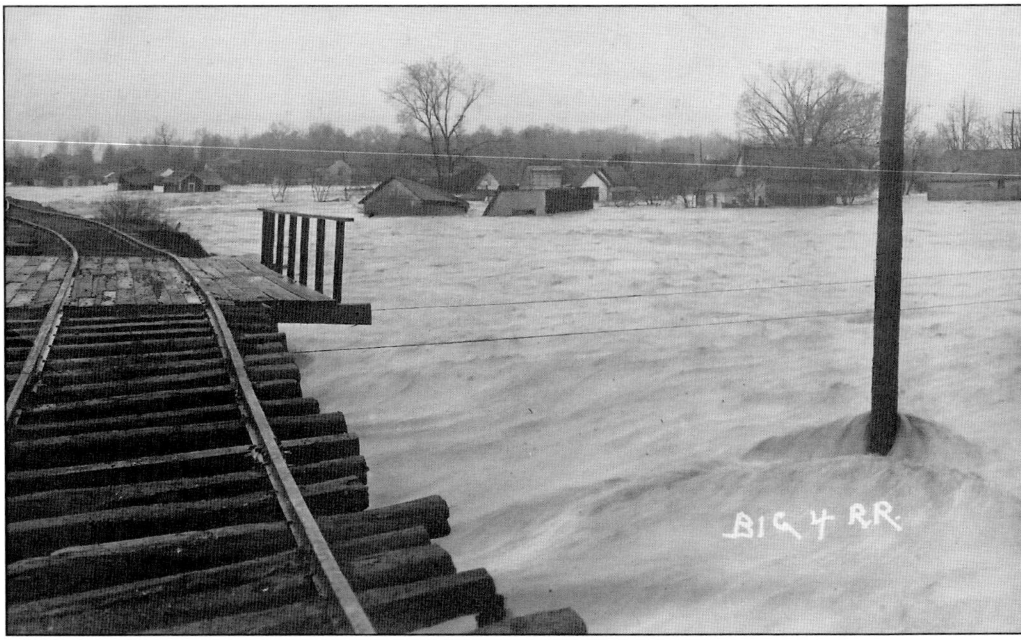

Against strong opposition from railroad employee Frank Colley, George Snyder and Muggins Kelley got dynamite from Peters Nursery and blew a hole was in the embankment. Snyder's grandfather, Civil War veteran Henry Van Tuyl, had separated from his wife and was living in a greenhouse near the blast site. Snyder had asked his grandfather to leave the building, but Van Tuyl refused. When the dynamite went off, the greenhouse turned over and Van Tuyl was killed. The greenhouse building is seen on its side above. The March 29, 1913, *Troy Record* reports that "Henry Van Tuyl lost his life thru his refusal to leave his home in the greenhouse at the east end of Halters' blacksmith shop on West Market Street. Later the house was lifted from its foundation and landed nearly on its side near the Big Four embankment. The water nearly covered the house Tuesday noon, and he was drowned." Nearby, the Peters Road cottage of George and John Glass was also destroyed, and both men drowned.

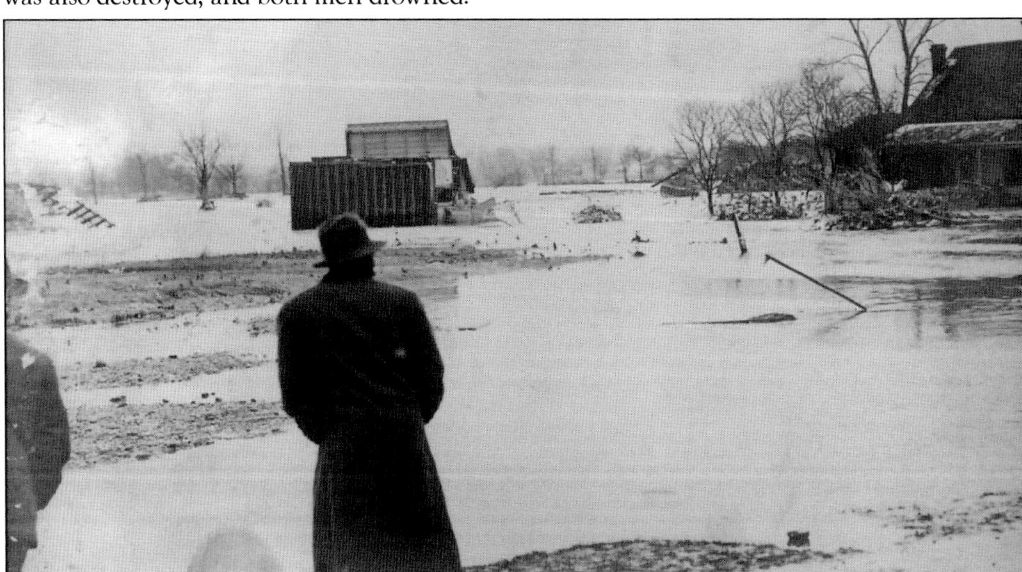

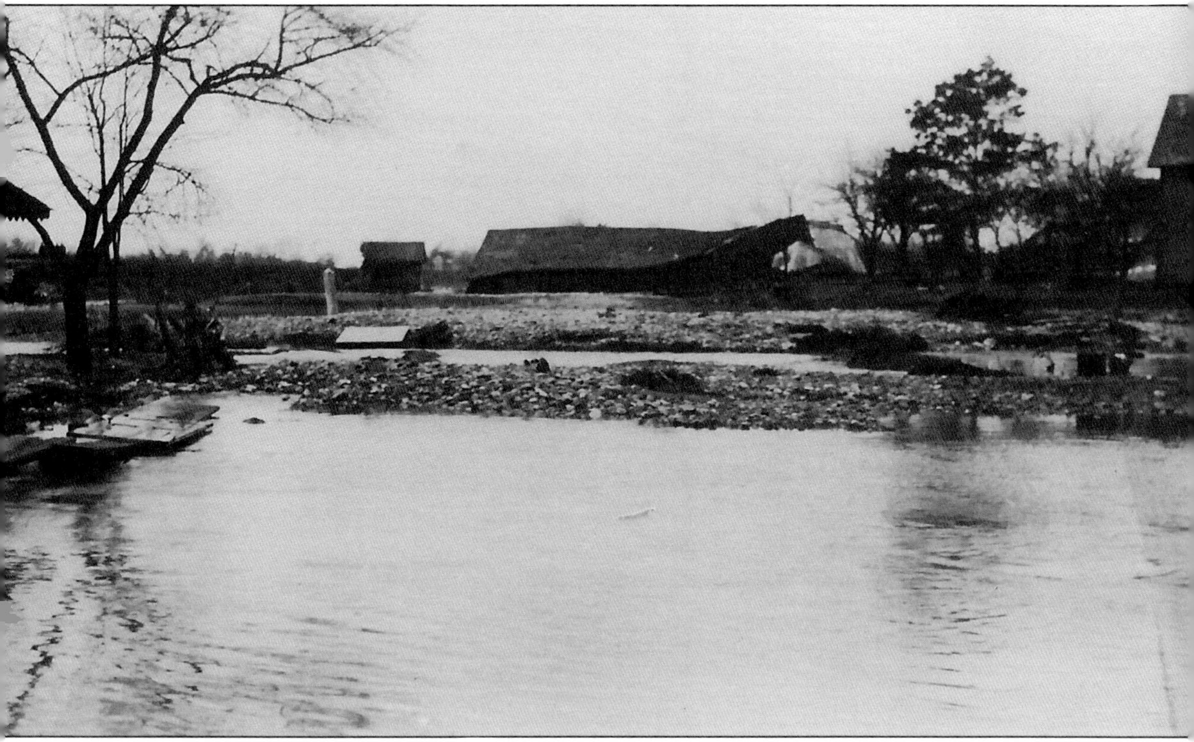

This view looks south from Race Street onto Garfield Avenue. Wilbur Curtis, Billy Quick, and Eugene Tilman rescued Aaron and Gertrude Smock and their one-year-old son Franklin from their home on Garfield Avenue. The rescuers had planned to row the Smocks up Garfield Avenue to safety, but the water current suddenly changed, and the boat moved south to West Market Street and toward the Big Four Railroad embankment. Anxious to stop the boat from heading south, the rescuers caught on to a small fruit tree and tied the boat to the tree. The strength of the water—and probably the weight of the boat and passengers—caused the tree to uproot and the boat to capsize in front of horrified witnesses. The Smocks drowned. Quick clung to a honey locust tree. He sat crying in the tree until the next day. It even snowed while he was in the tree. Tilman caught a floating rooftop and was rescued by Frank Sharits. Curtis took off his boots and swam with the current to the Francis family home on Swailes Road, where he was also rescued by Sharits.

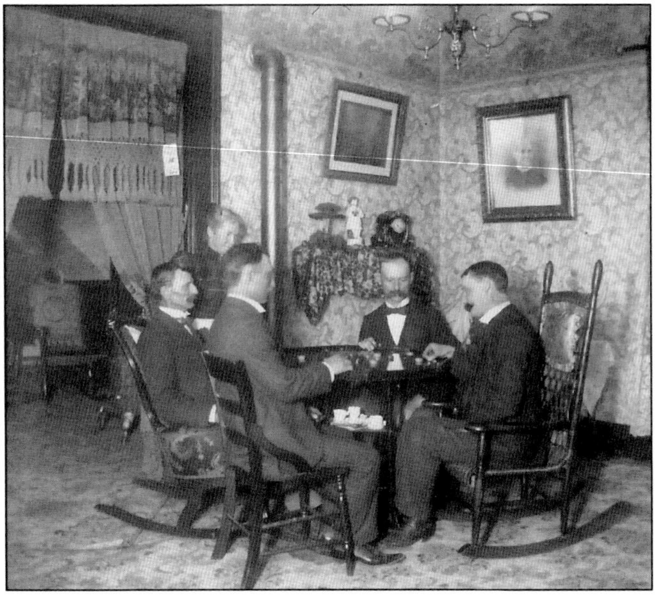

Two women had a difficult time trying to get to the home of Mead Stephey on Plum Street. The March 29, 1913, *Troy Record* relates, "While men were taking Mrs. Lablond of Grants (*sic*) Street, out of her house she missed the boat and fell in the water. She is a large woman, but by hard efforts was gotten into the boat, and taken to the home of Mead Stephey in a badly exhausted condition. A Mrs. Fellers had to wade thru water up to her armpits to get to Mr. Stephey's house. She nearly collapsed." In this undated photograph, Stephey (at right, in rocking chair) is seated with family members.

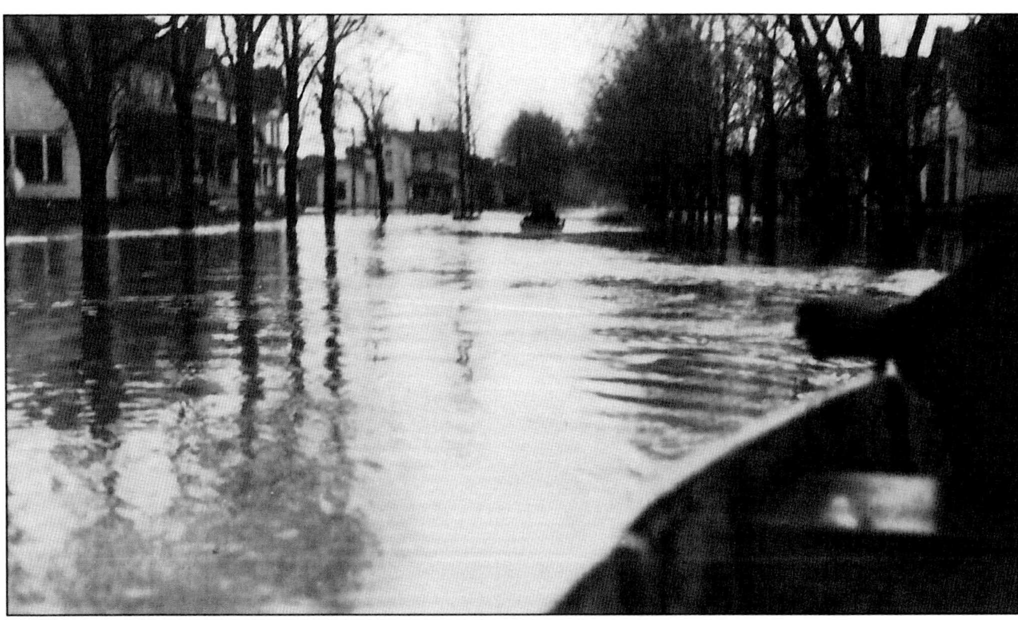

This photograph shows rescue work on Grant Street and appears to have been taken from a rescue boat.

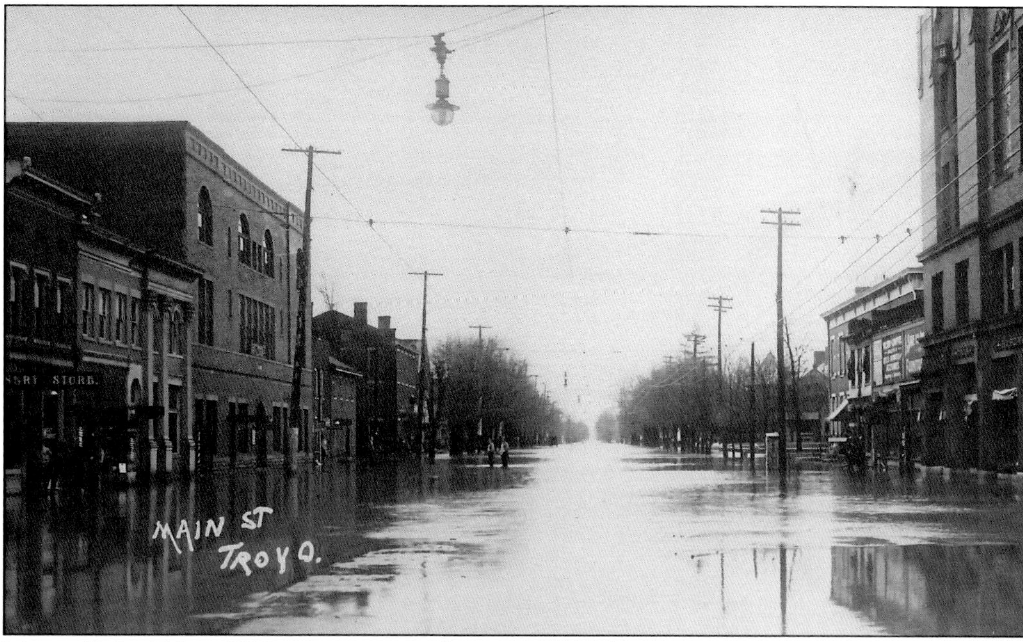

Mr. and Mrs. Edwin Wilson were waist-deep in water when a rescuer reached their West Main Street home. As they were leaving their home, Mrs. Wilson looked back and cried as she saw her new china cabinet fall over. Most homes on West Main Street had less damage than properties to the south of the street.

Harriett Pearson, 78, lived in a one-story house on West Market Street. When floodwaters came into her home, she had nowhere to go and drowned inside the house. Ruth Sharits Weaver said that her father, Frank Sharits, found Pearson. Weaver recalled that Pearson's body was taken out of her home on an ironing board and her valuable items were taken to Troy's city hall for safekeeping.

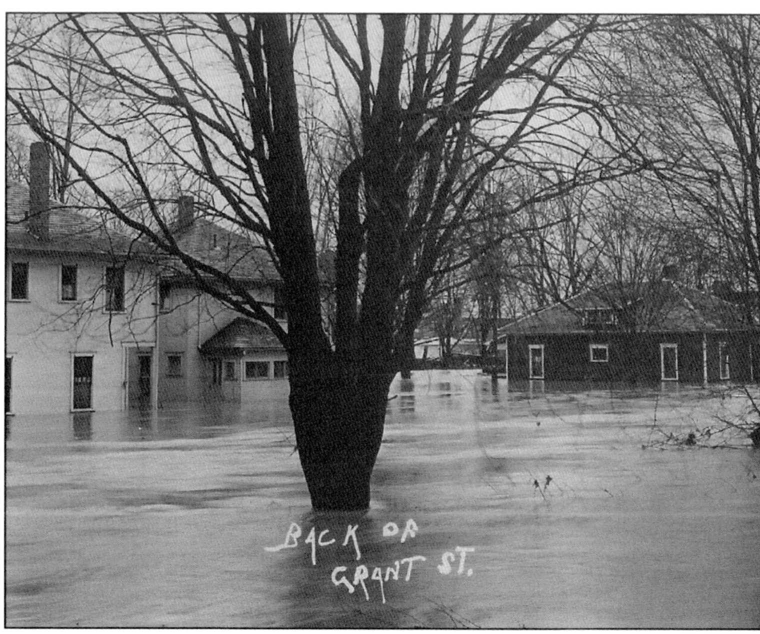

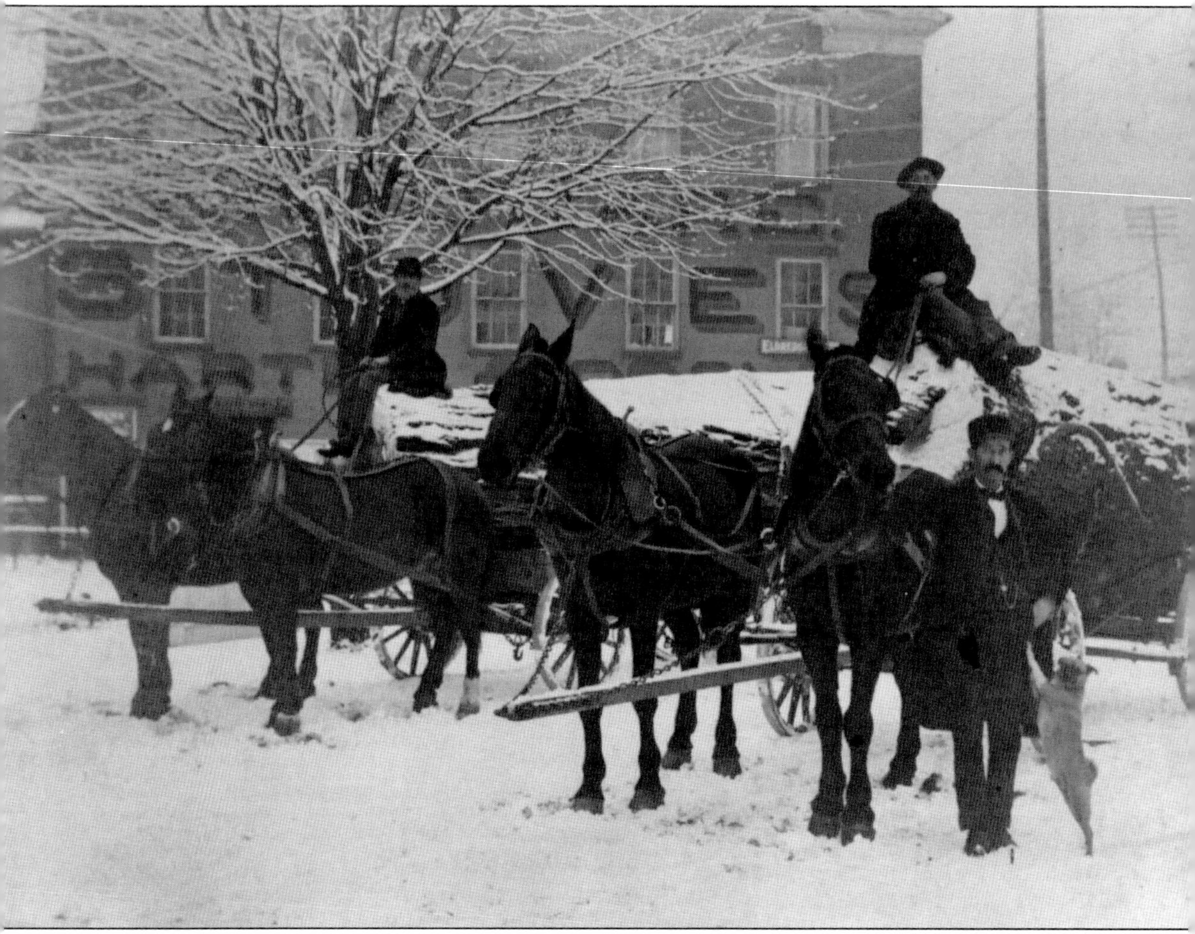

Animals had a large role in the town at the time of the flood. Aside from pets such as dogs, cats, and birds, horses were still used for transportation, chickens were kept for eggs and favorite meals, and family cows provided milk. As much as possible, owners moved their animals to places of safety during the flood. Ed McCurdy, the secretary to Troy mayor John McClain, had two valuable horses that he was unable to release from their stalls. The April 3, 1913, *Miami Union* newspaper reports that "both animals were found stretched across their stalls, one with its head extended over the feedway and the other with its head turned back into the stall and its hind quarters in the feed room, showing the terrible struggle made by the animals before they were overwhelmed."

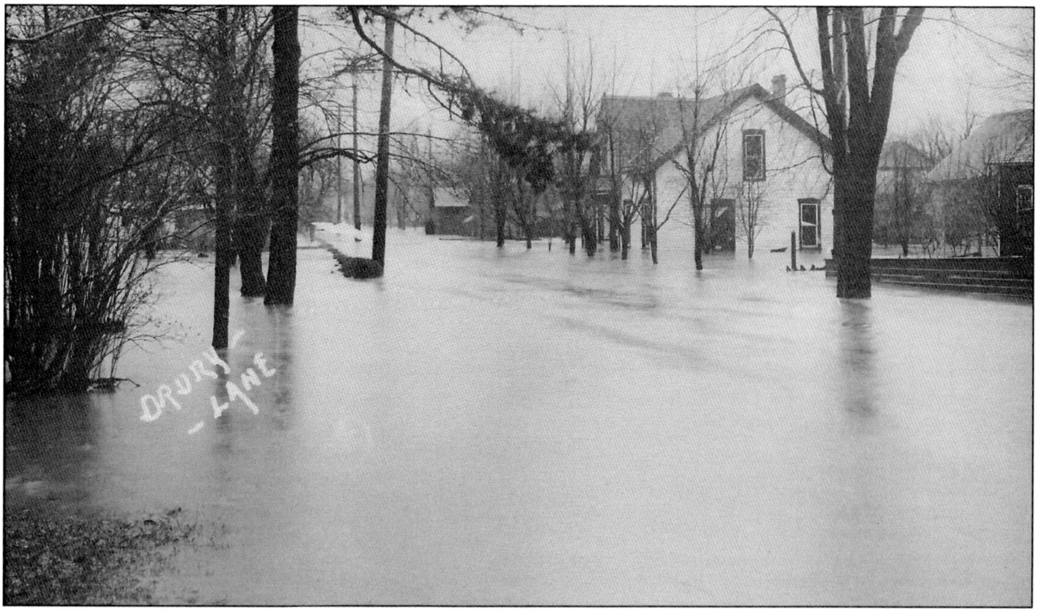

W.I. Tenney lived with his daughter, Mrs. Lee M. (Alice B.) Shellabarger, near South Plum Street and Drury Lane. As water surrounded their home, Tenney grew concerned about his horse in the barn behind the house. Despite protests from his daughter, Tenney went to the barn—walking in water up to his neck. His anxious daughter contacted their neighbor, Dr. B.W. Jones, who had a rowboat, for help. When Jones and Tenney got the horse, they tried to lead it while they remained in the boat. However, the horse tried to step in the boat, knocking Jones and Tenney into the water. Both men and the horse survived the spill. Shown here is a flood scene near the Shellabarger-Tenney home (above) and horses in the floodwaters (below).

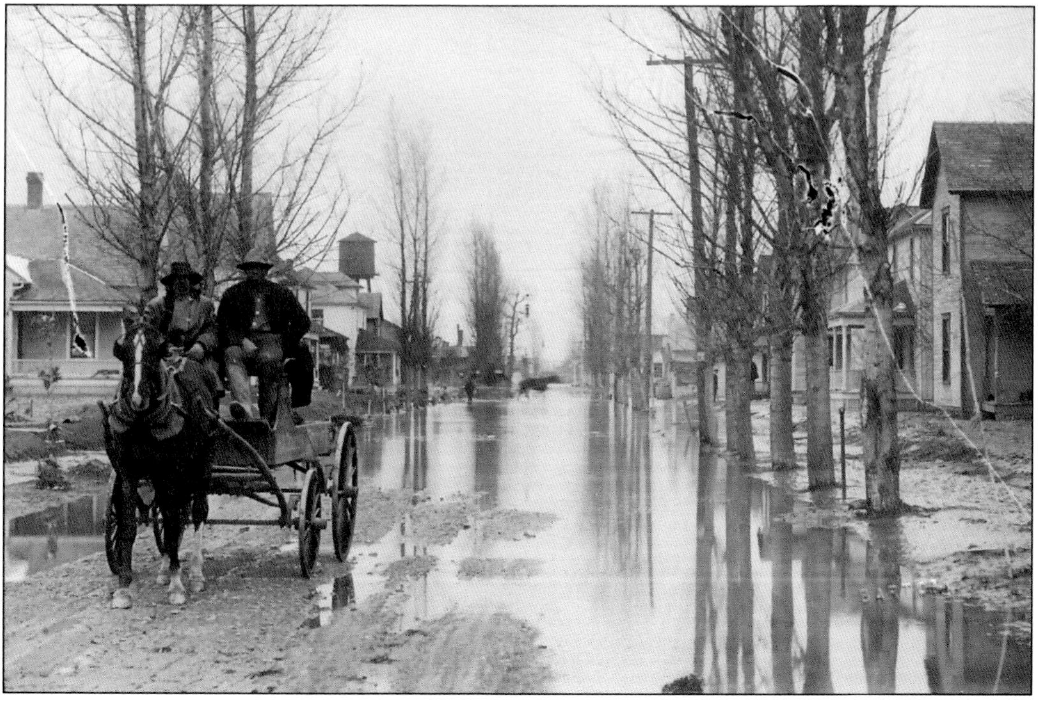

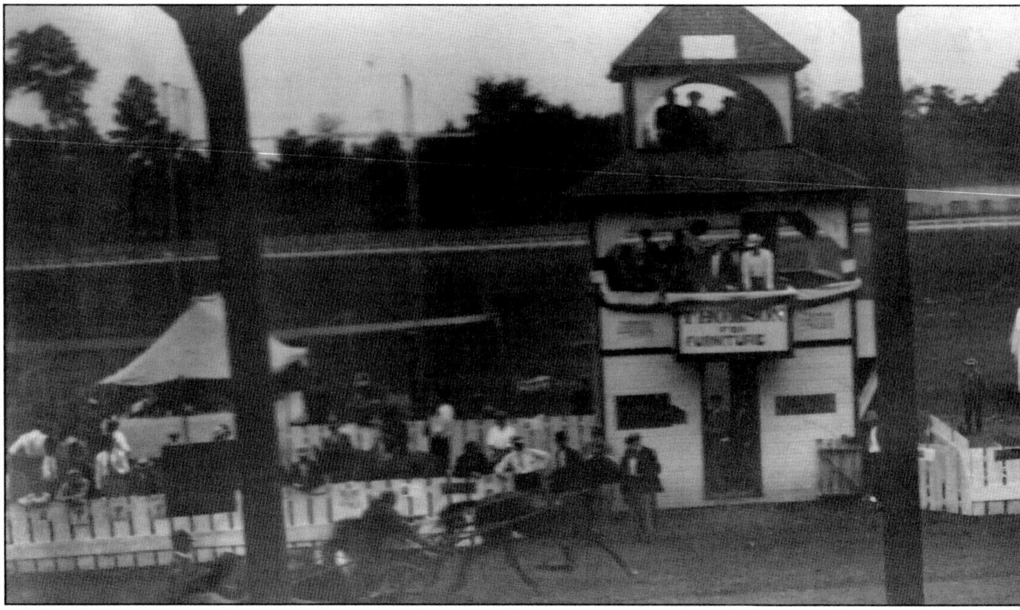

Upton B. Cook took the above photograph of a horse race at the Miami County Fairgrounds in 1912, showing the view from the grandstand of the track and what may have been the judging stand or press box. The photograph below was taken during the flood. The grandstand and judging stand can both be seen. As water flooded the fairgrounds, horse trainer Harry Hall took refuge in the fair secretary's office. When the water rose still more, he moved to the grandstand's reserved seat section on its south end. Hall became frightened as logs and building debris began floating by. Though he could not swim, he jumped into the cold water and drowned. Another man who died at the fairgrounds was George Boswell, about whom very little is known.

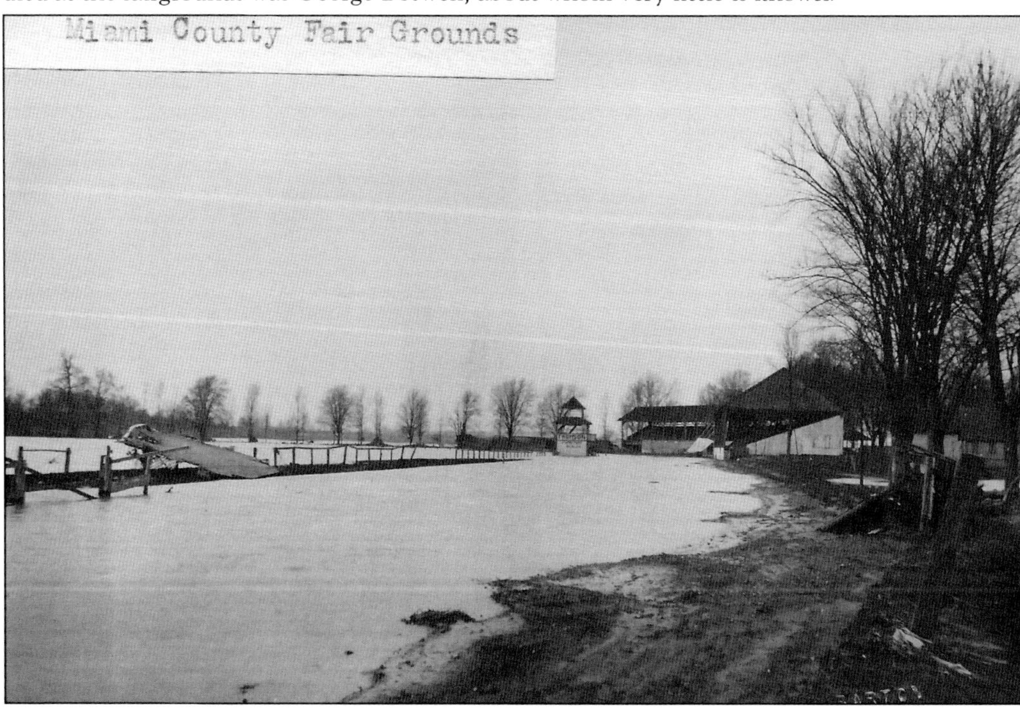

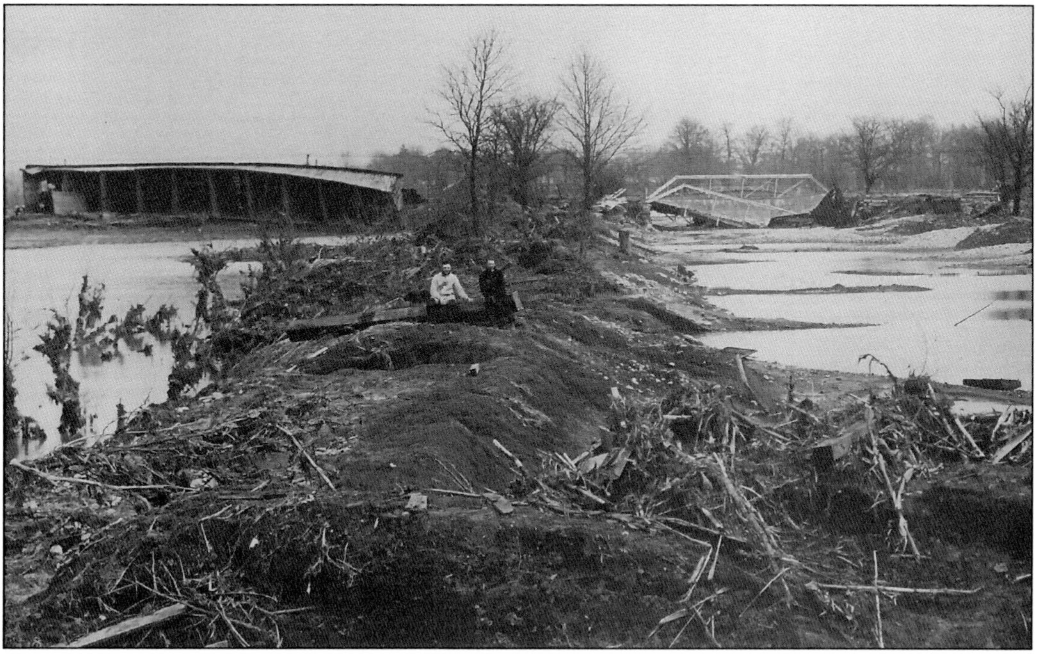

Most of the fairgrounds horse stables were destroyed. They are on the right side of this photograph. The March 29, 1913, *Troy Record* describes the destruction at the fairgrounds thusly: "The sheds at the fair grounds were entirely washed away and one end of the grandstand is also gone, 14 head of horses belonging to F.M. Sterrett at the fair grounds (*sic*) perished."

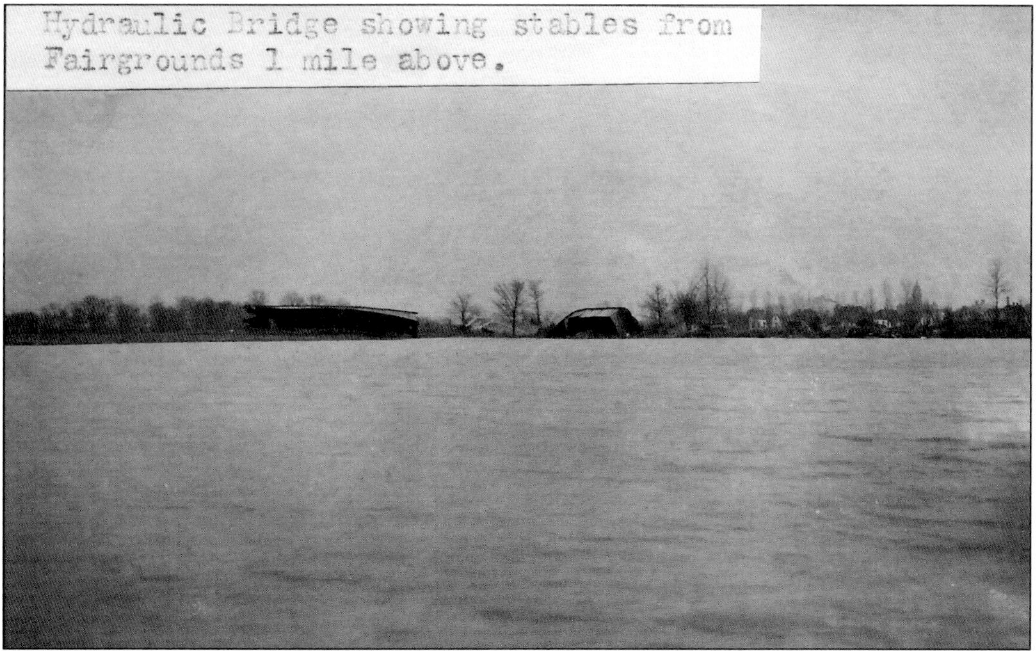

Debris floated nearby and into the fairgrounds from northern Miami County. A trunk was found with the name of a Dr. McCarty on it. Other items recovered in the area were a box of jewelry, wearing apparel, linen, and dishes. Some of the items were identified as the property of William Graef of Piqua. This photograph shows the amount of water.

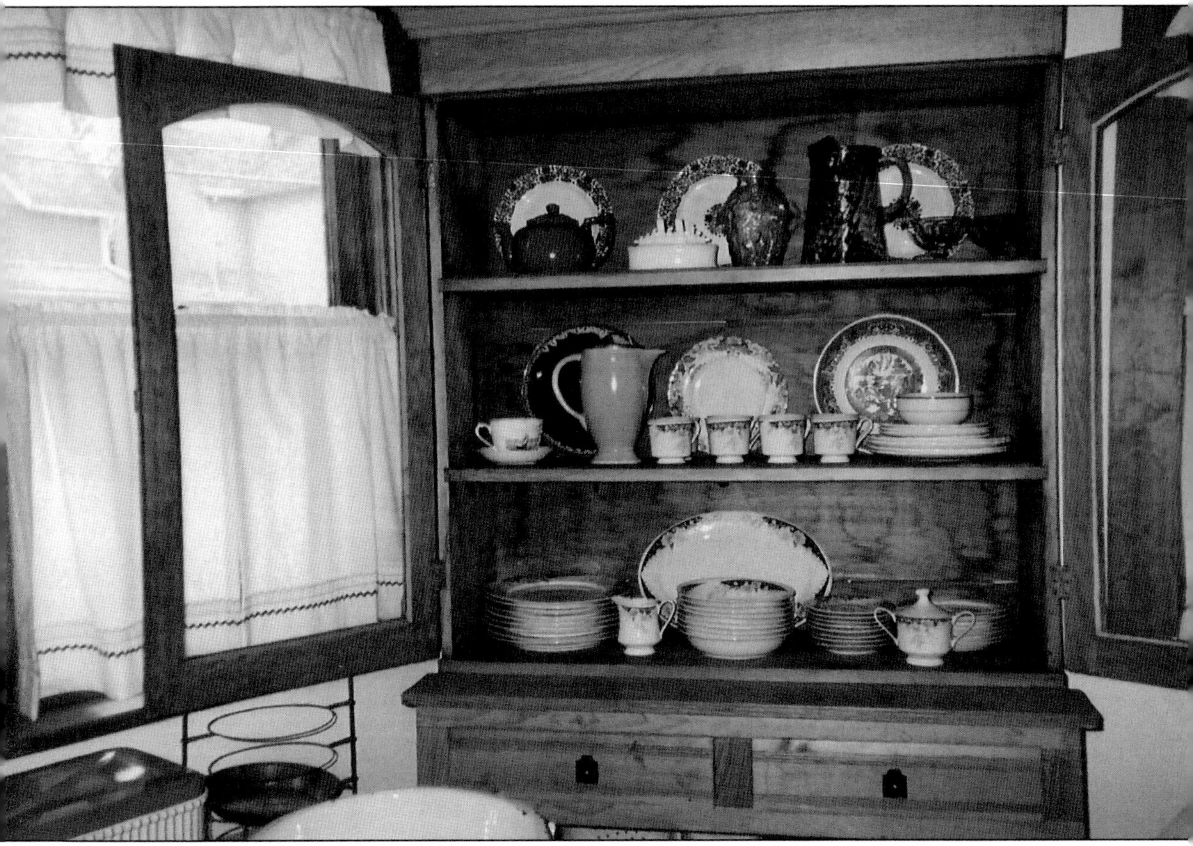

In a 1975 interview, Troy residents Scott and Jenny (Eccard) Sayers told stories about horses during the flood. Scott said that many horses ran loose in the streets and remembers a nearby house with a big front porch, which served as shelter for seven horses. Jenny recounted, "A horse rammed his head through our dining room window where we had taken mother's good Austrian ware dishes out of the cupboard and put them on the dining room table. We sat on the stairs and watched the dishes float out the window." The horse bled to death in the yard. The dishes shown in this china cabinet at the Museum of Troy History are typical of early-20th-century dinnerware. (Courtesy of Judy Deeter.)

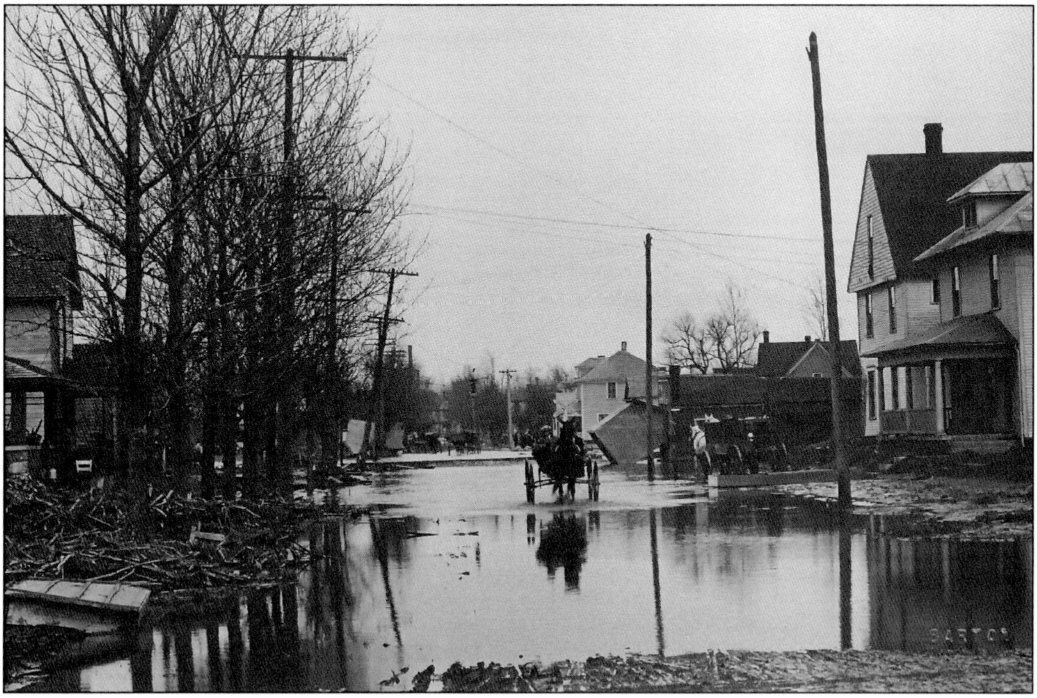

Dorothy Strasser Holler was four years old when the flood came to Troy. Her family lived in a two-story house on Race Street. As the floodwaters rose, she watched the muddy, churning water on Race Street from an upstairs window. She later remembered, "Then I began to see livestock. I saw a horse. All that showed above the water was just the horse's head. I think it was trying to swim, but it wasn't very successful because the water kept moving it right on down the street. Then . . . here came a chicken house, and it had two or three little chickens sitting on top. They were just sailing along like riding to the moon." No one could rescue them. These scenes show horses after the flood (above) and the water on Race Street east of the Strasser home (below).

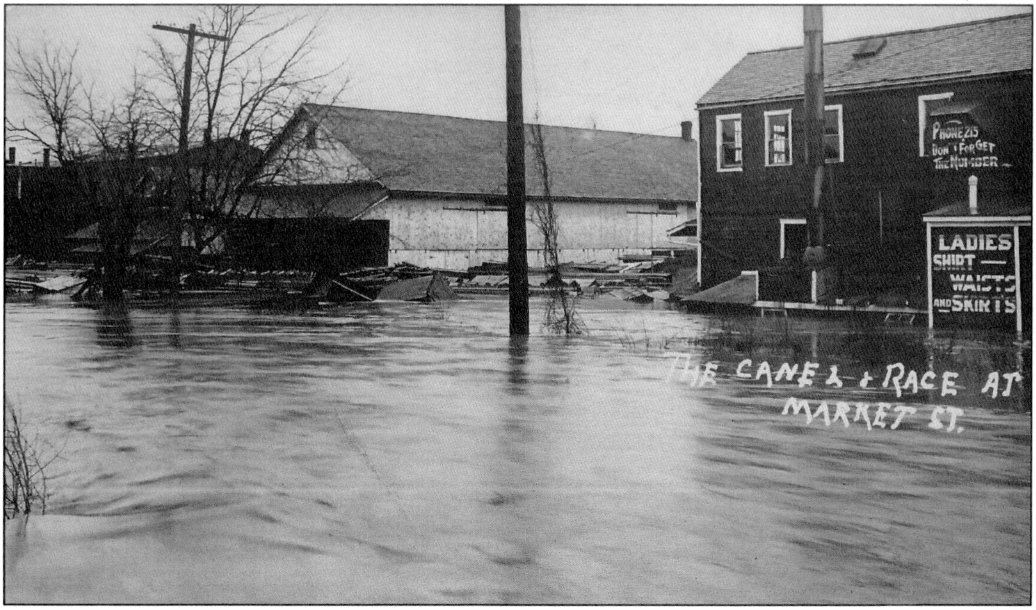

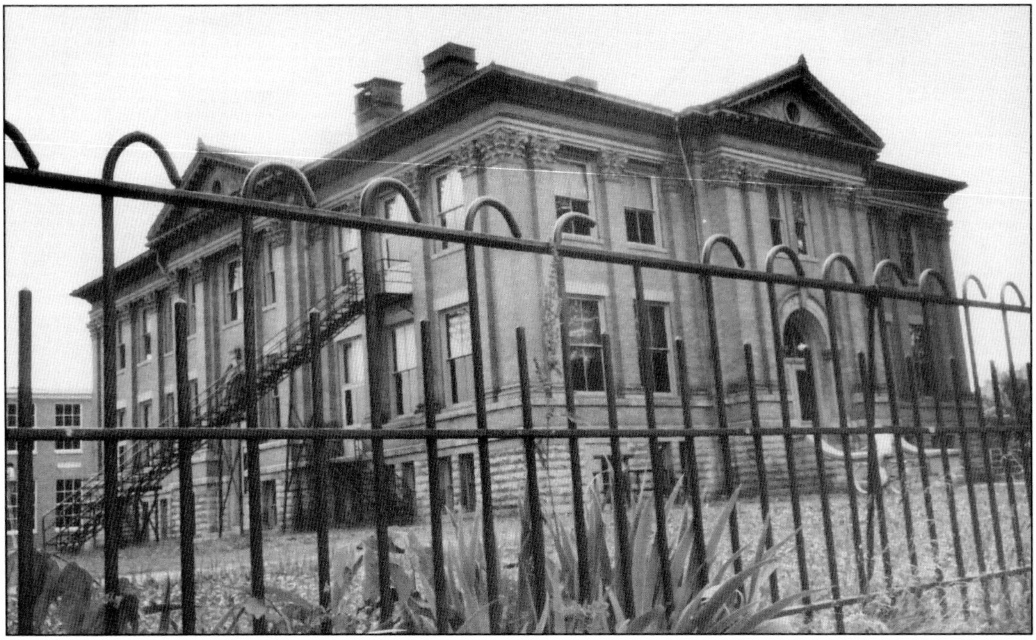

Persis Johnson Faust recalled that a child at her school—Forest School, seen here—told a story about his family canary. The family had sought shelter on the second floor of their home, but for some reason, the canary was left downstairs. As long as they could hear the canary chirping downstairs, they knew he was still there. When the chirping stopped, they that knew the bird had drowned.

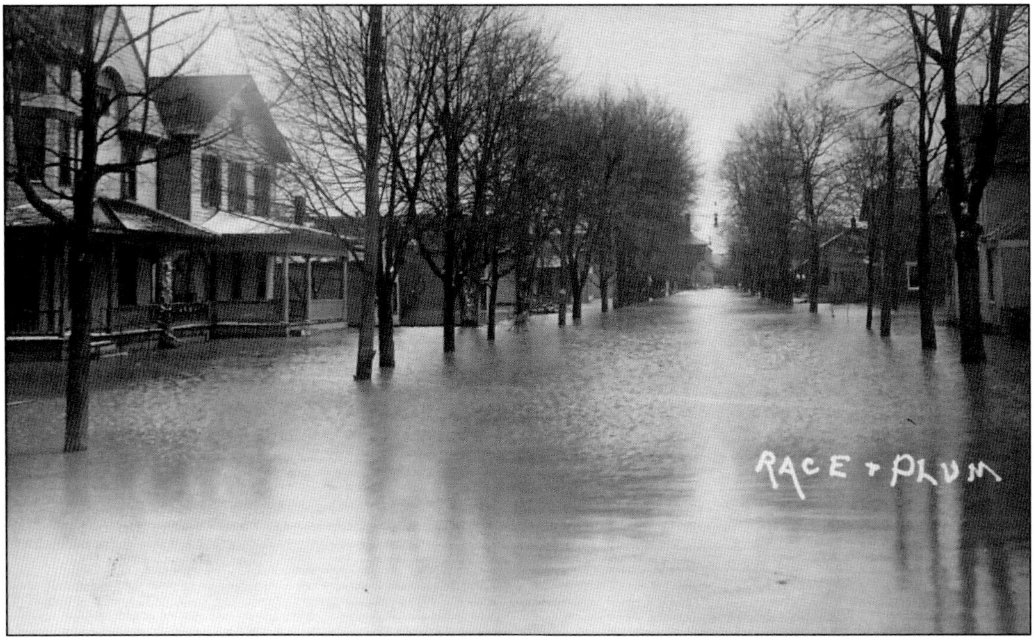

Dorothy Strasser Holler remembered that when her family evacuated their Race Street home, the family dog did not go along. Her father, David Strasser, put the dog in an upstairs closet so it would not go into the flooding part of the house. Every day, he returned to the home and checked on the dog.

Four

Shelters, Healers, and Helpers

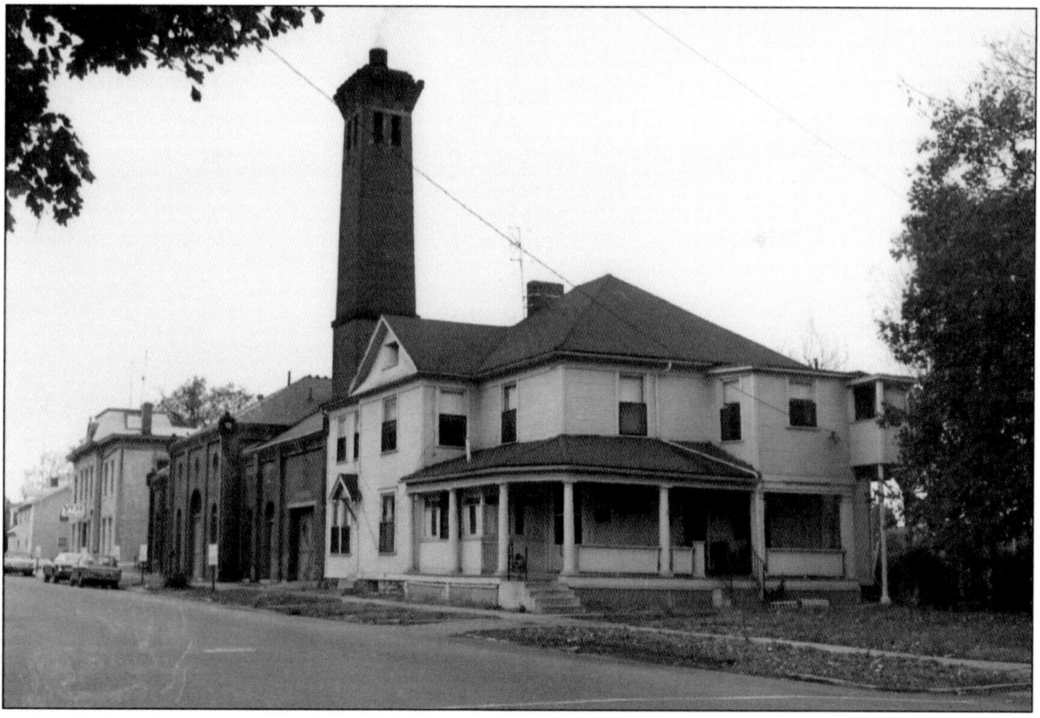

Many flood victims needed shelter or medical attention after they were rescued. Some sought food and a place to stay, while others needed medical assistance. Temporary hospitals were set up in the Ridge Avenue homes of L.H. McConnell and J. Wesley Morris. Public places of shelter were established at Edwards and Forest Schools, First Methodist Church, and the Troy Manufacturing Company plant. The white building in the foreground was a private hospital located on West Water Street and owned by Dr. Warren Coleman.

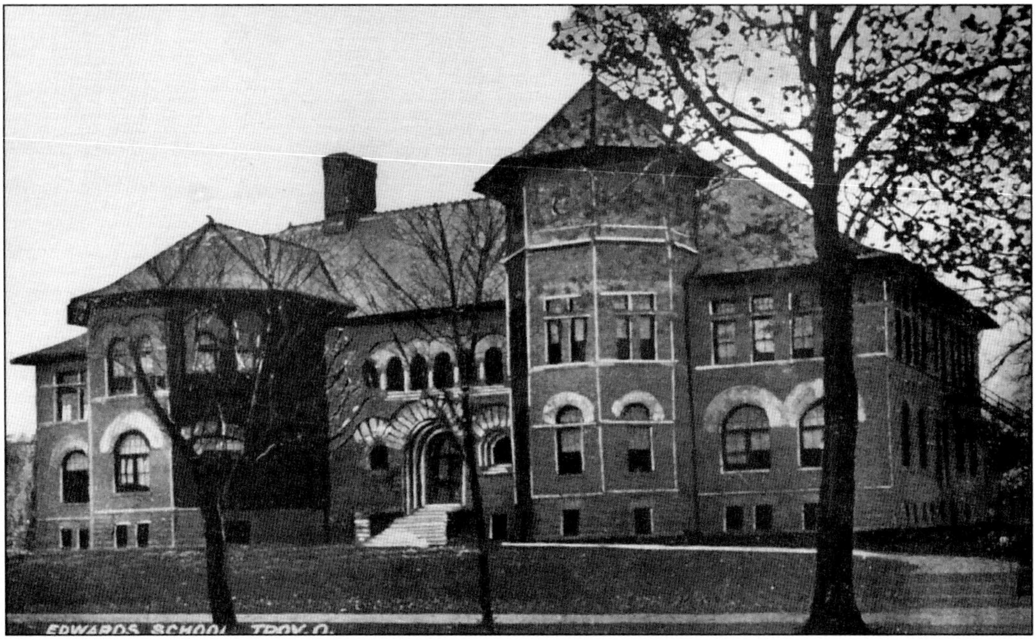

The Edwards School, at 401 West Main Street, was used as an emergency hospital and refuge for people who were stranded and ill from the flood. The first high school graduation at this school (and the 38th for the Edwards School) was held in June 1893 in the newly rebuilt school. That same building was Troy's sole large entertainment space until Van Cleve School opened in 1931. The Troy-Miami County Public Library now occupies the former Edwards School site.

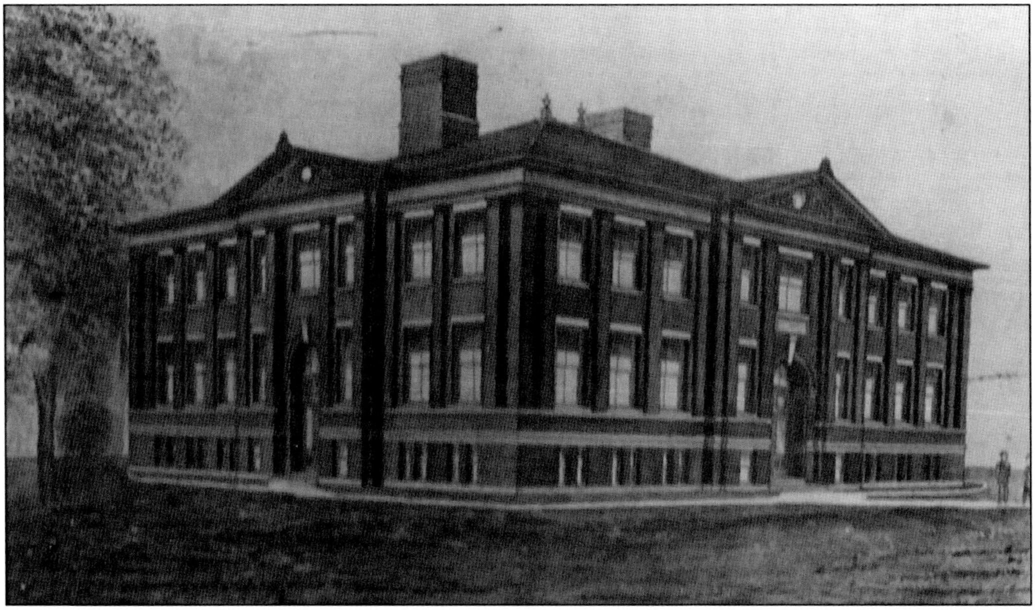

Forest School, on East Franklin Street, was a place of shelter and care for flood victims on the east side of Troy. According to flood survivor Persis Johnson Faust, "Families in the east part of Troy who were underwater stayed in the old Forest School." Doris Kathlyn Sowry, the two-month evacuated baby of Nell Stoner and Harry Sowry, died at the school. In a 1975 interview, Faust remembered, "One pregnant woman birthed a child while at the school."

First Methodist Church was used as an emergency hospital and refuge for people stranded or ill because of the flood. The church is at 11 West Franklin Street, at the intersection with South Cherry Street. Church records mention that more than one-third of church families were in the flooded districts and 75 families had water on the first floors of their homes.

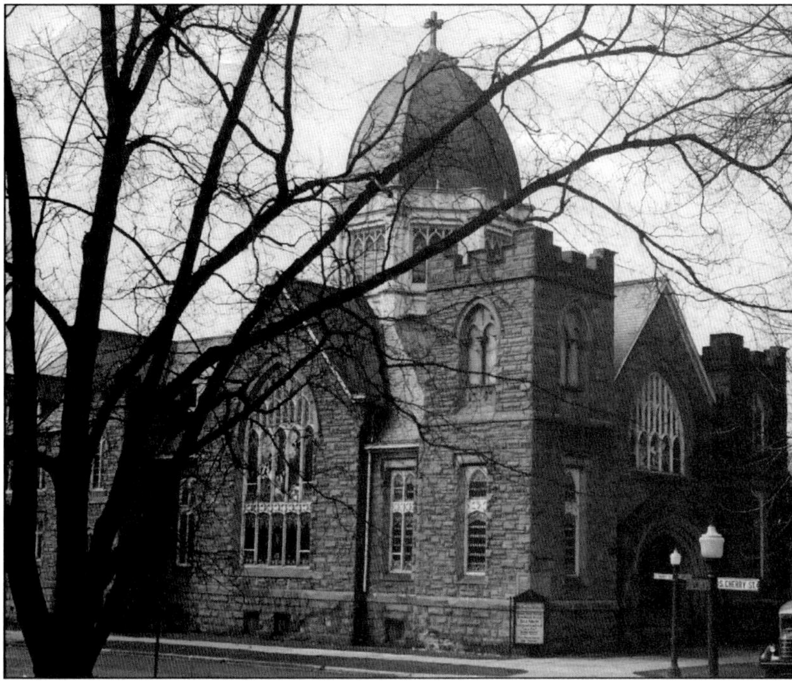

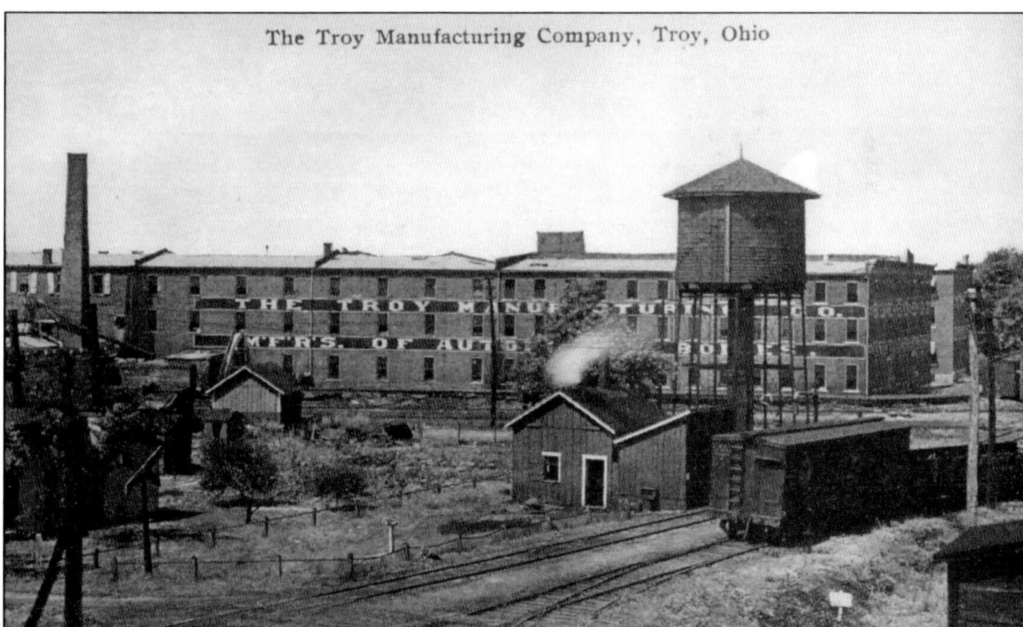

The Troy Manufacturing Company plant, opposite the Big Four Railroad south of Troy, served as a place of shelter and care for flood victims. The company was incorporated in 1909 to make automobile bodies, tops, and other automobile accessories. During World War I, the firm made 100 different parts for airplanes. In 1919, its name was changed to Troy Body Works.

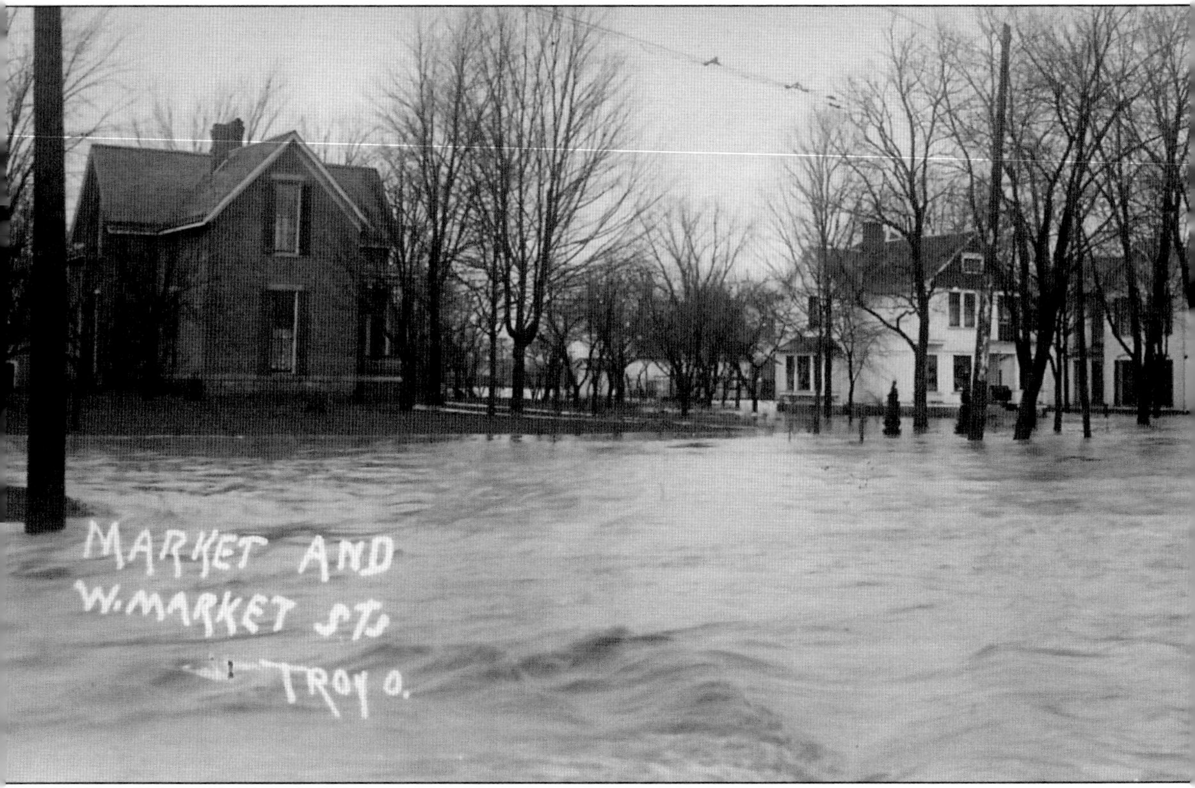

The home of Edwin and Carrie Cairns at 644 South Market Street was used as a way station for flood victims. Because the house had a high foundation, water did not get inside, though it came up to the back door. People rescued from the rooftops of nearby homes came to the house by rescue boats. The Cairns's daughter, Hortense Cairns Mumford, described how their house was used: "They had been up there in the cold rain, some for two days and two nights. Some had pneumonia, some were not alive but they would bring them to our back door and lay them on the floor of our living room wrapped in blankets furnished by merchants uptown . . . My mother and grandmother kept 'wash-boilers' boiling on an old cook stove making heavy, strong hot coffee for these victims as they were brought in, and under doctors' direction, a teaspoon of whiskey was added . . . this was to give them strength and revive them. Dr. [Joseph W.] Means and Dr. [Thomas] Wright were the doctors who checked victims in our home."

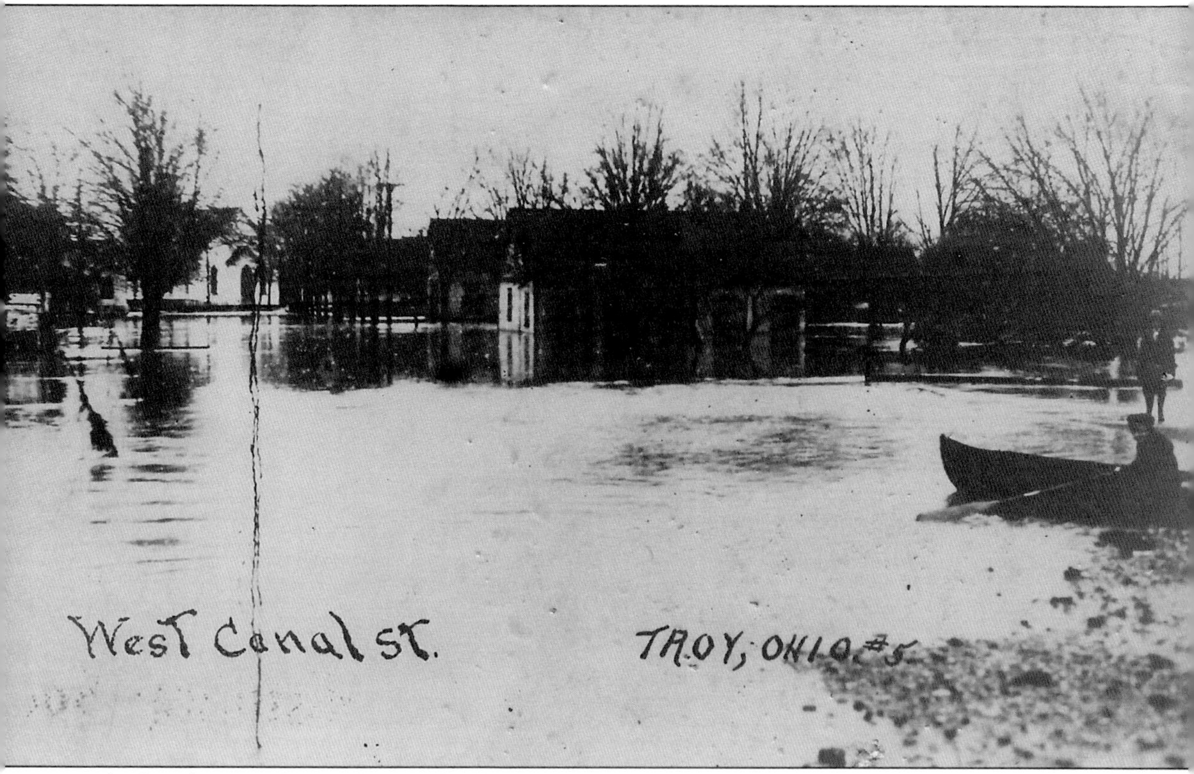

Very little is known about what medical treatments were provided to flood victims, except that they were given hot drinks and warm blankets. Most were exhausted, cold, and hungry. Two rescued babies died after they were removed from their homes: two-month-old Doris Sowry and six-day-old Byron Humberger. Nineveh rescuer and Casstown resident Raymond Harrison sat for hours in a tree after a nearly fatal rescue attempt. He was put to bed to recover. For months after the flood, rescuers Wilbur Chaffee and Al Bretland suffered from cramped and paralyzed hands and feet after spending hours rowing in the cold rain. According to a story in the *Troy Daily News* on March 24, 1947, Bretland said that doctoring his hands and feet took much of his time and money. At Christmas 1913, the Elks Club slipped an envelope under his door with $25 and a note that said, "From those who don't forget." In this photograph, people watch rescuers.

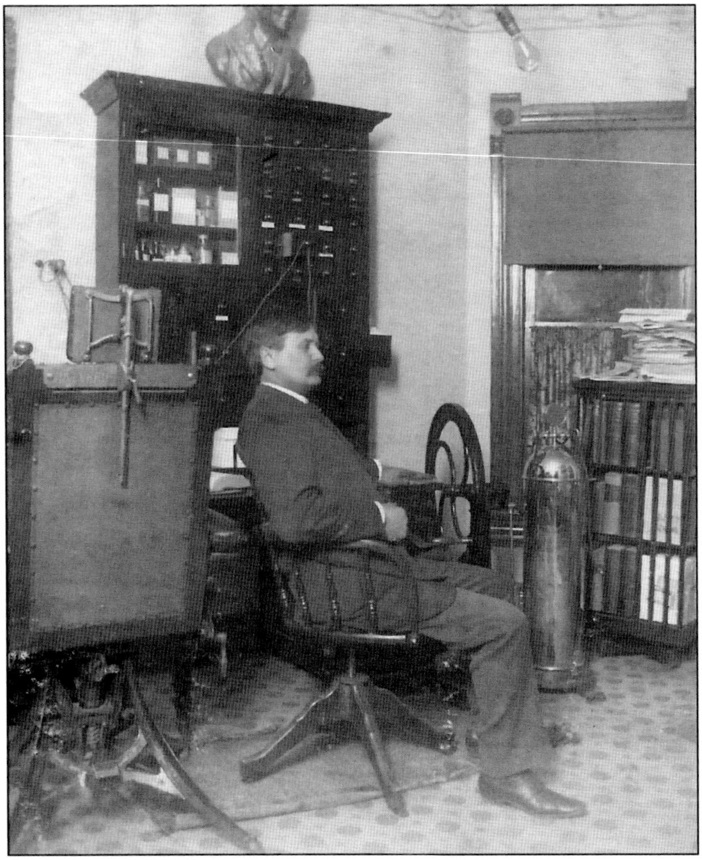

On March 30, Troy physicians wrote a resolution announcing that they would give free medical services to "needy sufferers" of the flood until May 1, 1913. The resolution was signed by Dr. Wilbur R. Thompson, Dr. Lauren Lindenberger, partners Dr. Warren Coleman and Dr. Harry Shilling, Dr. George McCullough, a Dr. Shroyer, Dr. Roy Wolcott, Dr. Thomas M. Wright, Dr. Peter Eagle, Dr. Joseph Shinn, Dr. Jess Francis, and meeting chairman Dr. Joseph W. Means, who is seen here in his office.

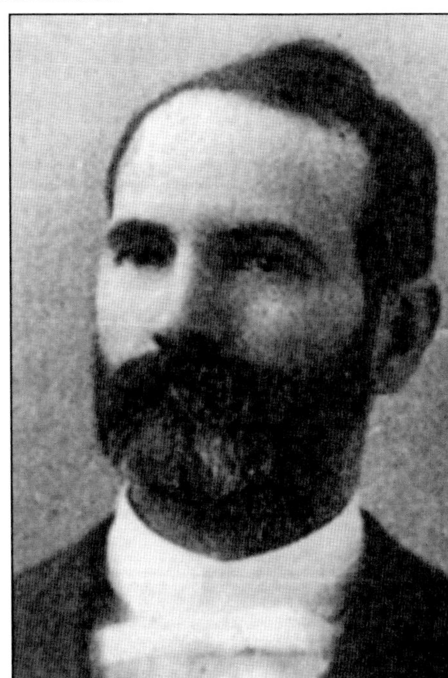

Dr. Thomas M. Wright, pictured here, helped many flood victims and was one of the doctors who signed the resolution to give free services to flood victims. He began his medical career in Troy in 1876, and by the time of the flood, he was well known in the town.

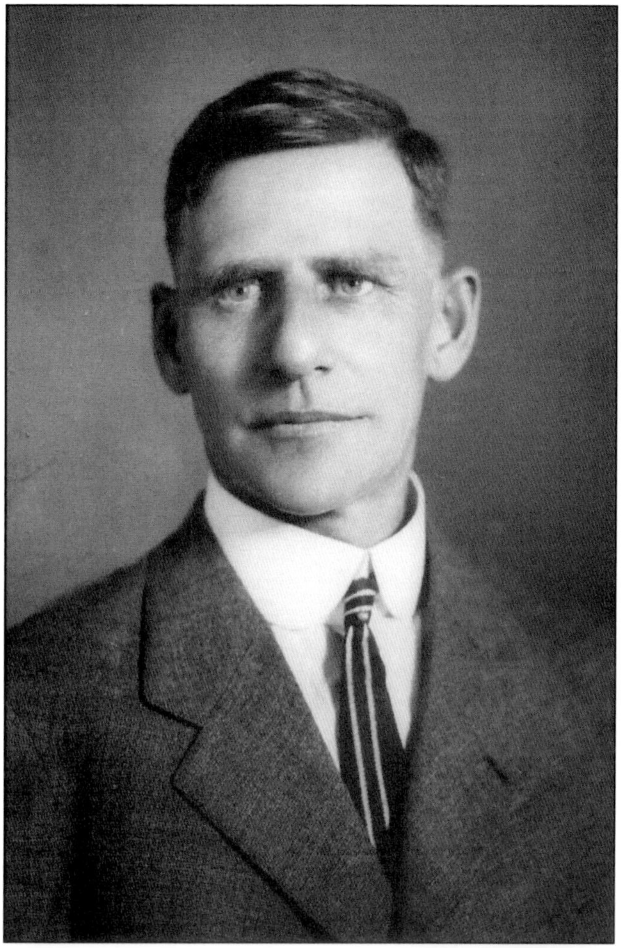

This portrait of Dr. Harry Shilling was taken around 1920 by C. Butterworth. Dr. Shilling treated many flood victims. According to his daughter, Lois Shilling Davies, he treated some flood victims at the Colored Odd Fellows Lodge in the Mayo Hall Building on South Market Street. Shilling was the 1905 valedictorian of the University of Cincinnati's College of Medicine. In 1906, he began his partnership with Dr. Warren Coleman, whose office was on West Water Street in Troy. Davies recalled that during the flood, Shilling went out the front window to get on his horse. The Shilling home, at 113 North Market Street, is seen below.

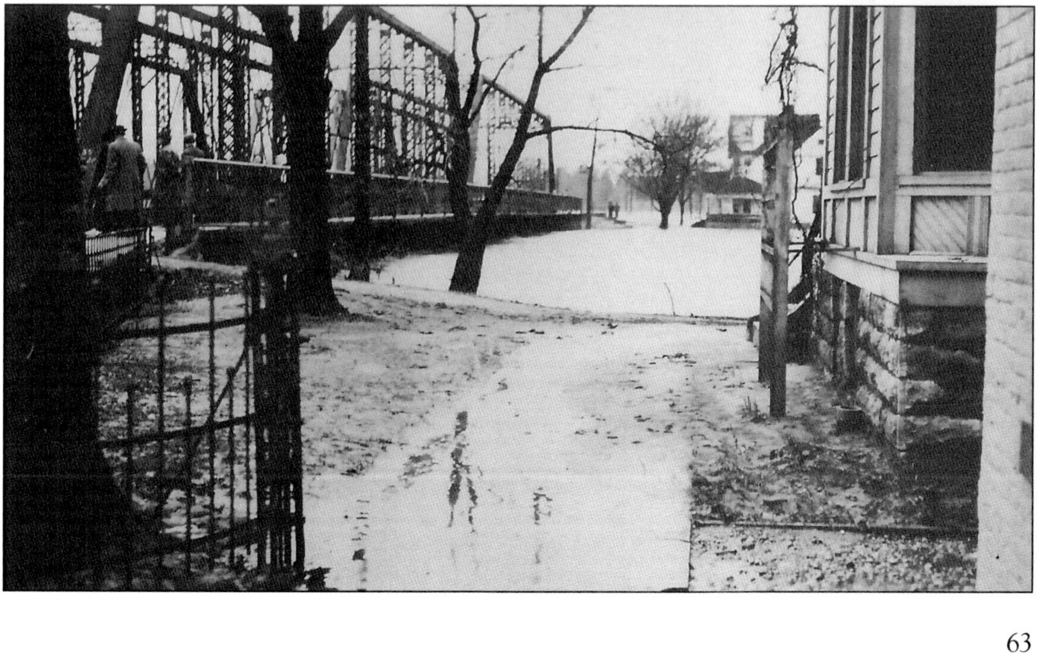

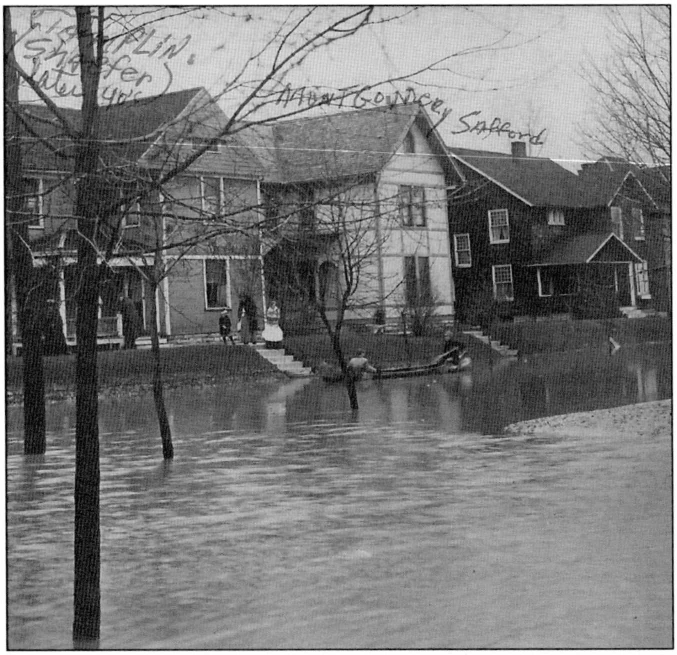

Many young children had a difficult time during the flood, and two evacuated babies died. Doris Sowry, the two-month-old daughter of Harry Sowry and Nell Stoner, died at the Forest School evacuation center, and Byron Humberger, the six-day-old son of professor Frank Humberger and his wife, May, died after being evacuated. It is believed that the Humberger baby died at one of the temporary hospitals on Ridge Avenue. Charles Croner of Piqua was found just north of Troy. He was 13 months old. Here, an unidentified family watches a rowboat pass by Cherry Street and Raper Street.

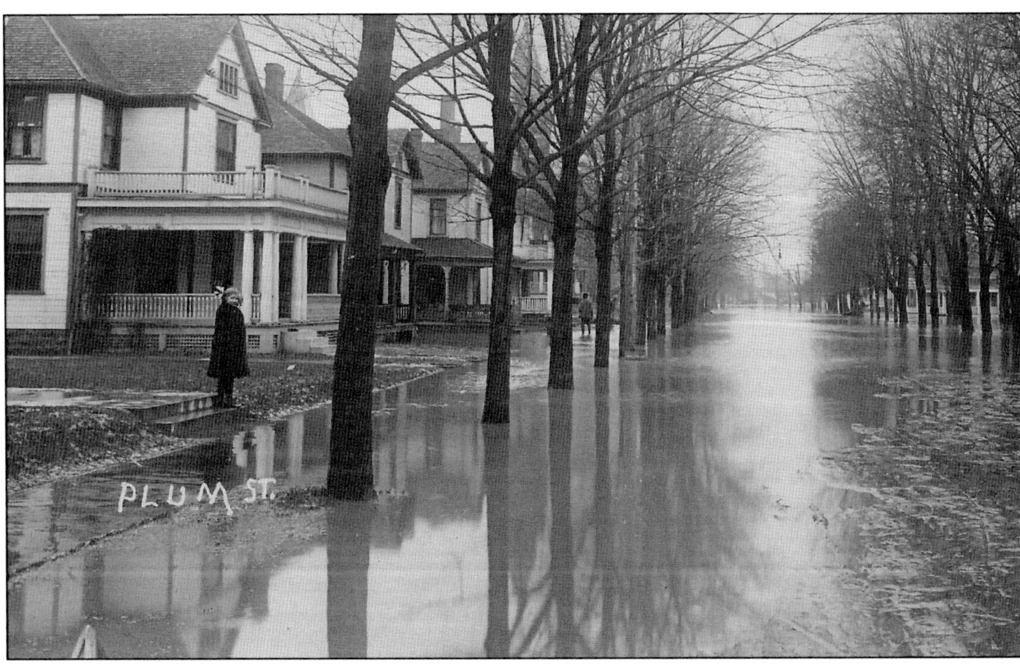

In this image, an unidentified young girl looks at a flooded Plum Street.

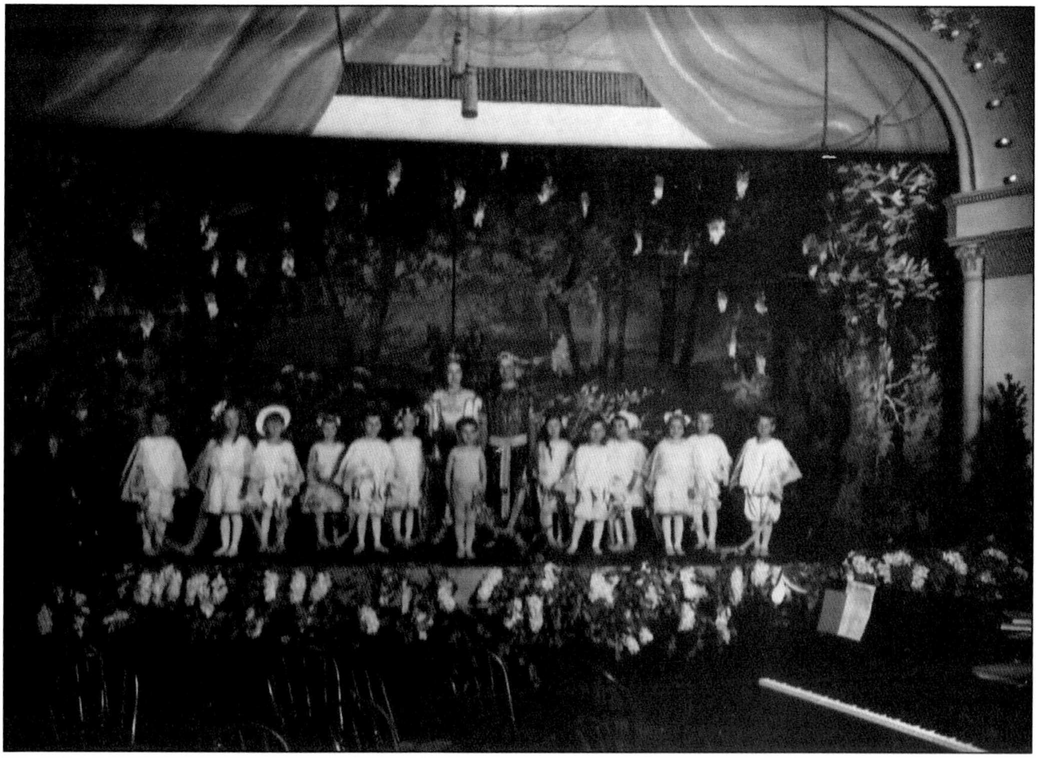

The above photograph was taken at Edwards School, on West Main Street, before the flood, in 1911 or 1912. The Troy-Miami County Public Library was later built on the school site. It is believed that most of these children lived in or near Troy during the flood. Children found their lives turned upside down because of the great rain. Their homes and possession were ruined, and family members, friends, and pets became sick or died. The 1911 postcard at right depicts the style of clothing worn by girls in the early 1900s. (Right, courtesy Judy Deeter.)

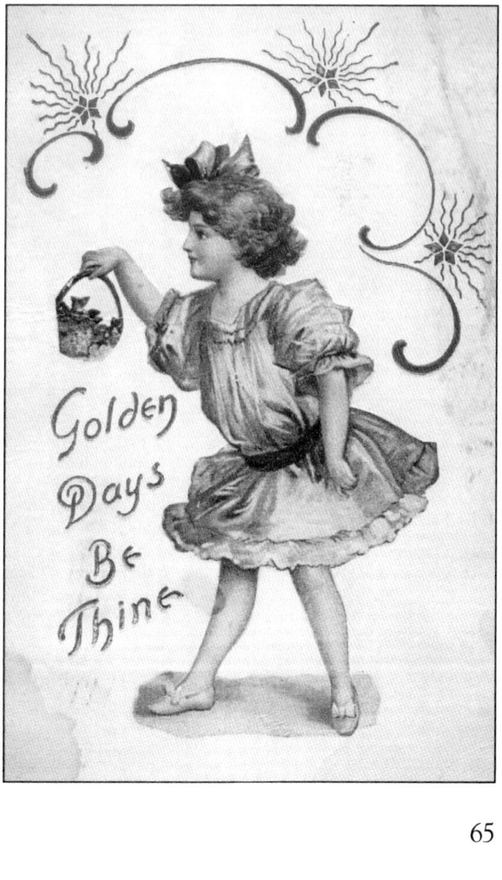

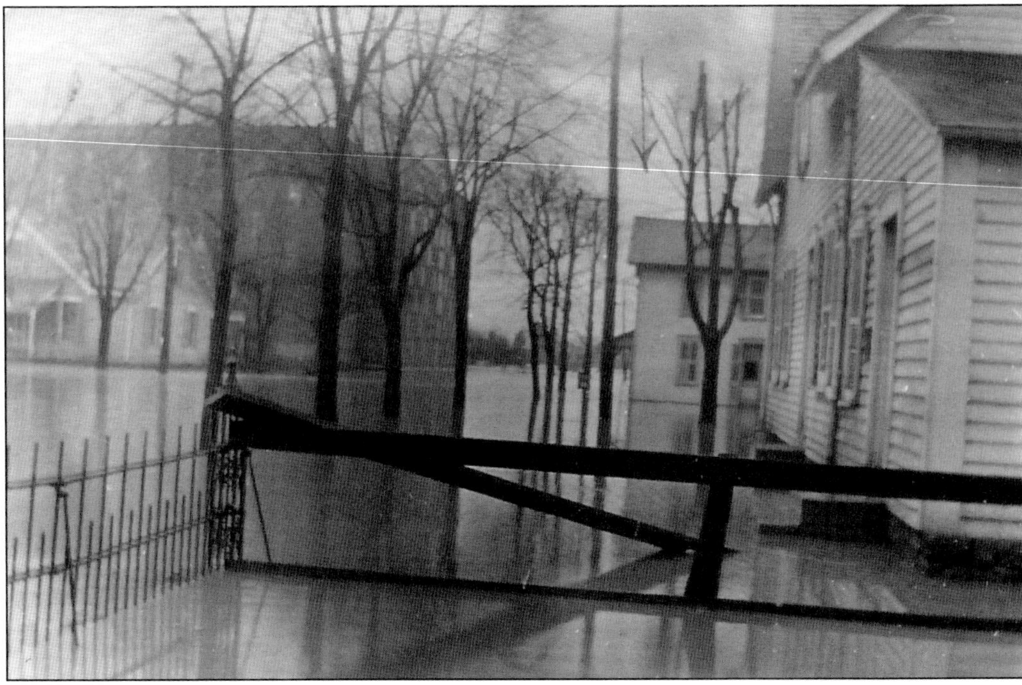

The people of Troy, including 18-year-old Clara Henne Loop, who lived at 107 East Water Street near the huge Hayner Distillery buildings, grieved for those who died. Loop recalled that as soon as she could leave her house, "I went right down to the distillery where my father told me not to go because they were bringing all the dead and laying them on the platform. There was a big platform on the distillery. They had them covered with a tarp, but I can still see them. They were bloated so terrible that I gave one look and turned around and ran off." The above image shows the large Hayner Distillery buildings along Water Street in the left center. Below, a body is pulled from an area near the Big Four Railroad tracks.

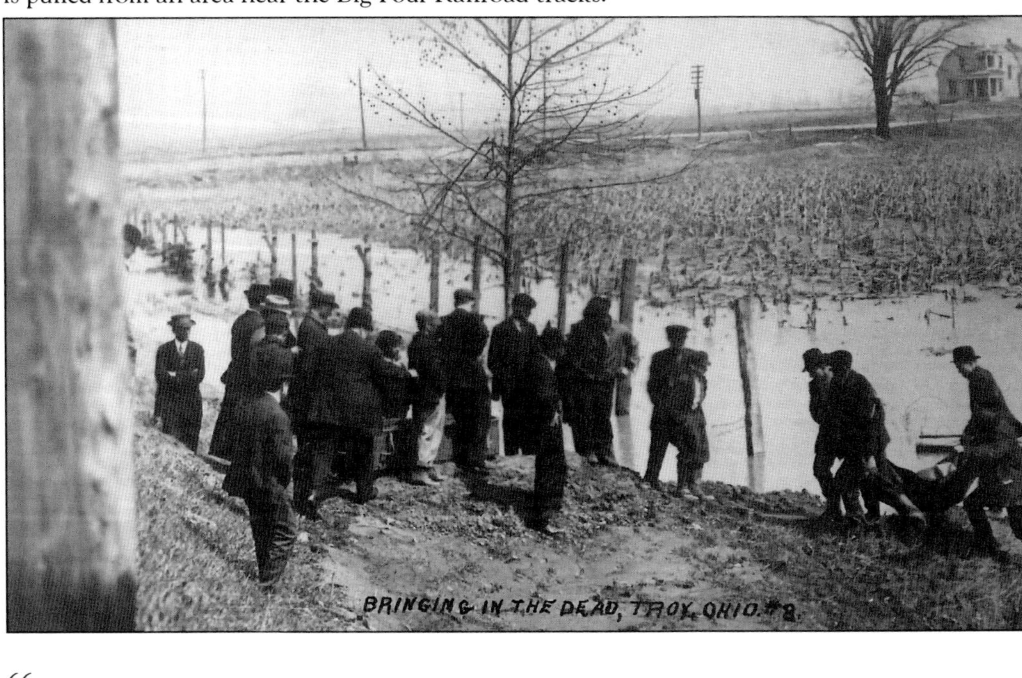

Five

Sharing Flood Stories

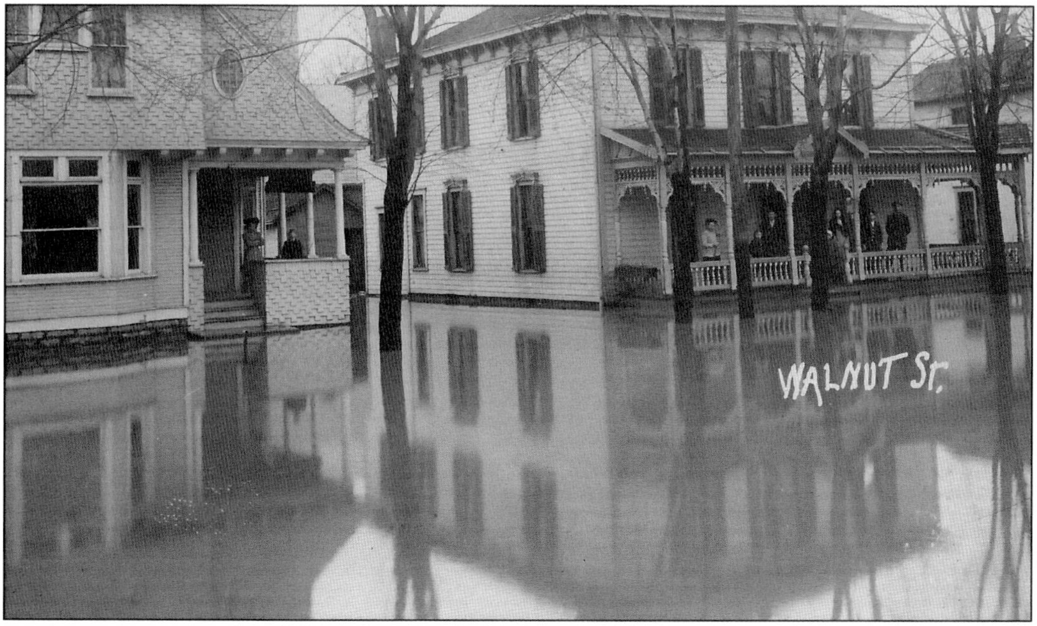

As the rain continued to fall, Trojans fearfully waited in the uppermost spaces of their homes to be rescued or for the rain to end. Some residents talked to neighbors from windows or porches. For days, many sat hungry in their darkened, cold homes. Long after the flood, survivors remembered Troy as "eerily" quiet, with silent and dark nights.

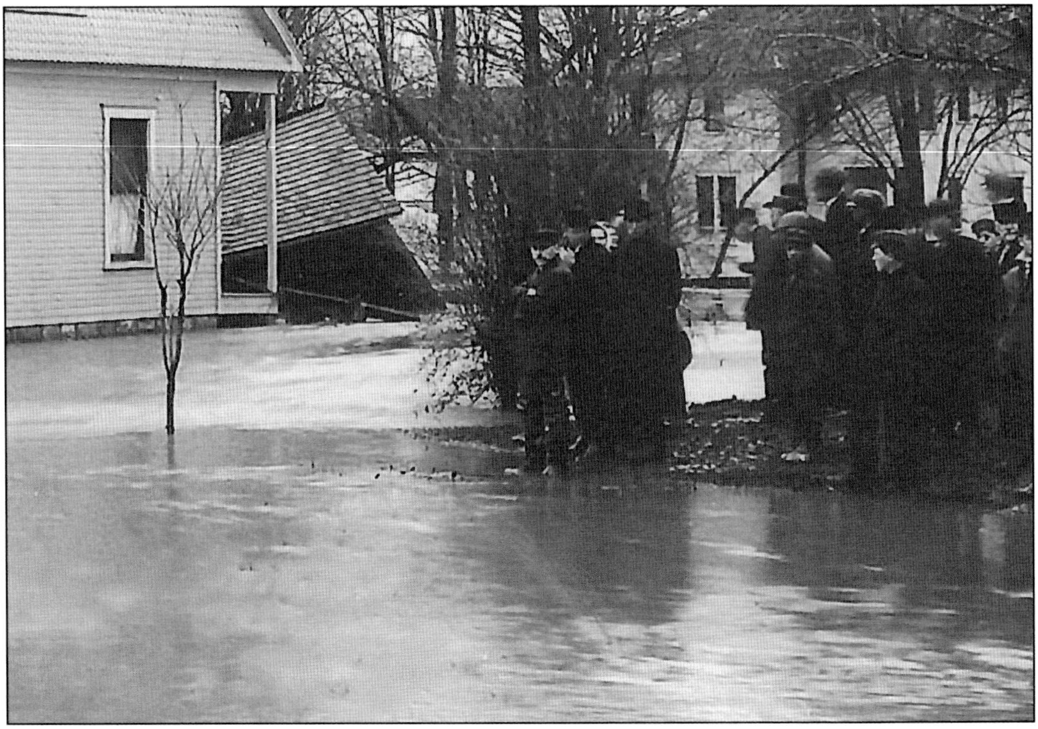

People who were able to leave their houses to watch rescue operations often did so, observing rescue boats go by their homes. Ned English, who was 18 and lived south of Troy on Dye Mill Road, walked into Troy from his home and watched several rescue operations take place. Here, a crowd is gathered near Peters Avenue and West Market Street.

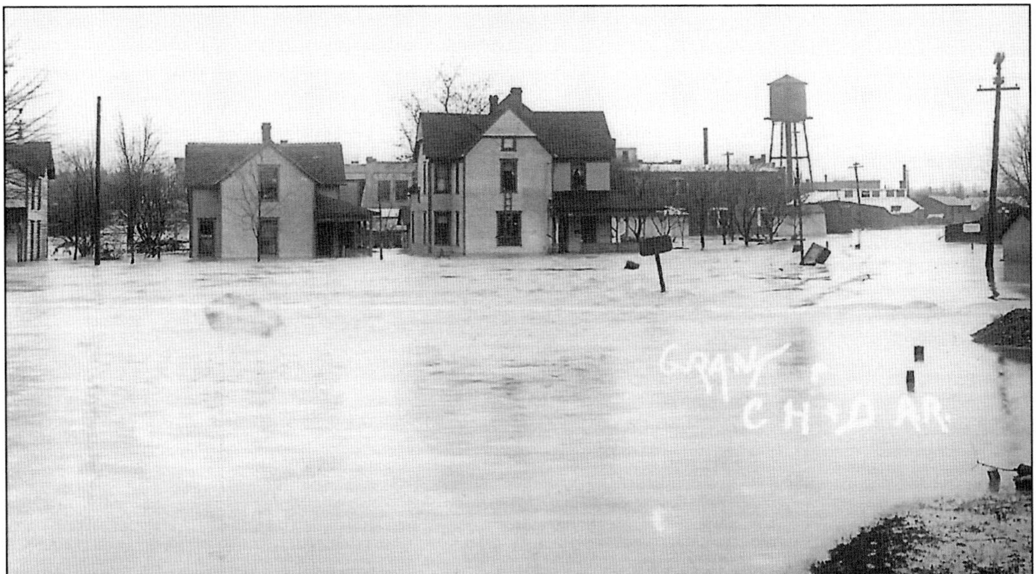

Photographers sometimes walked on top of railroad embankments to capture flood scenes as the elevated tracks provided a passageway across flooded Troy. Trains did not run during the flood. This view of Grant Street was taken from the Cincinnati, Hamilton & Dayton Railroad tracks.

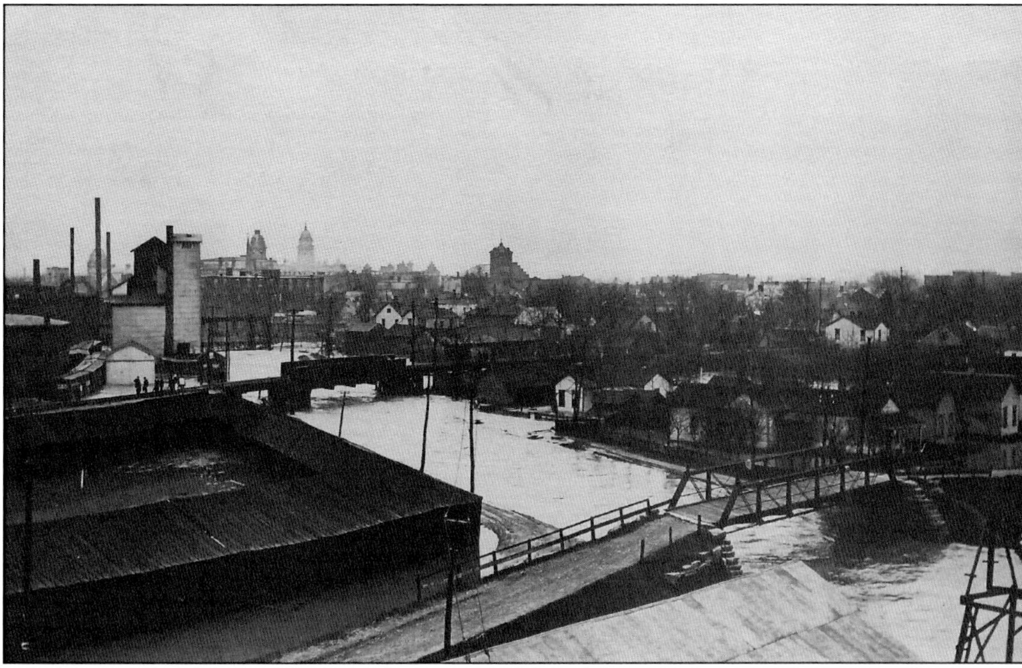

Photographers also documented Troy's flooded streets and waterways by taking pictures from high buildings. In 1913, the airplane was still a new invention and aerial photography was not in general use. Troy flood photographs were taken from the tops of the Miami County Courthouse on West Main Street, the old Kyle School building on South Plum Street, and the Troy Wagon Works plant on South Crawford Street, from which these images were taken. The *Miami Union* newspaper sold 30 flood views of scenes in Troy and Piqua at 5¢ a copy or six for 25¢.

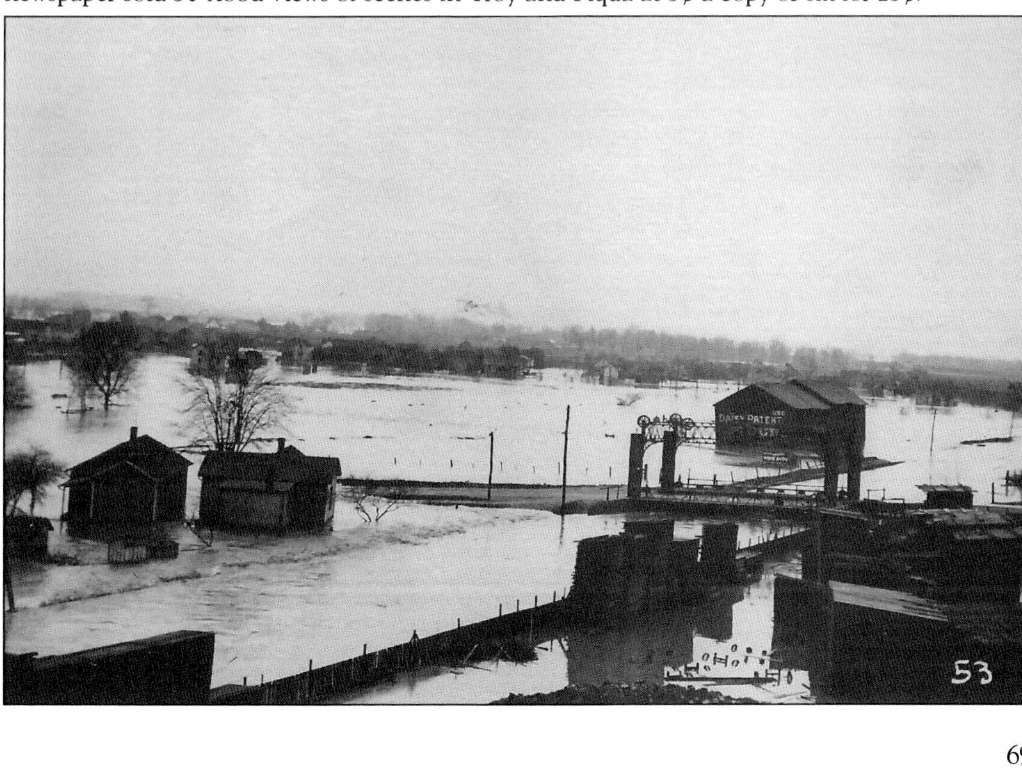

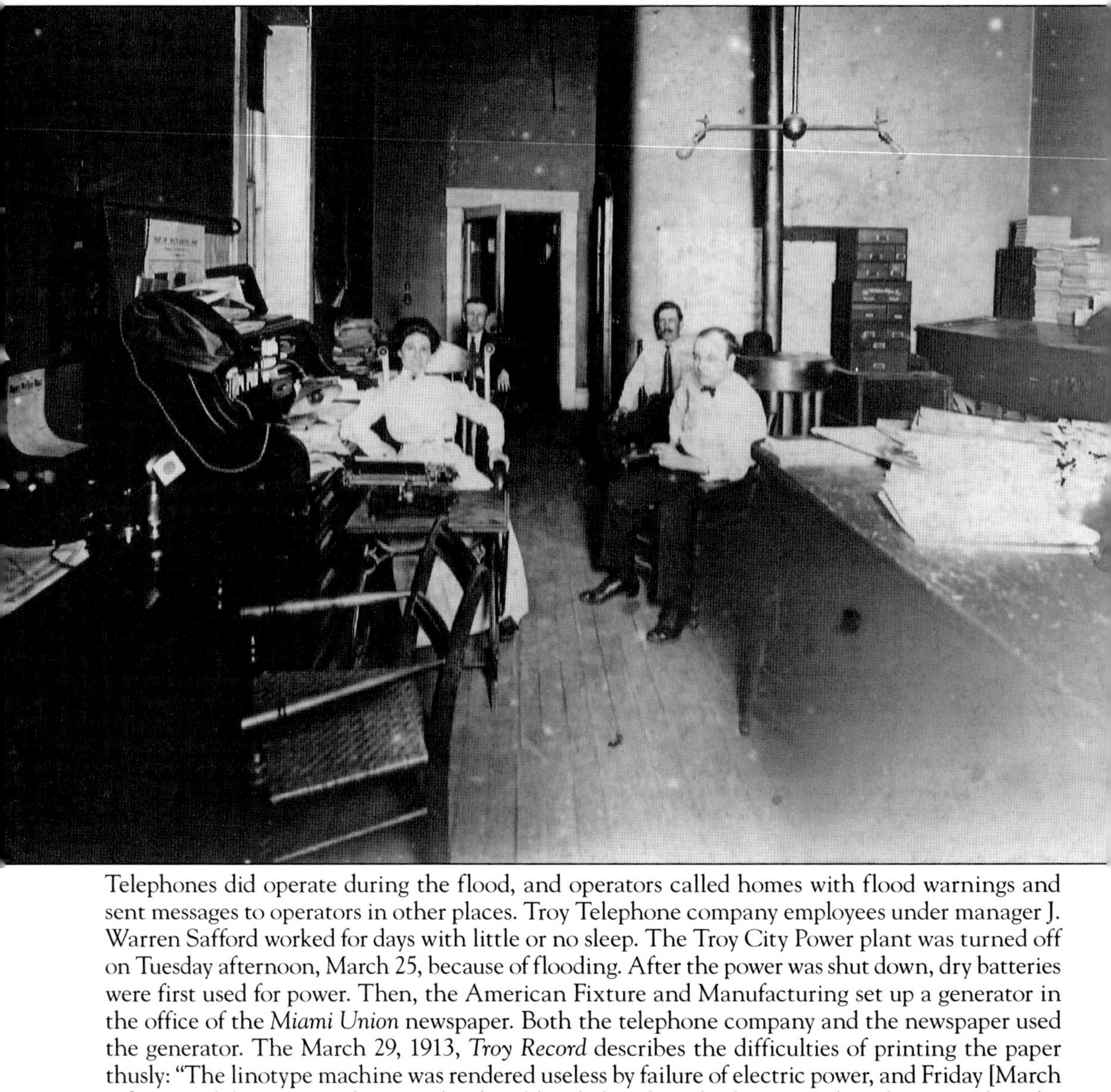

Telephones did operate during the flood, and operators called homes with flood warnings and sent messages to operators in other places. Troy Telephone company employees under manager J. Warren Safford worked for days with little or no sleep. The Troy City Power plant was turned off on Tuesday afternoon, March 25, because of flooding. After the power was shut down, dry batteries were first used for power. Then, the American Fixture and Manufacturing set up a generator in the office of the *Miami Union* newspaper. Both the telephone company and the newspaper used the generator. The March 29, 1913, *Troy Record* describes the difficulties of printing the paper thusly: "The linotype machine was rendered useless by failure of electric power, and Friday [March 28] most of the type used was set by the old style hand method. Late Friday afternoon thru the kindness of managers of the electric light plant an independent line was run over to the *Record* office, providing light power for the machine, permitting its use Saturday, tho handicapped to some extent." This rare image is a 1910 photograph of the shared office of the *Troy Daily News* and the *Miami Union*. Today, the *Troy Daily News* is Troy's only hometown newspaper.

Six

BAD DAYS FOR BUSINESSES

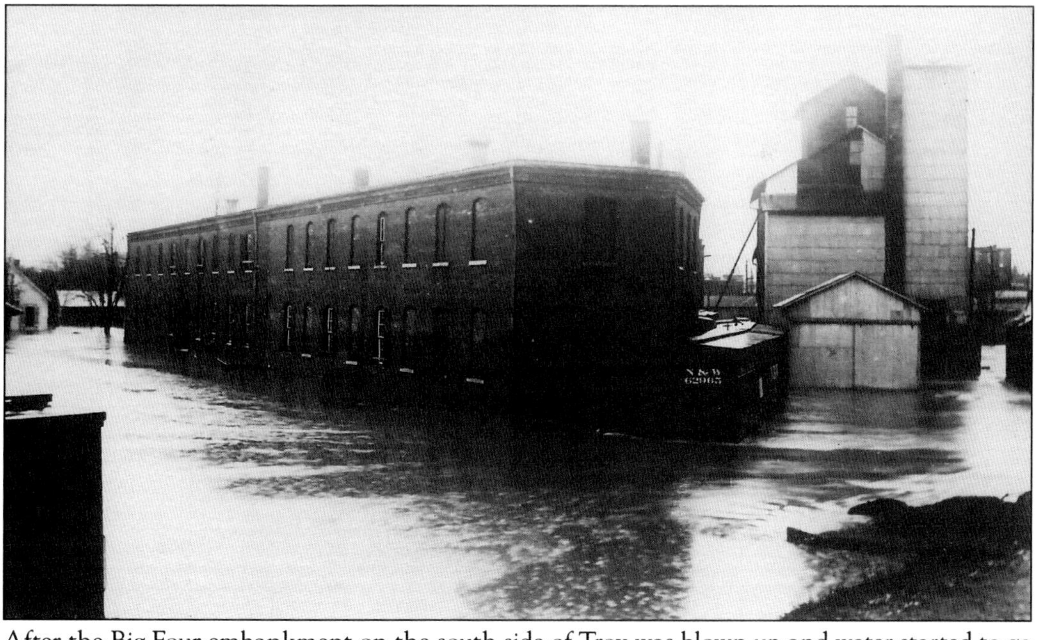

After the Big Four embankment on the south side of Troy was blown up and water started to go down, local businessmen began evaluating their damages. Lists of business losses were published in the local newspapers. The March 29, 1913, *Troy Record* reports, "It is estimated . . . the loss from the flood in the Miami Valley will exceed that caused by the earthquake at San Francisco." Shown here are buildings of the Allen and Wheeler Company. The tobacco warehouse is the long structure on the left, and the company elevator is at right.

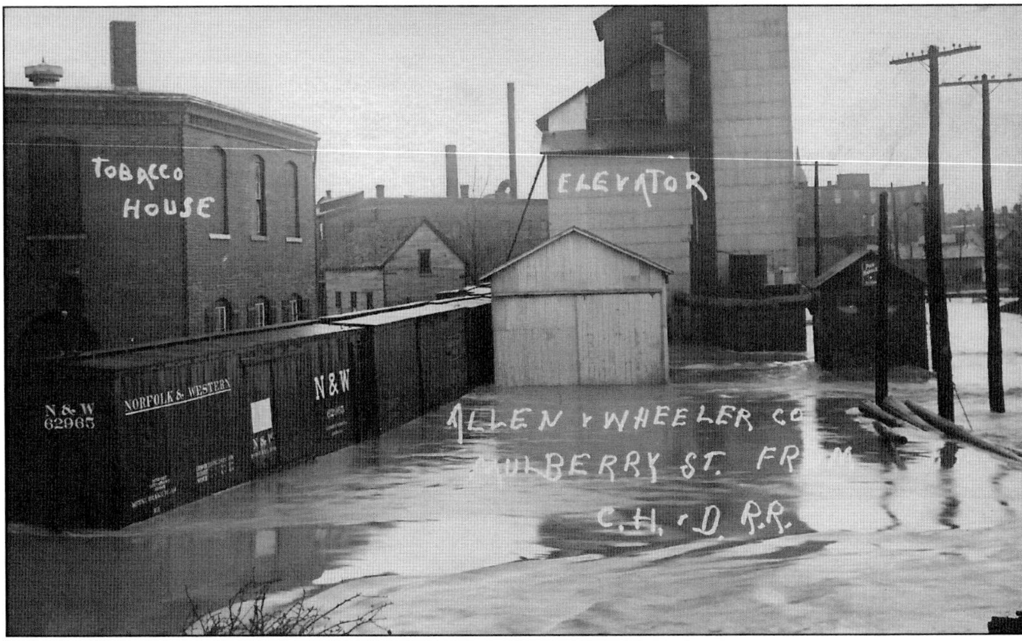

This photograph shows the Allen and Wheeler Company elevator at Market Street and the Miami and Erie Canal, tobacco warehouses at the packing plant on Mulberry and McClung Streets, and a storage house at Market and Canal Streets. The plant estimated its loss as between $30,000 and $60,000. The principal loss was the large inventory of tobacco stored in the various warehouses. Officials expected that, after the flood, much of their finest tobacco would be fit only for fertilizer. At the company's Eldean Mill, about $3,000 worth of damage was done to machinery.

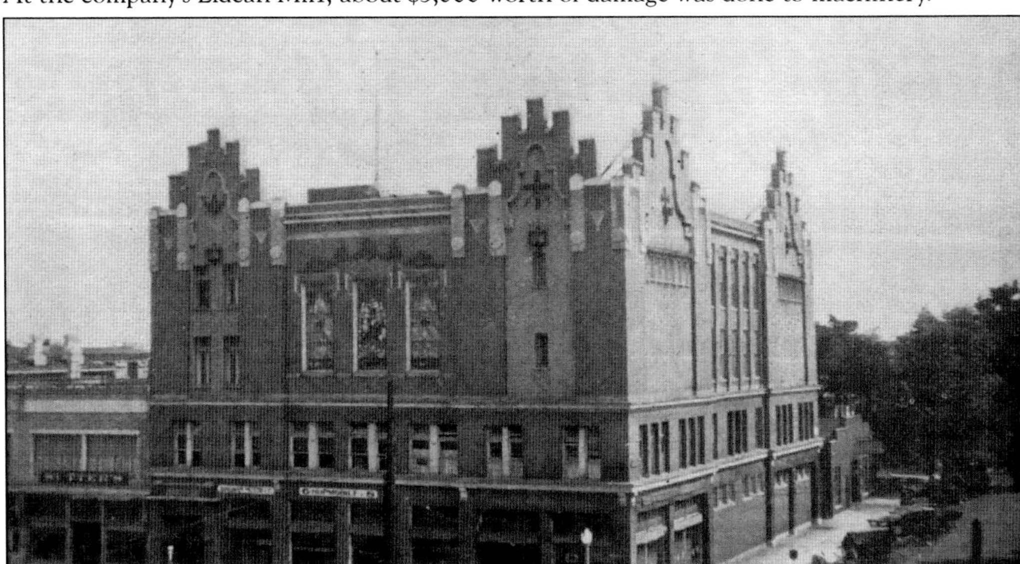
Masonic Temple, Troy, Ohio

The H.A. Cosley hardware store, located in the Masonic Temple Building, posted a notice in the April 3 edition of the *Troy Record* stating that "$4,000 of flood-damaged goods would be sold at a great sacrifice." Everything from washing machines to lawn mowers was offered for sale. Cosley said that he would dispose of products "to your advantage and my loss."

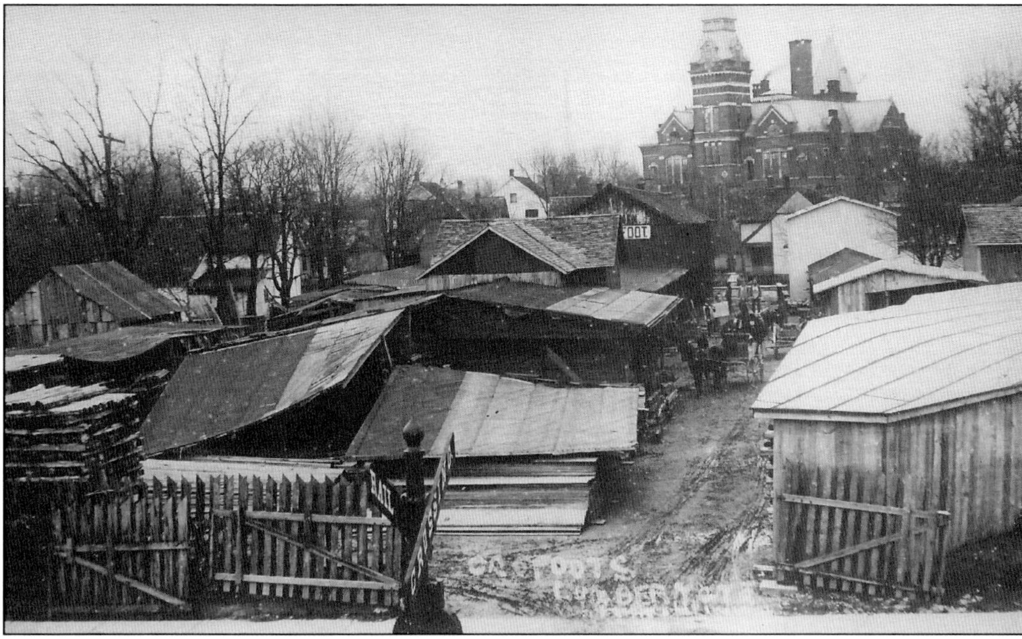

Water covered the desks and counters of the R.W. Crofoot Lumber Company at 528 Grant Street. In the yards, lumber piles were toppled over and there was considerable damage to buildings. Luckily, the yard was enclosed, so little, if any, of the lumber got away.

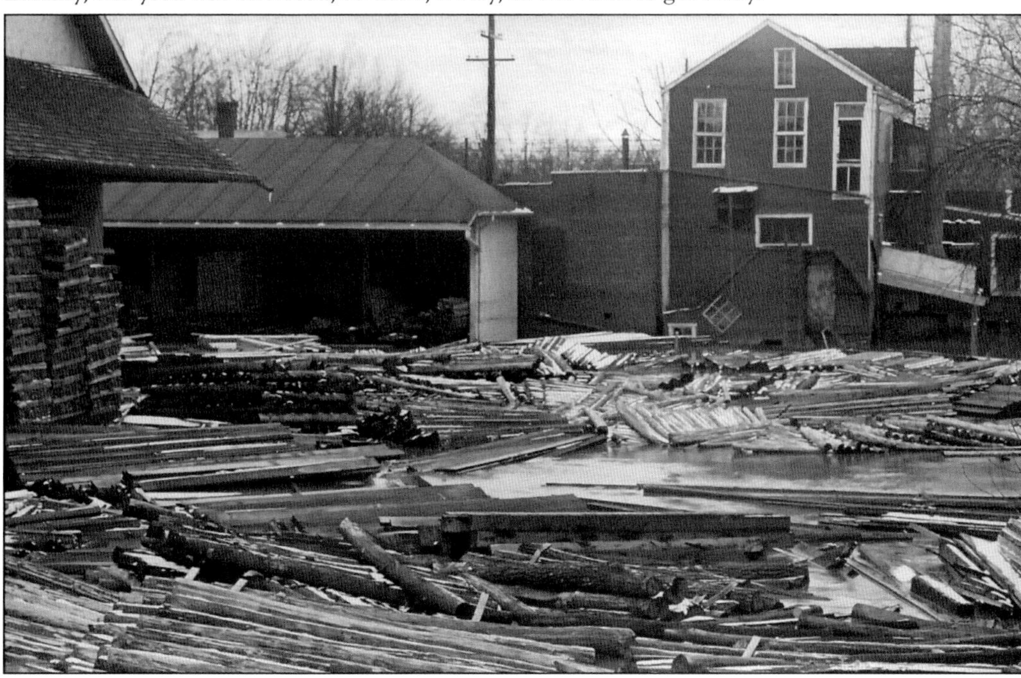

The Francis and Clemm Company lost thousands of dollars worth of lumber and shingles. A March 25, 1963, article by Dale Francis in the *Troy Daily News* states that "stacks of lumber floated away from Francis and Clemm's Lumber yard at Walnut and Race. 'There goes our new house,' one fellow said as he saw a big stack go by on South Walnut." Lumber from the company was scattered all over southeastern Troy.

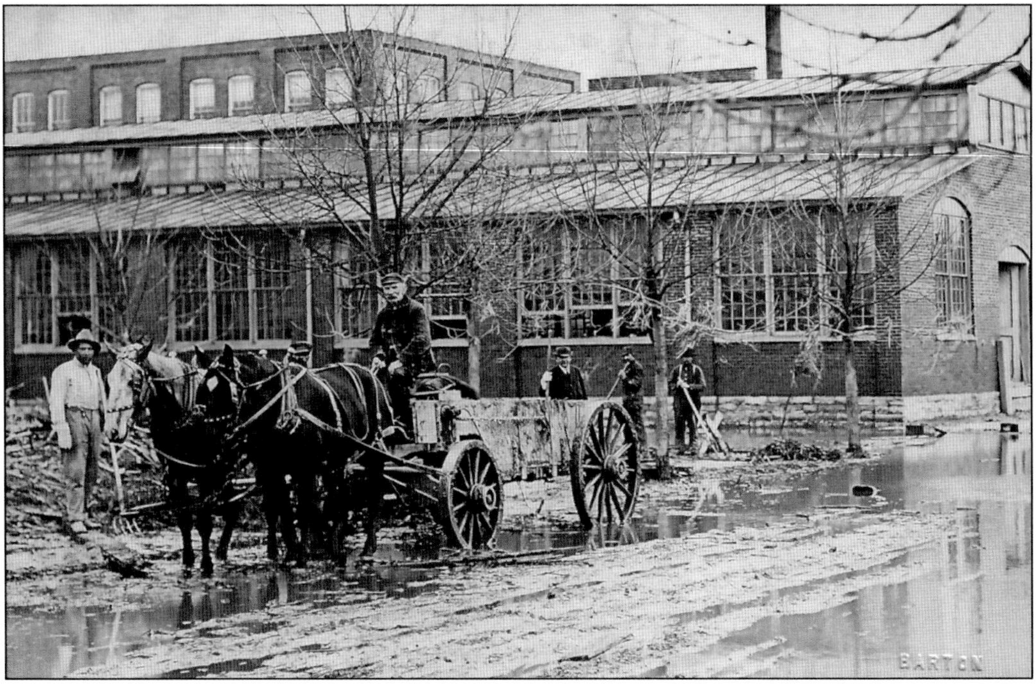

The Hobart Electric Manufacturing Company, a food equipment company, had reincorporated as Hobart Manufacturing Company only days before the flood. The company offices stood in seven feet of water, and years of records were destroyed. The April 3, 1913, the *Miami Union* reports that "all of the books, records, office forms, and advertising matter were soaked and not a single piece of office furniture was left standing . . . In the Hobart machine shop, there are many thousands of dollars worth of expensive lathes and other machinery, the water was the same depth as in the offices and no estimate of loss can be made until the machinery is thoroughly dried. Fortunately, the finished coffee mills and meat choppers, ready for shipment, were high and dry." The photograph below was taken on Pennsylvania Avenue looking south from Race Street.

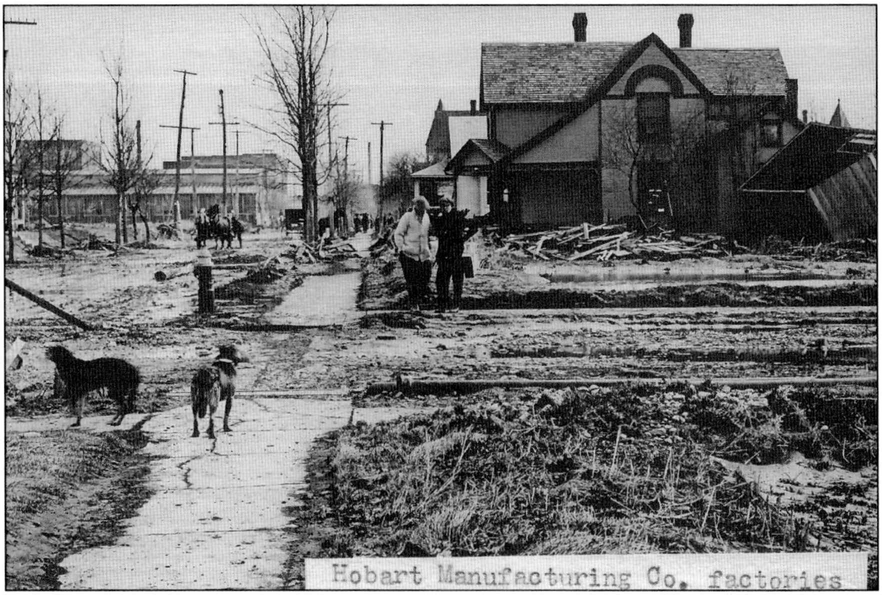

Augustus Stouder was the president of the Hobart Manufacturing Company at the time of the flood. Stouder, H.L. Johnson, and E.E. Edgar bought the company from its founder, C.C. Hobart, in 1904. Stouder is remembered in Troy for his generosity. He established the Troy Foundation and provided funding for Troy's former medical facility, Stouder Hospital.

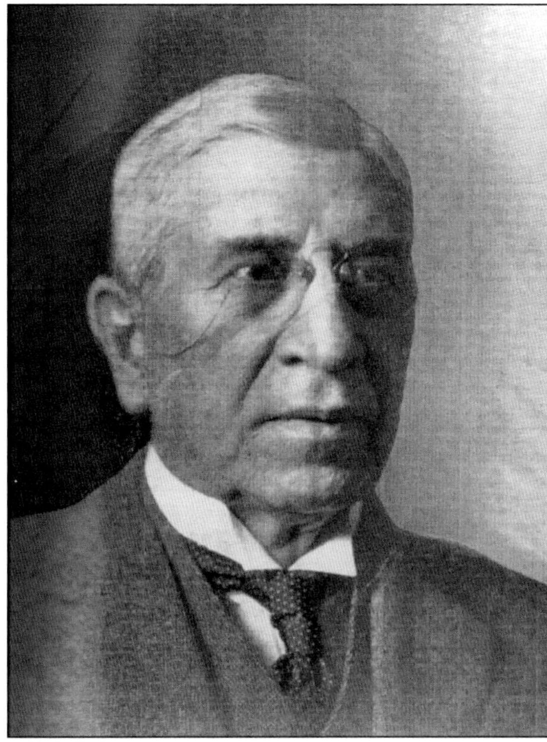

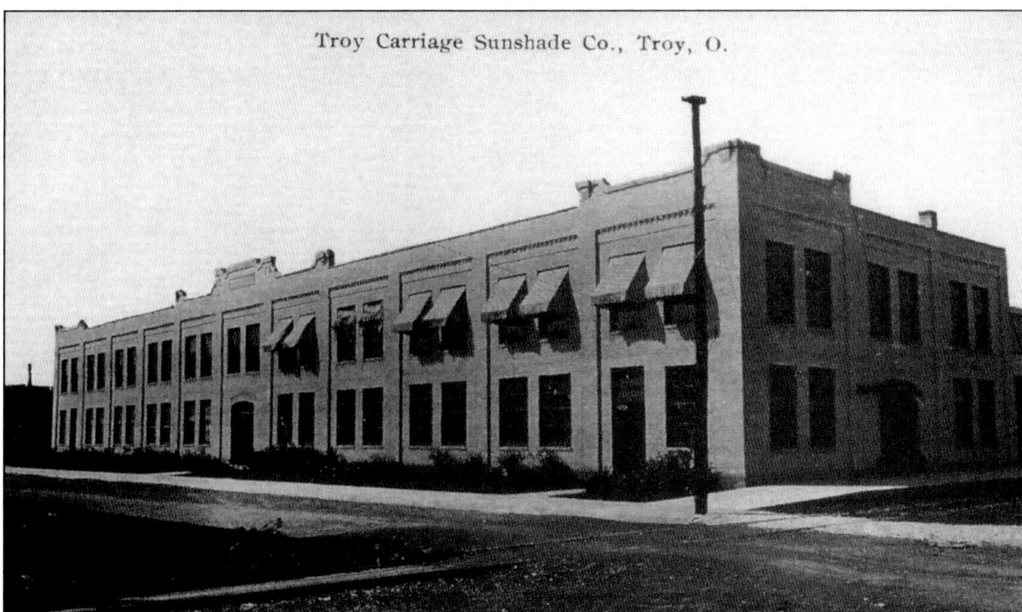

Troy Sunshade Company was located on Lincoln Avenue and Raper Street. Company offices were located on the building's second floor, so no books or records were lost. The company originally made sunshades for surreys, but over time it produced a variety of products. In its automobile windshield factory, water was seven feet deep, covering finished windshields, tons of plate glass, pieces of brass, and polished wood with thick mud. Many machines were damaged, and the company reported a loss of $25,000.

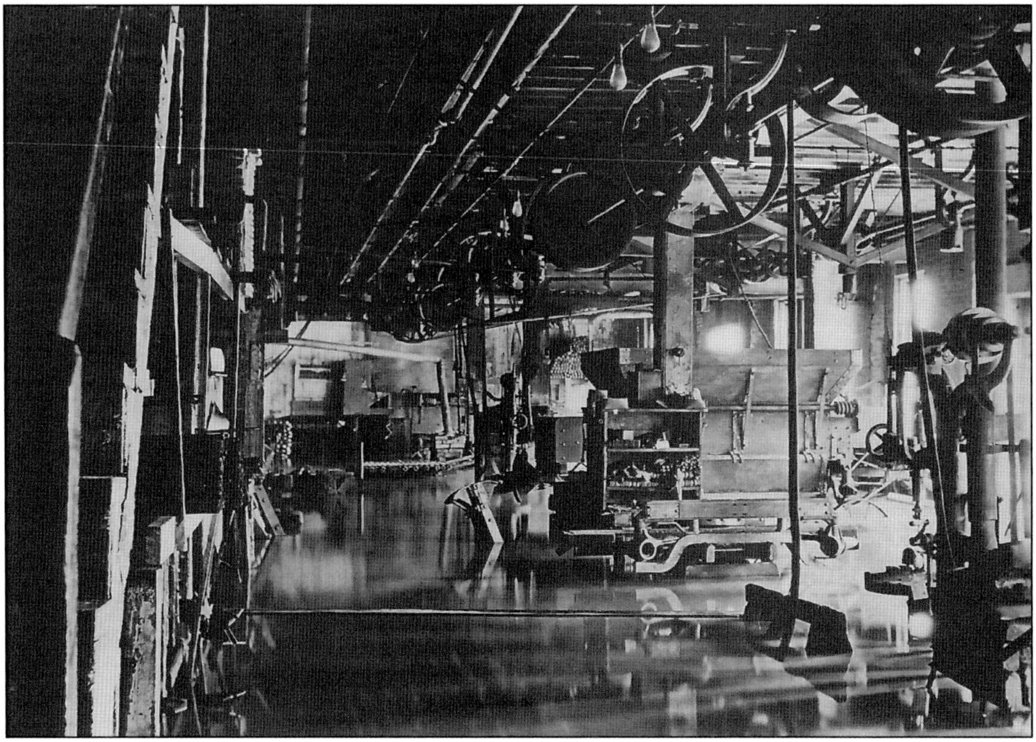

Troy Wagons Works had two Troy locations, with company offices at Race and Mulberry Streets and the plant on South Crawford Street. As a hard rain fell and water rose in the streets, employees frantically carried company records and advertising materials from storerooms in the basement to ground-floor offices. By Tuesday morning, however, water had reached and destroyed many of the documents. Large inventories of hardwood lumber stored at company yards were washed away or damaged beyond use. Several pieces of heavy machinery were submerged. These photographs show water inside the plant (above) and debris outside the company building (below).

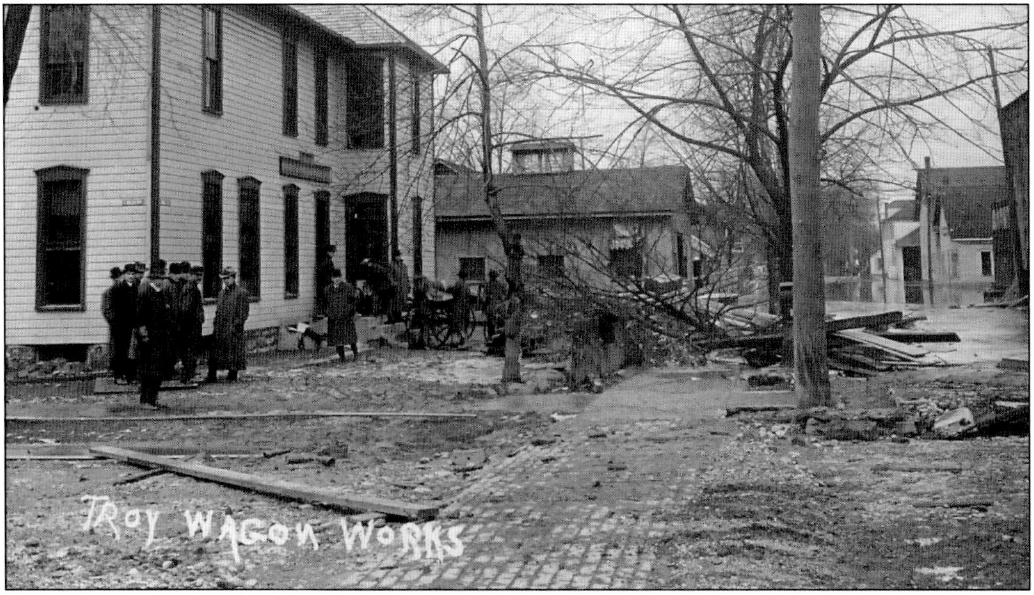

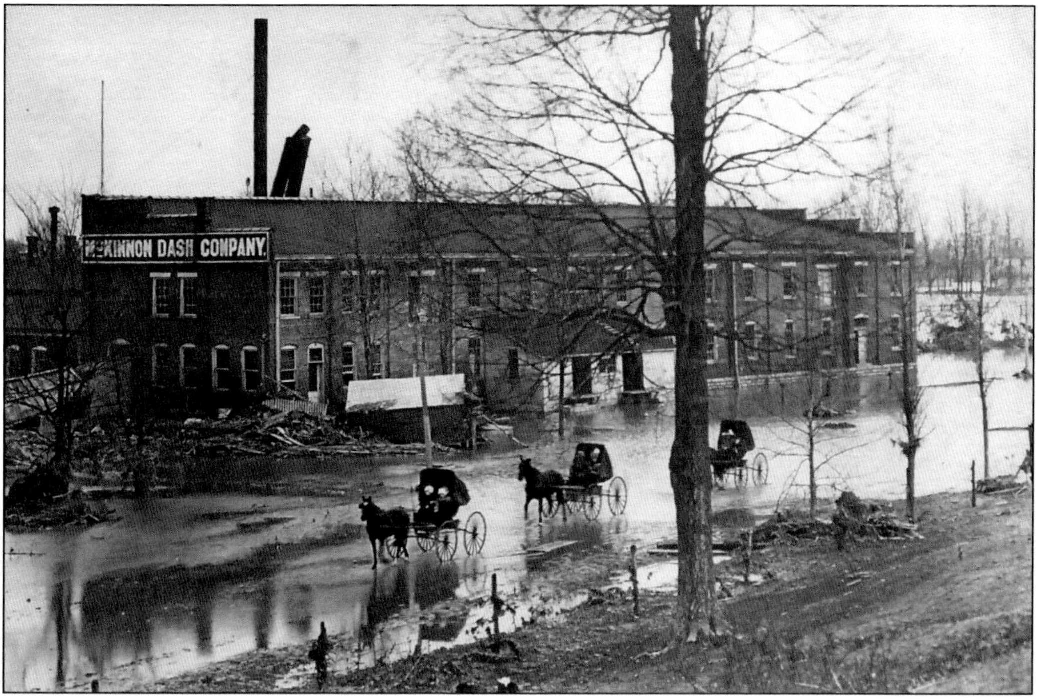

McKinnon Dash Company, at Ridge Avenue and Olive Street, manufactured dashboards for buggies and automobiles. As the floodwaters receded, company official L.H. McKinnon stated that he could not even guess at their losses. Water had reached 12 feet deep, and it was only possible to enter the plant from the roof. About $14,000 worth of finished work was ruined.

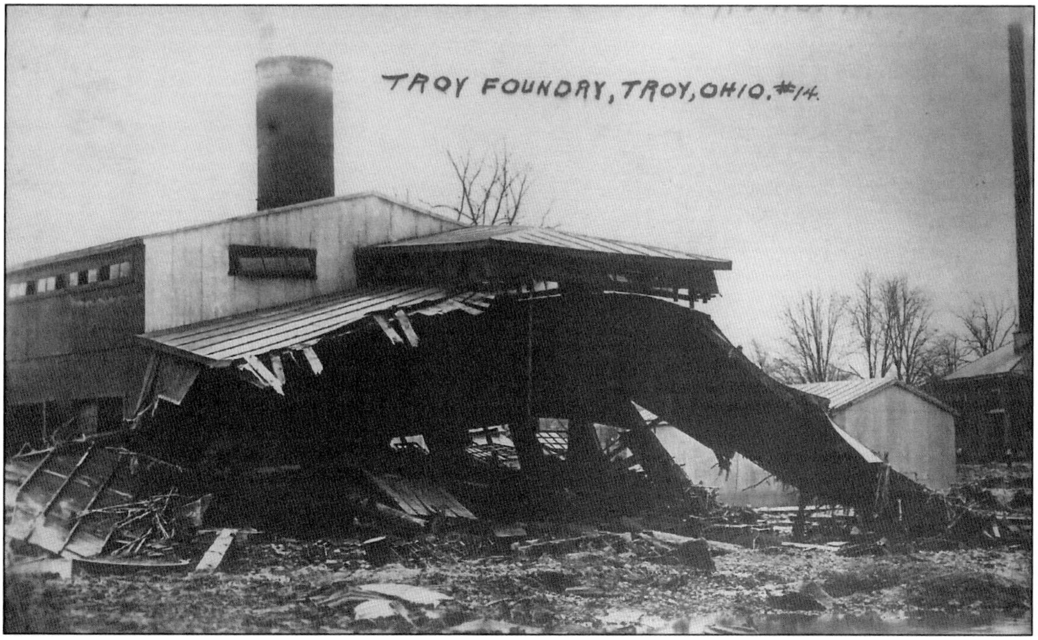

The Troy Foundry Company was damaged at the north half of its plant, as seen in this photograph. It was torn from its foundation on Monday by swift currents of water, and pieces of the building were scattered. Other parts of the plant were also damaged.

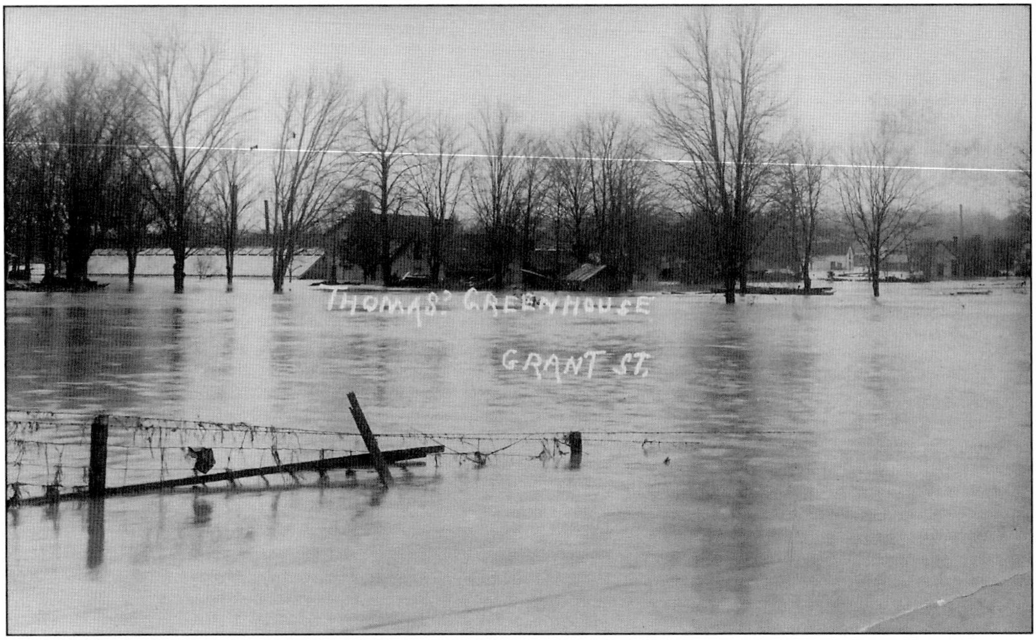

Troy florist L.A. Thomas suffered heavy damage to his South Grant Street business, reportedly losing around $5,000. The April 13, 1913, *Miami Union* states, "His immense greenhouses were directly in the path of one of the most destructive currents of the flood and it is considered miraculous that they were not entirely swept away. Quantities of debris sweeping down with the current crashed into the west ends of several of the greenhouses crushing them in and allowing muddy water full sway across great beds of carnations, which were Mr. Thomas' especial pride." The Thomas family was forced to seek shelter in a nearby packing shed. Eventually, rescuers in a boat took them to a place of safety. These photographs show the strong water current near the greenhouses (above) and a damaged greenhouse (below).

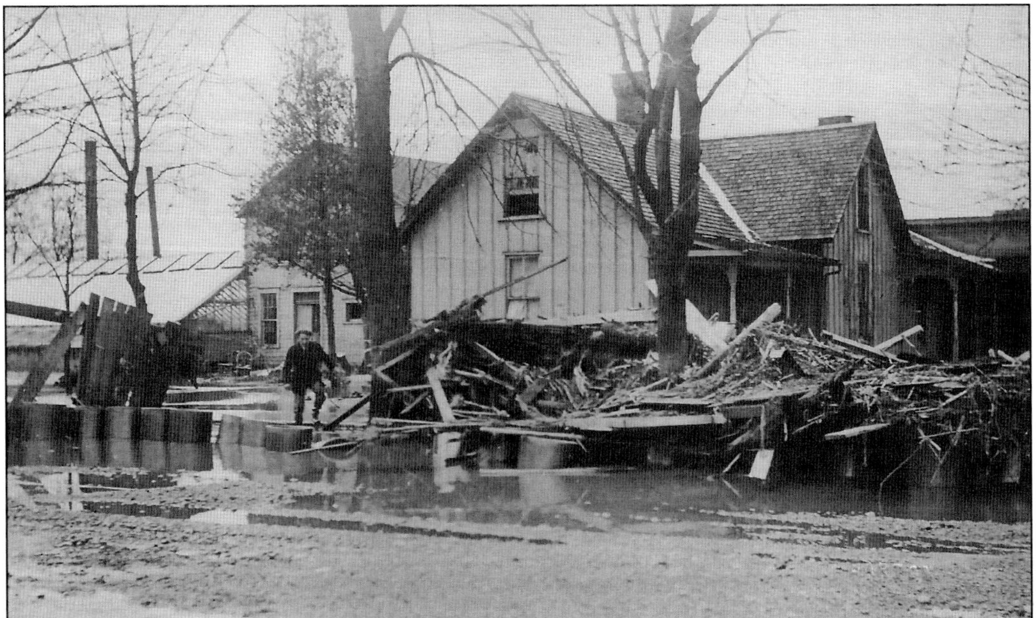

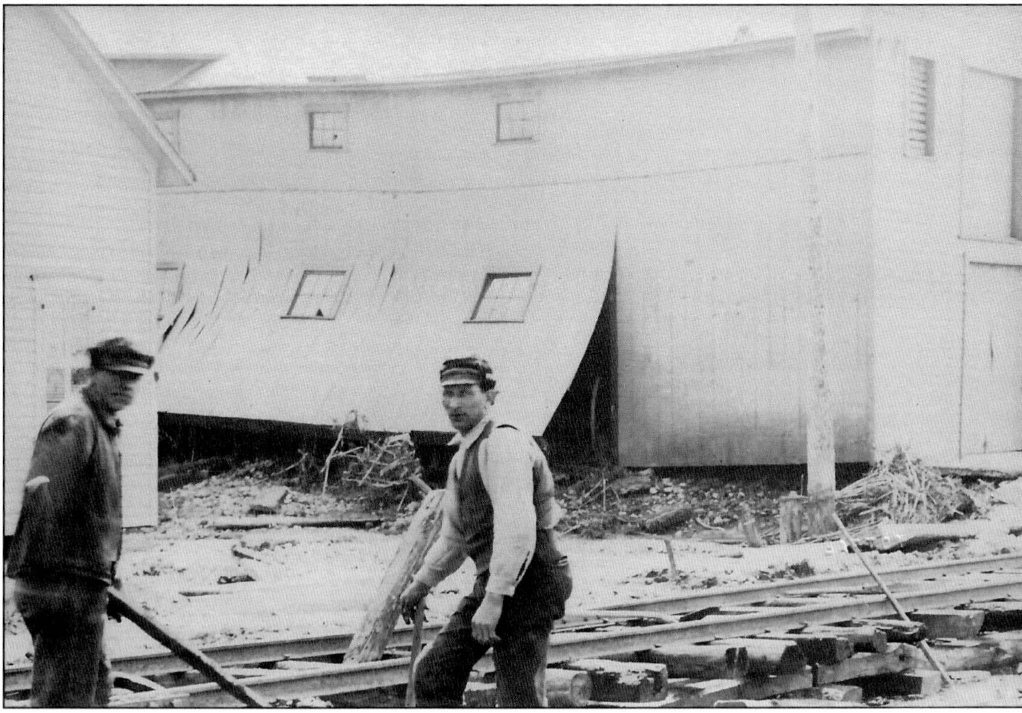

The Cortez N. Smith livery barn in Nineveh, on the southeast corner of the intersection of North Market Street and Staunton Road, was badly damaged. The horses, normally kept in the barn, had been evacuated to Troy as the waters rose. Here, a cleanup crew works at the barn after the floodwaters had receded.

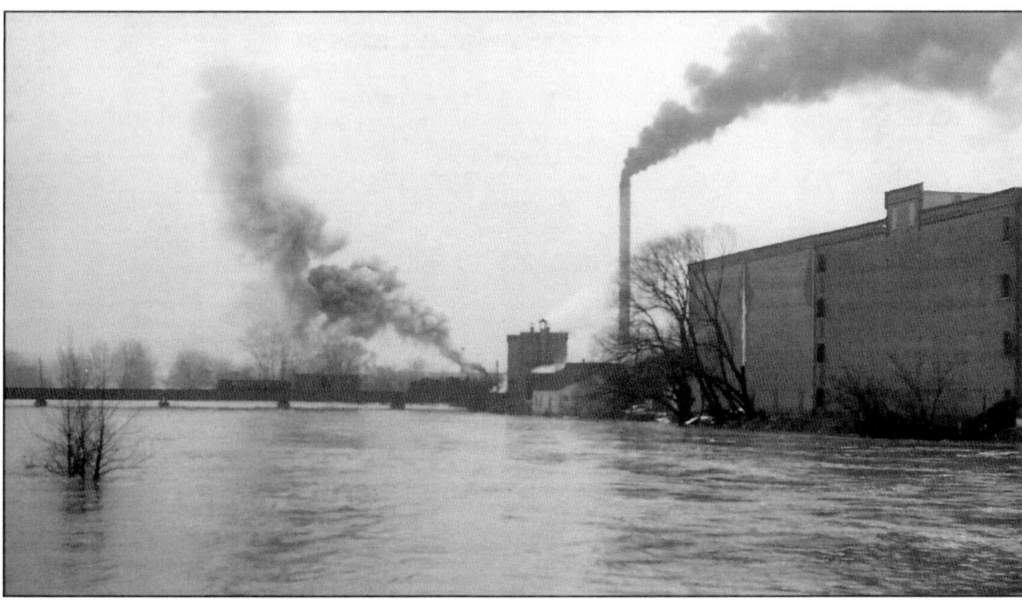

Across the Great Miami River from Nineveh was the Hayner Distillery. There were reports of some water in the building's lower levels, but there was not heavy damage. Company officials had hoped to keep the distillery open during the flood, but they could not find enough employees available to support operations.

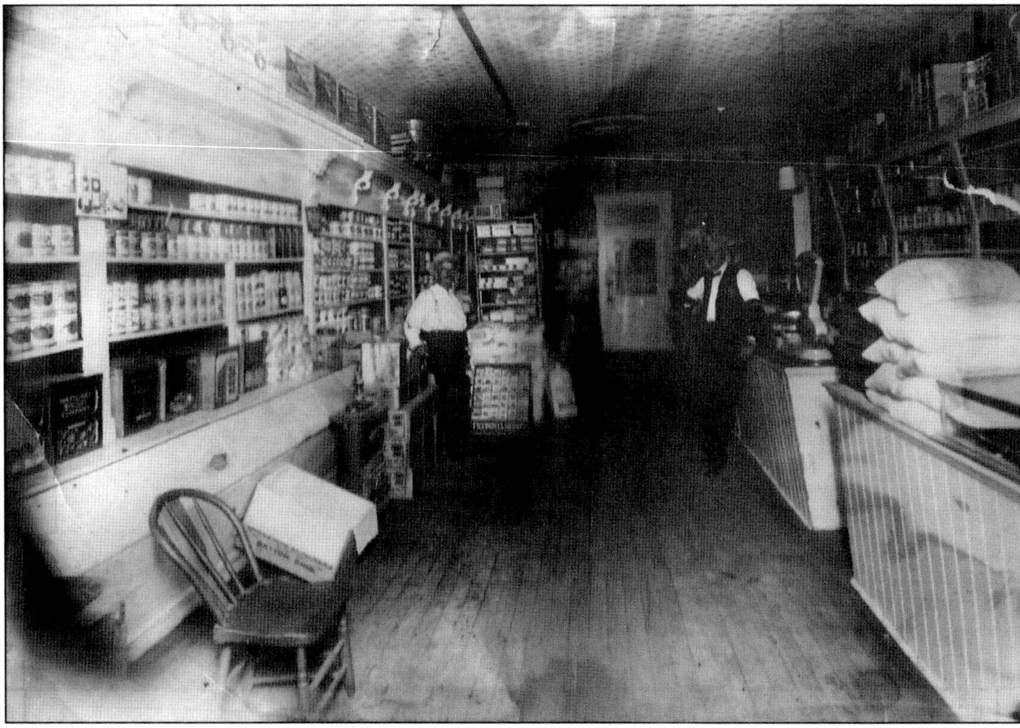

Troy had several neighborhood markets, many of which suffered substantial flood losses. Young's Grocery store, seen here, was on Garfield Avenue, a badly flooded street. Jenny Eccard Sayers recalled that "the grocery store was across the street [from her home]. We'd look out the window and see cranberries and stuff floating down the street."

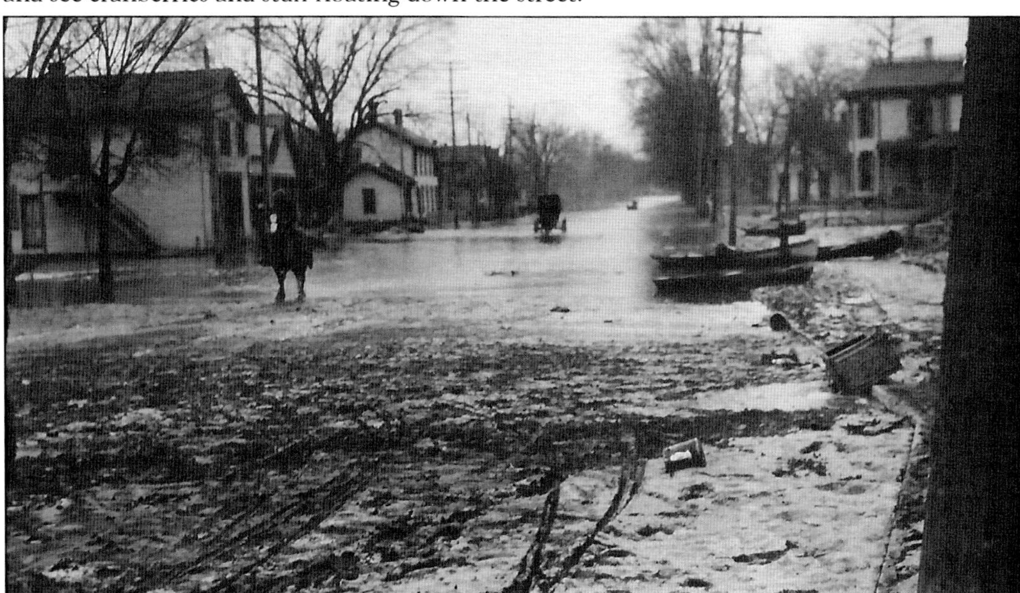

The Adam Long grocery store on West Main Street is the first building on the left in this photograph. Long's home is across the street on the right. It was reported that the store was hit by a current of water six to eight feet deep and was heavily damaged.

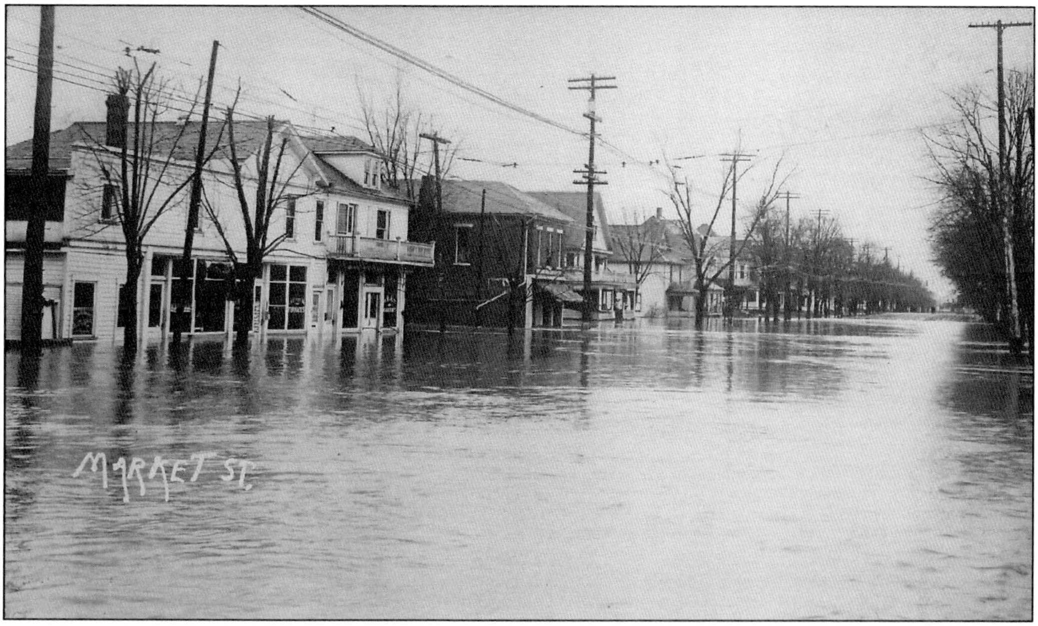

H.W. Doppler and Company was a grocery store at the corner of South Market and Race Streets. The store was caught in the middle of a strong current, and water ran across the tops of the counters. Just before the flood, Doppler had received a shipment of a ton of sugar, which was underwater for several days. This photograph shows South Market Street near the Doppler store.

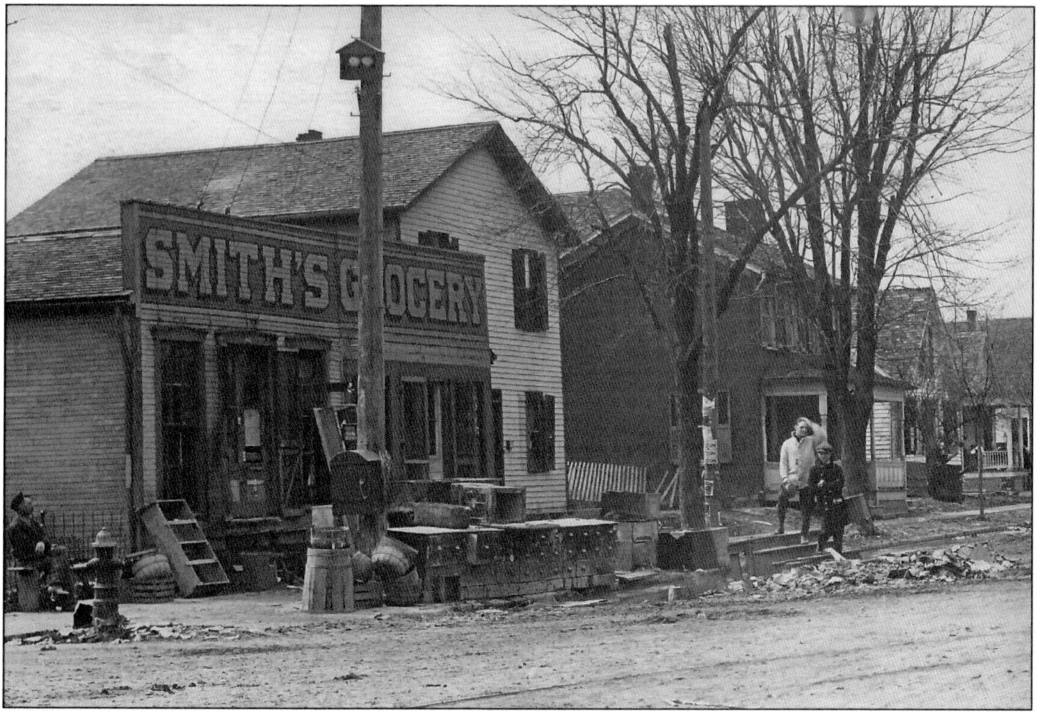

Otto Smith owned a store at West Main and Elm Streets. He rowed a boat to the store and ducked his head to get through the front door, finding only the items on the store's top shelves untouched by water. Smith loaded all the items that were not ruined into his boat and rowed out.

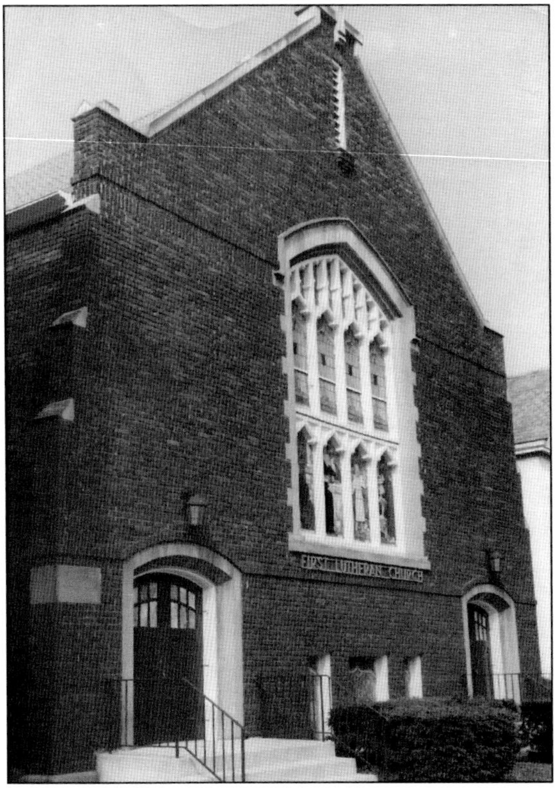

The First Evangelical Lutheran Church of Troy had just built a new church on West Main Street and had planned to dedicate the new structure, when the flood struck. The new church building sustained some damage, delaying the church dedication ceremony until June 1, 1913. The church still stands at 214 West Main Street but is no longer used by the Lutheran church.

Floodwaters damaged the Rosehill Cemetery at the northeast corner of North Market and Staunton Road. The April 10, 1913, *Miami Union* reports, "The sidewalk to the Rosehill Cemetery was carried away in most places while the ground was excavated in places deep enough to hold a small house. The street is covered with gravel and earth in places and at other points is washed out for several feet."

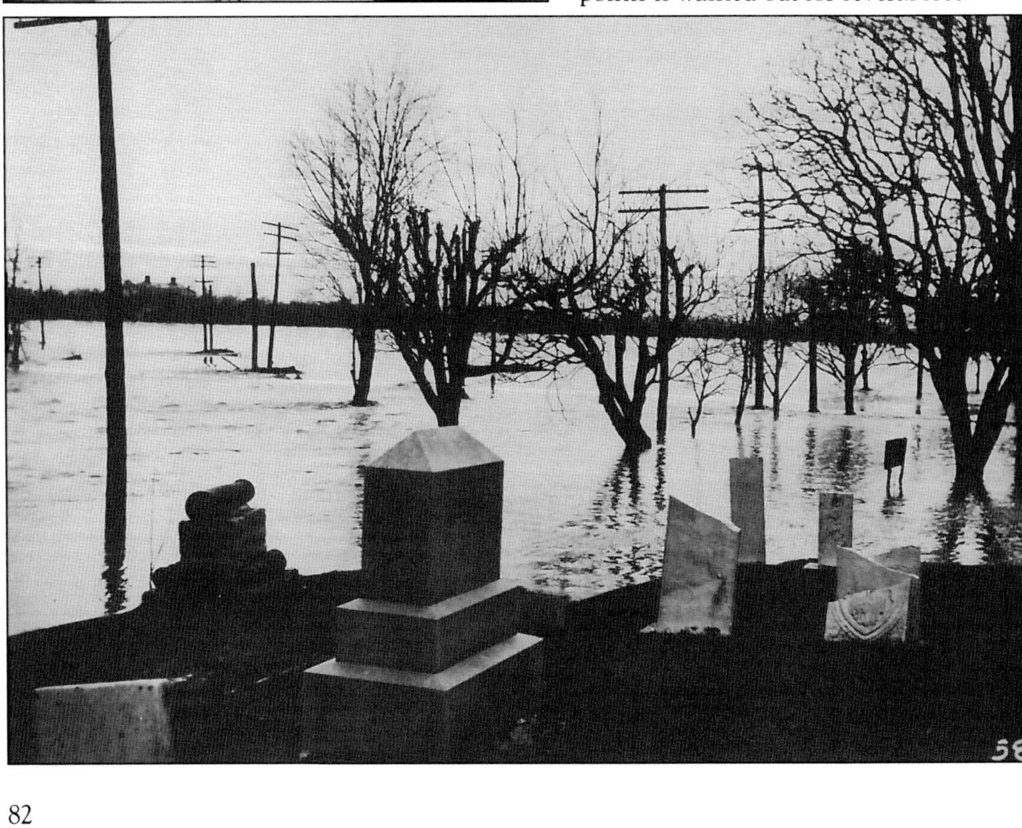

Seven

Wrecked Railroads

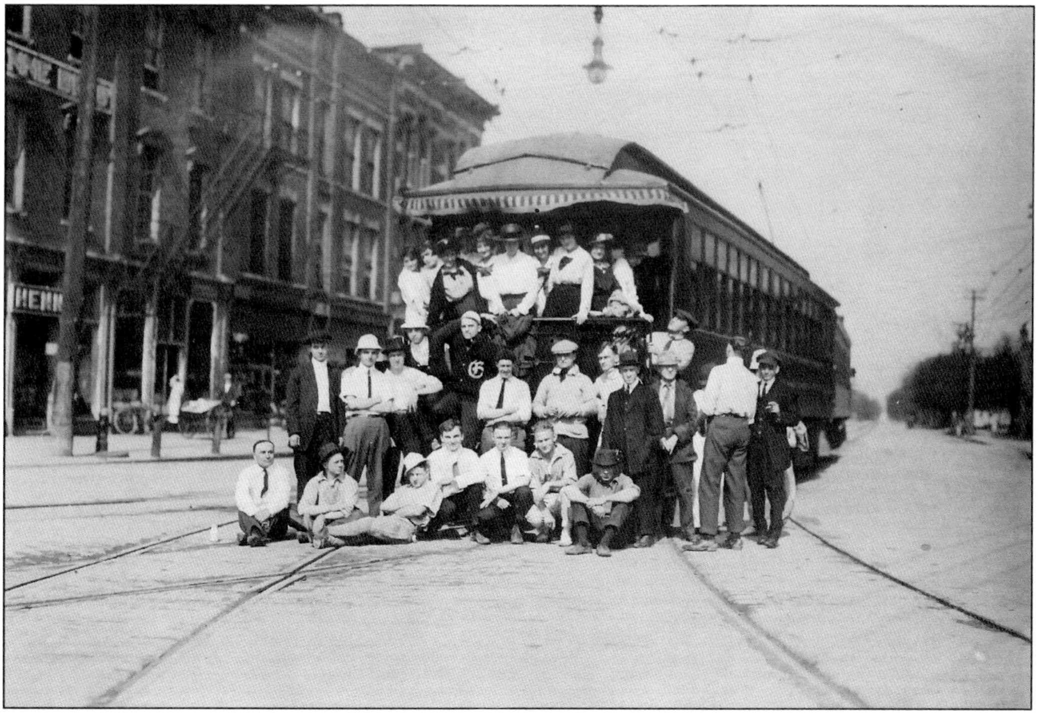

At the beginning of the 20th century, railroads played an important role in Troy life. Before the general use of the automobiles and the birth of the trucking industry, railroads provided transportation for business and social travel and the shipment of goods. When the flood hit, train service to Troy came to a halt, stranding passengers and freight in Troy.

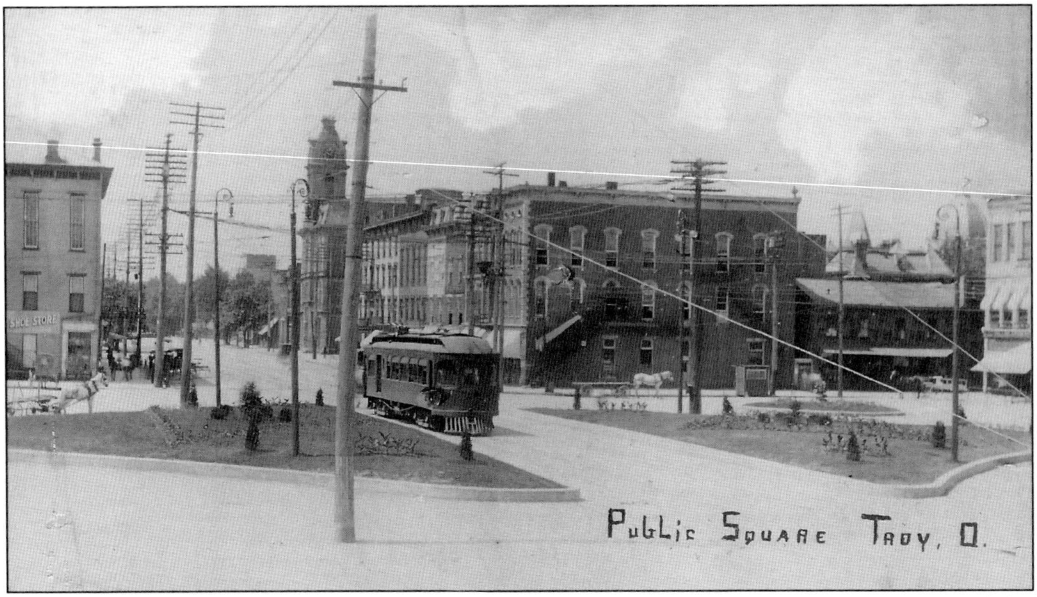

In 1913, two interurban lines operated in Troy—the Dayton & Troy Electric Railway and the Springfield, Troy & Piqua Electric Railway. Interurban lines were trolley cars that operated between towns as short-distance railways. Interurban cars ran so frequently that people could have dinner or see a show in Dayton and come back to Troy in one evening. Young men especially liked to use them for a night out with a favorite lady.

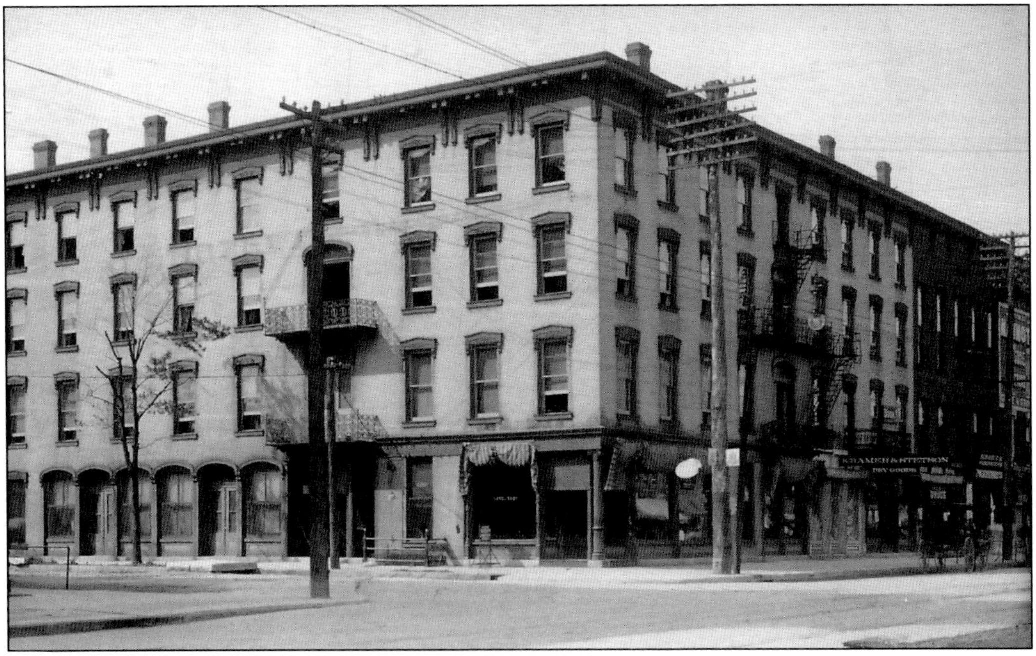

Three men tried to go from Dayton to Sidney on March 24, but the interurban car stopped somewhere in Troy because water was coming over the tracks, marooning the men in a Troy hotel for two days. They eventually decided to walk from Troy to Sidney. On their way north, they saw people drown near the Market Street Bridge. They may have stayed at the Lollis Hotel, seen here. The Lollis Hotel building still exists as Morris House on South Market Street.

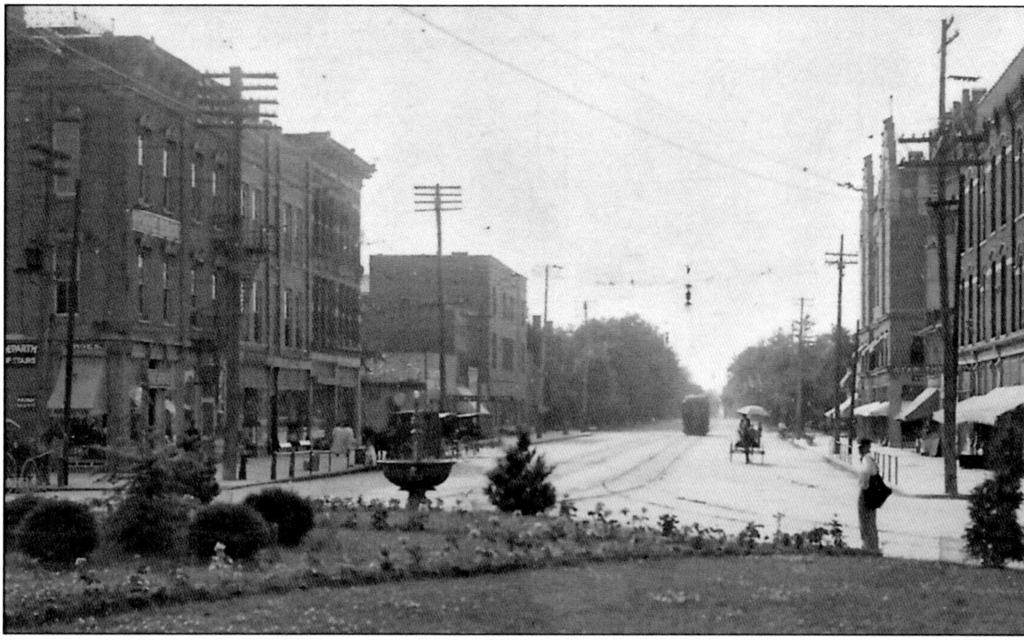

Though the interurban train tracks are now gone, some railroad tracks are in the same places they were 100 years ago. The Cincinnati, Hamilton & Dayton line ran north-south on the east side of town and the Big Four ran east-west was on the south side. The railroads intersected near South Crawford Street, where there were two depot buildings and a restaurant. This photograph shows an interurban train near downtown Troy.

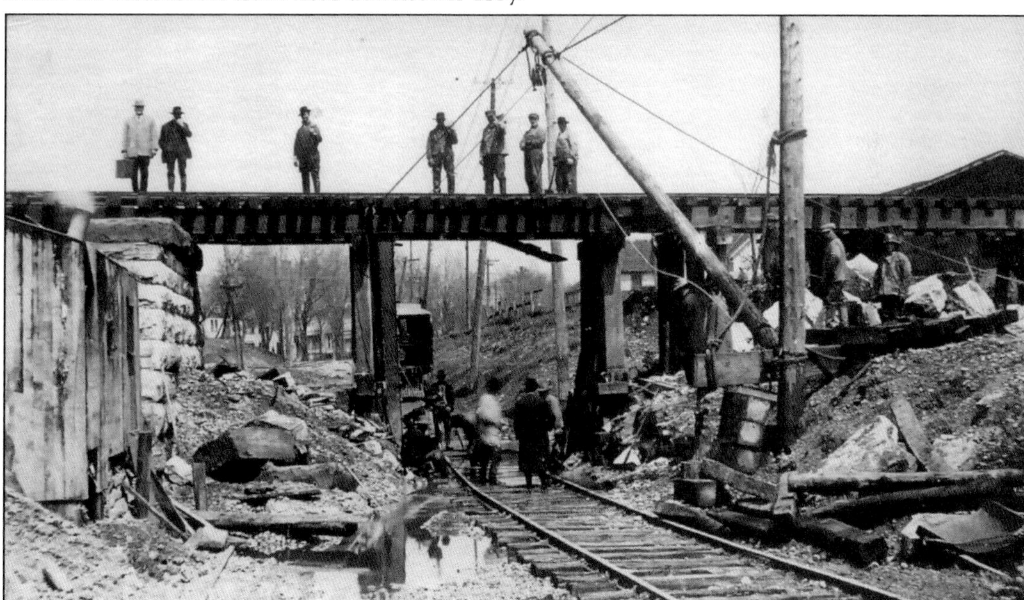

The Dayton & Troy Electric Railway recovered quickly from flood damage. The April 3rd edition of the *Miami Union* announces that cars were leaving Troy for Dayton on the half hour. Passengers would be able to enter flood-stricken Dayton without passes, but not after 6:00 p.m. This photograph shows where the Dayton & Troy Railway passed under the Big Four Railroad tracks near South Market and West Streets.

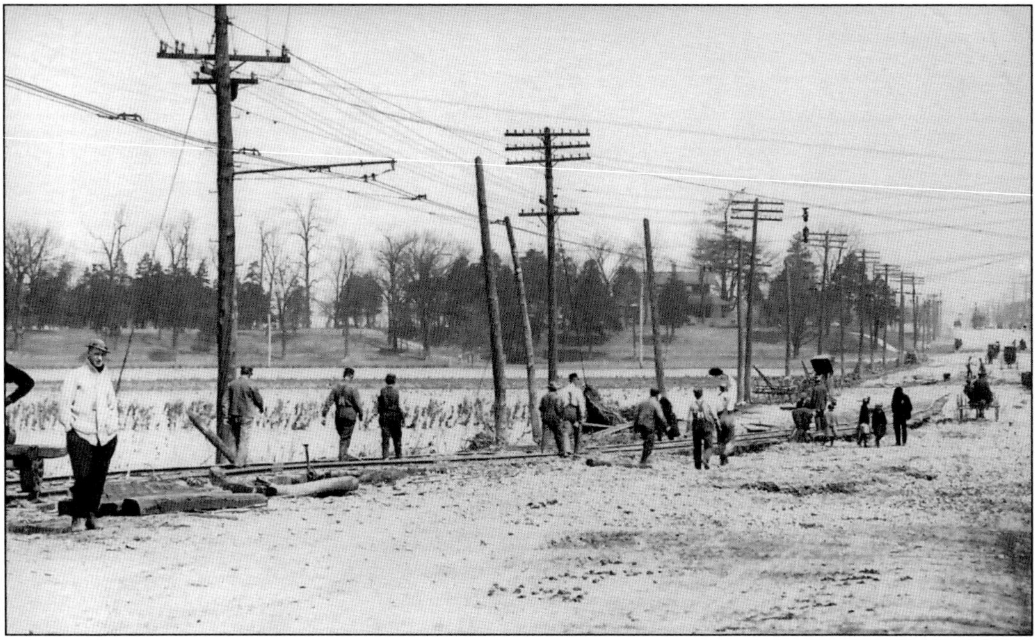

The Dayton & Troy Electric Railway lost no bridges, but the tracks did have some problems with washouts south of Troy. The railroad offered to pay men 40¢ per hour to help repair the tracks, but only a few responded. An article in the March 31, 1913, *Piqua Daily Call* describes the work as "clearing the tracks of gravel and wreckage and repairing the breaks in the grade." These photographs show men working on the tracks. Information written on the back of the photographs indicates that the work crew is under the direction of Ernest Holler, but it does not specify which line they are working on.

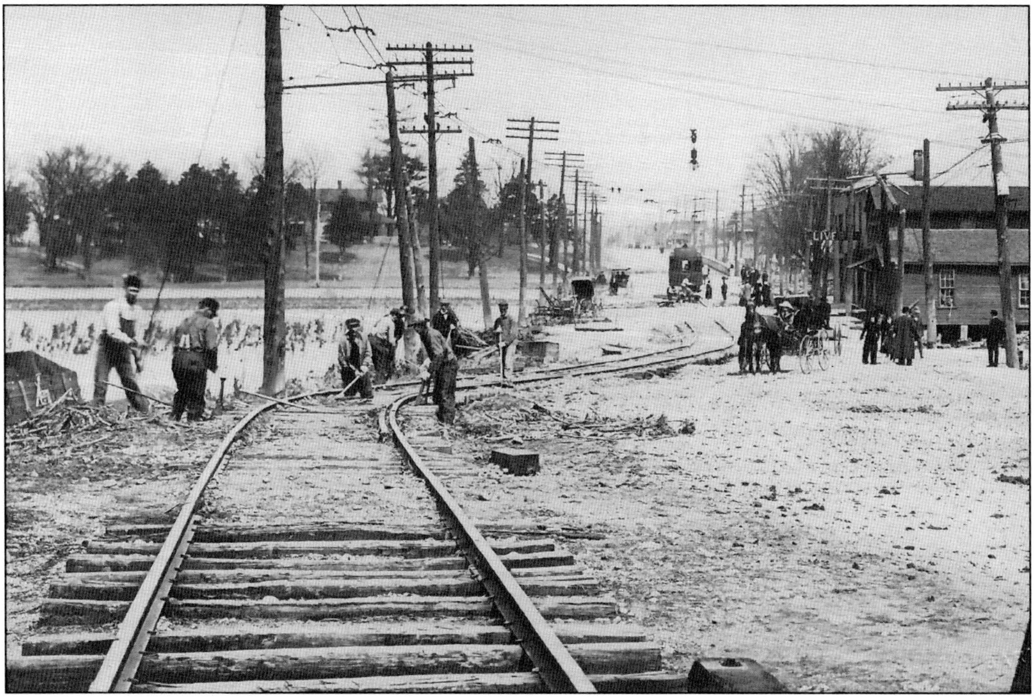

The Cincinnati, Hamilton & Dayton Railroad Bridge over the Great Miami River underwent repair work after the flood. Here, a railroad crew works on the bridge. The span still crosses the Great Miami River near North Clay Street today. The buildings in the background of this photograph are believed to be part of the Hayner Distillery, which was located along the south bank of the river.

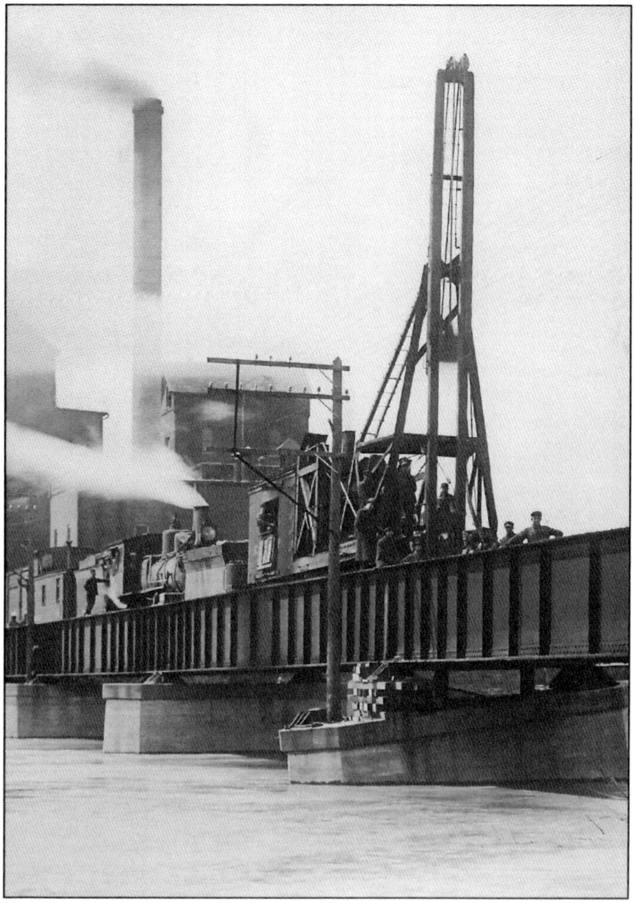

Troy railroad embankments were both a help and a hindrance during the flood. Residents walked the Cincinnati, Hamilton & Dayton Railroad embankment to get through Troy, but the Big Four embankment in the south part of Troy acted as a wall, keeping water in the Troy streets and causing damage. This 1909 photograph of a Big Four Railroad wreck shows the height of one such embankment.

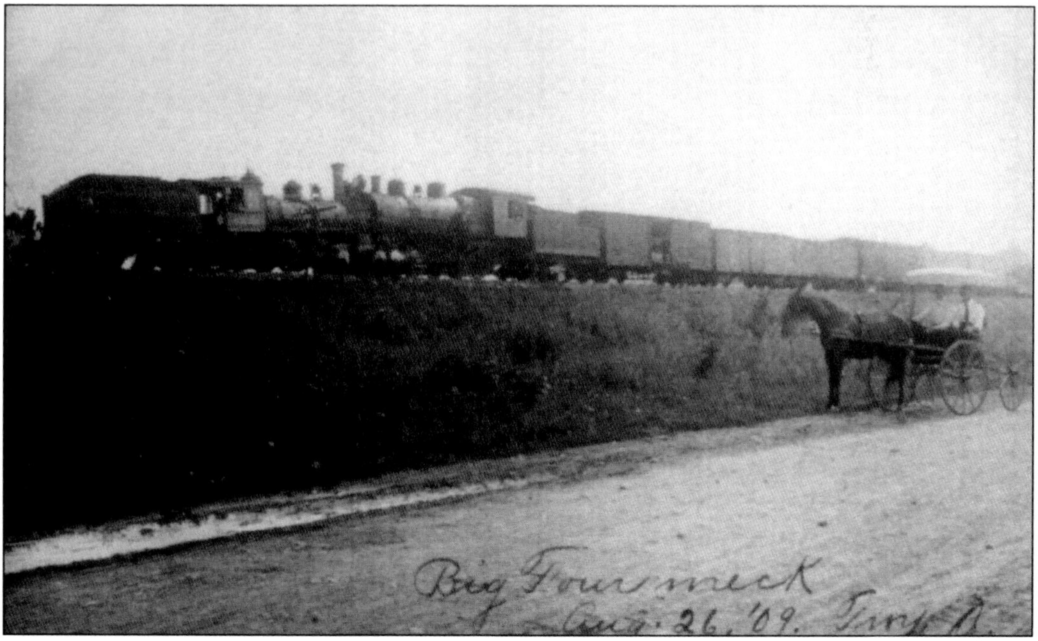

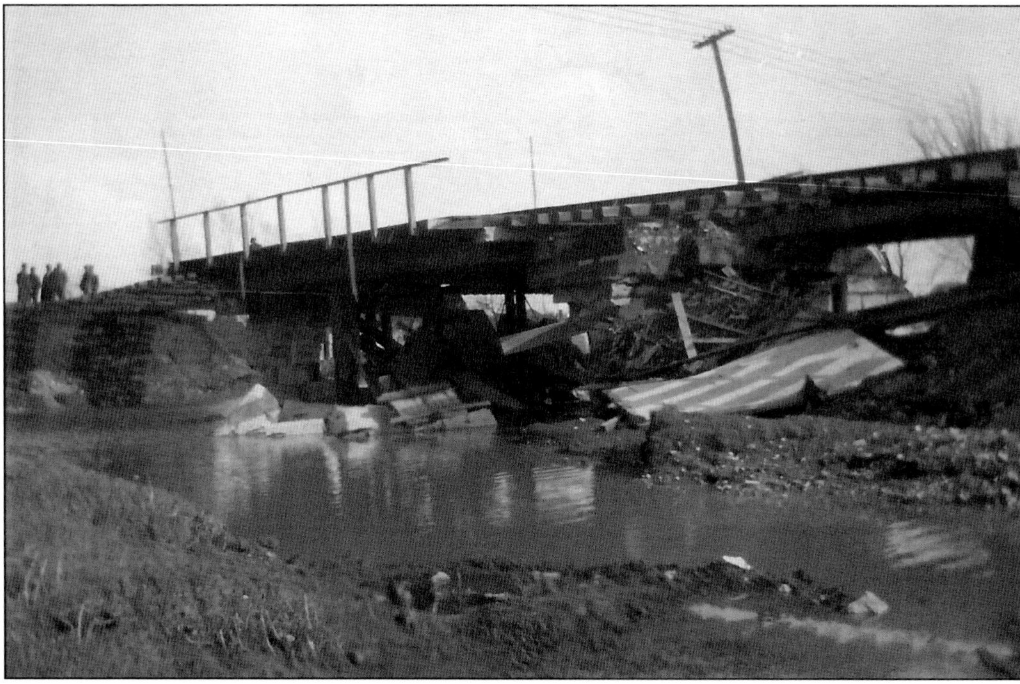

This is the Big Four Railroad embankment south of the intersection of West Market Street, Grant Street, and Peters Avenue. The embankment stopped floodwaters from flowing out of town, causing it to back into the streets and homes of southwest Troy. Using dynamite, a hole was blown in the side of embankment. While the water receded in Troy, its fast rushing through the opening resulted in the loss of both property and life.

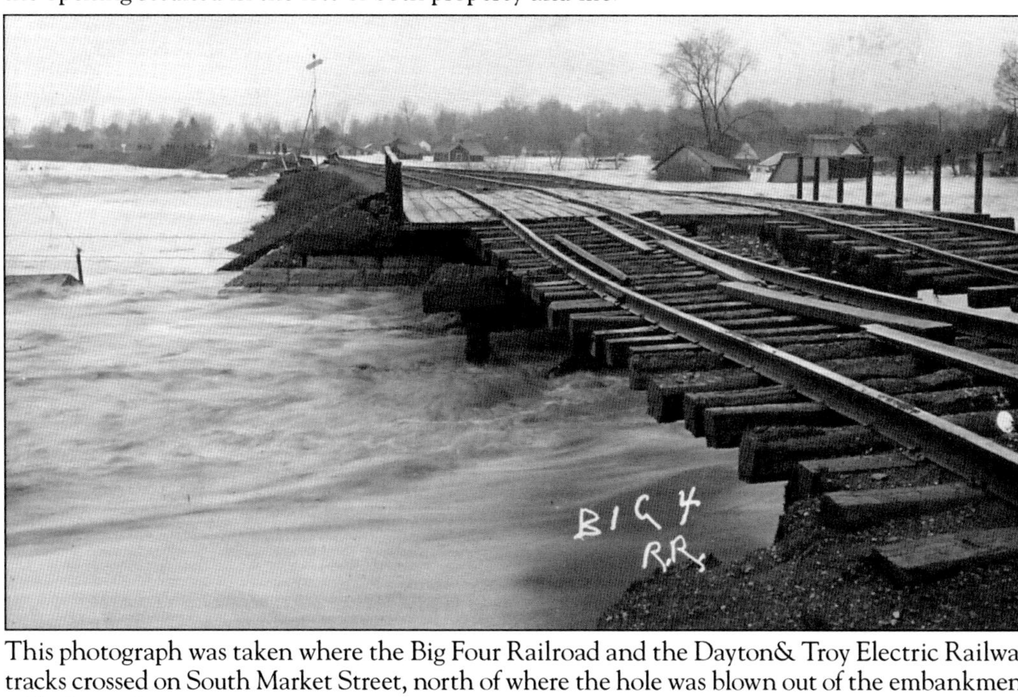

This photograph was taken where the Big Four Railroad and the Dayton& Troy Electric Railway tracks crossed on South Market Street, north of where the hole was blown out of the embankment with dynamite.

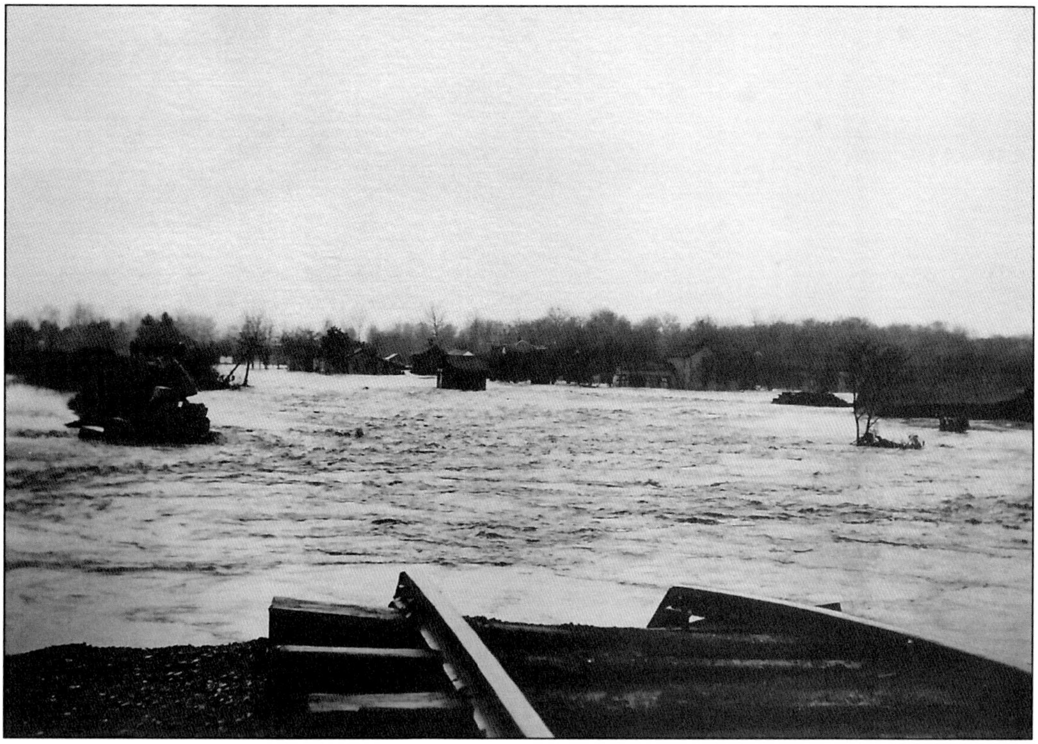

The April 1, 1913, *Troy Record* reports that "the board of health held a meeting Monday night to go over the local situation. They passed a resolution asking the state not to allow railroads to build up their embankments on both sides of town to the extent they were before the flood, but allow openings that will prevent flood conditions in Troy."

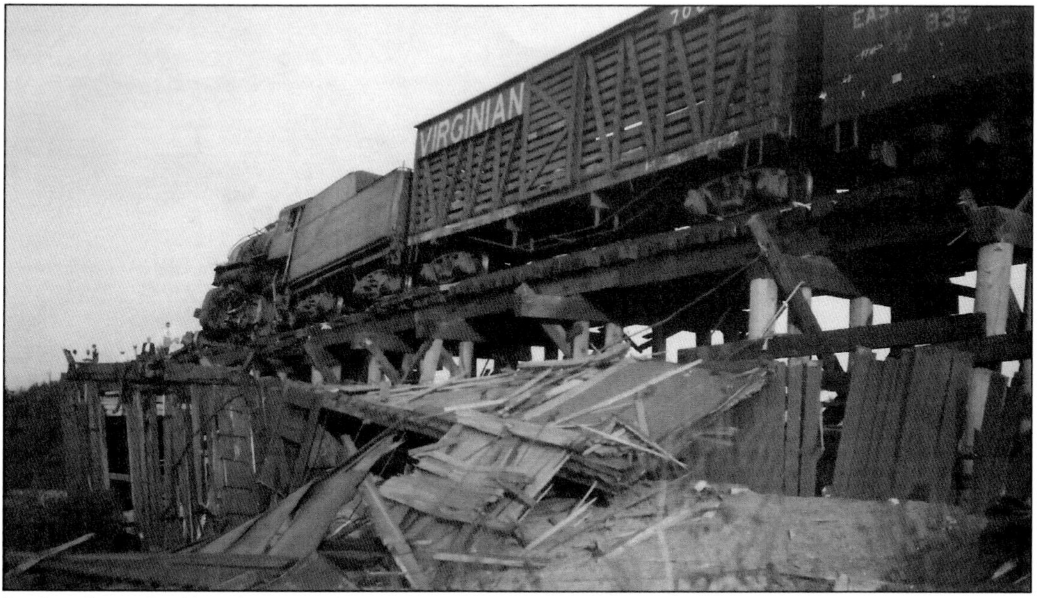

Railroads worked hard to save their property during the flood. In this photograph, a railroad train was pulled out onto tracks to keep them in place and to prevent a bridge from washing away. This photograph was taken near Troy.

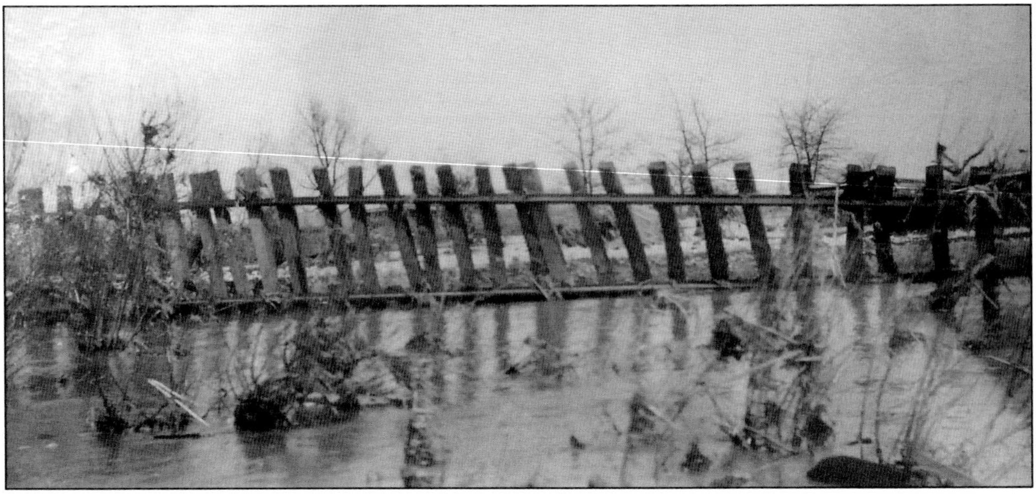

The Cincinnati, Hamilton & Dayton tracks were washed out near the Miami County Fairgrounds. The March 29, 1913, *Troy Record* reports, "The C.H.&D. railroad near the fairground for the distance of nearly three squares, was lifted from its position and turned almost entirely over, a part lying on the ground and a part sticking in up in the air." People compared the sight of the railroad ties to a picket fence.

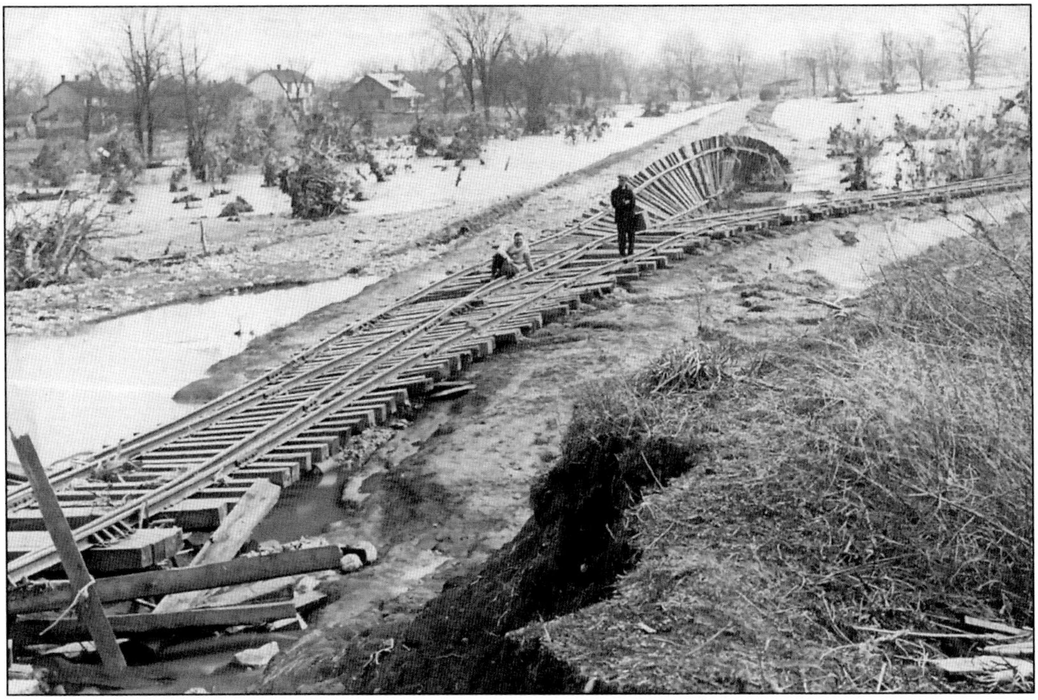

This photograph shows train tracks that were washed out near the Miami County Fairgrounds at Troy. It may be a long-distance view of the scene pictured at the top of this page. In her book, *Golden Jubilee History of the Troy Central Women's Christian Temperance Union*, Anna Stillwater writes the following about the organization's county president returning to Troy from Delaware, Ohio: "On the way, a wash out on the railroad was encountered, and she walked a mile on the trestle, under earnest protest from men, who gave her efficient help in the way our splendid American men are accustomed to do."

Eight

Rebuilding from Ruin

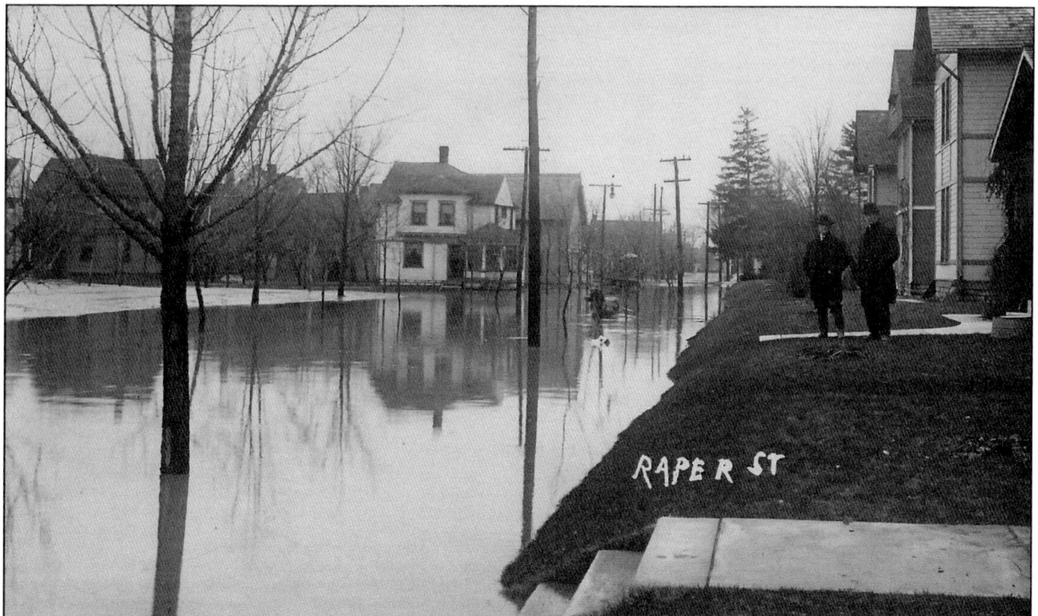

From the beginning of the flood, Troy's leaders—elected officials, business people, and volunteers—organized to care for the town and its people. They sent out warnings, formed rescue teams, and set up shelters, temporary hospitals, and food and clothing distribution centers. When the water was as at its peak on Tuesday, they met to consider how they would lead recovery efforts. There was never a doubt that Troy would be rebuilt and reinvented. The men at right are probably discussing flood conditions.

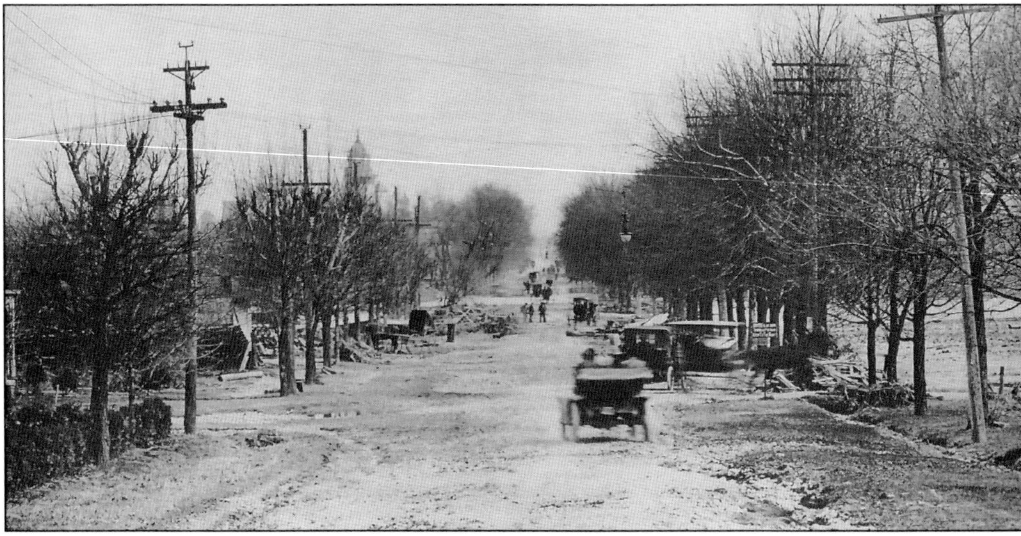

Robert Smallenbarger remembers, "It was scary to look out over old familiar areas, one that had always seemed so reassuringly pleasant and free of drastic change, and then overnight, as it were, have daylight reveal a monster in possession of your little world, using it as a playground for total disaster." This West Main Street view looks east toward the Miami County Courthouse.

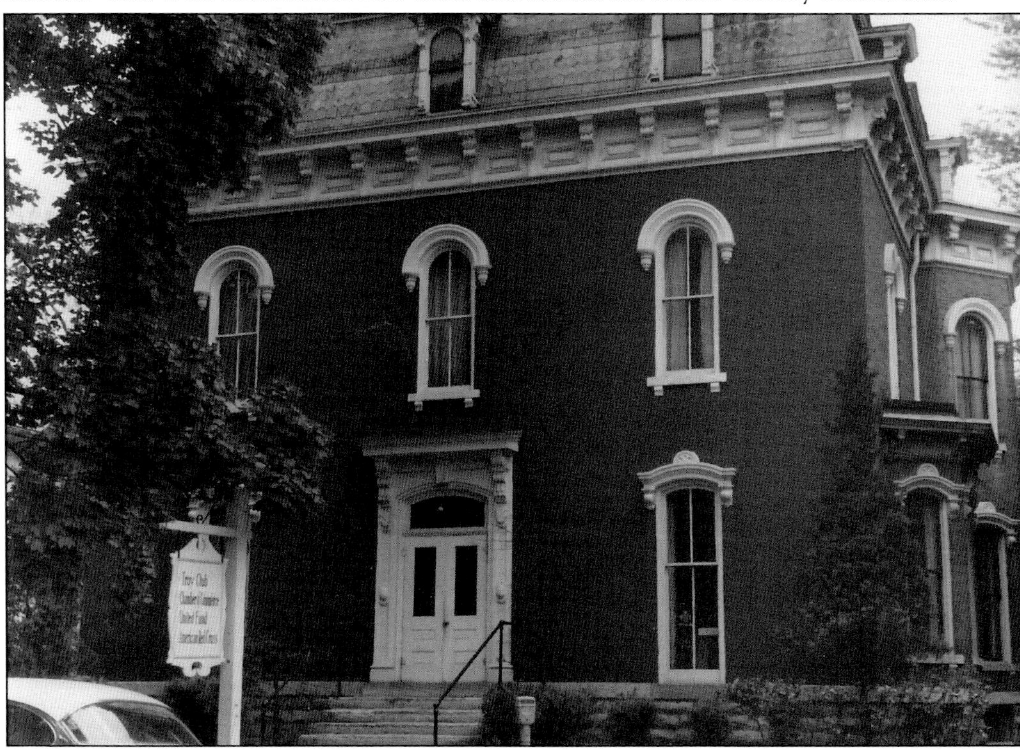

On the evening of Tuesday, March 25, several residents gathered at the Troy Club, seen here, to organize what was termed "a systematic relief committee." Civic leader Walter E. Bowyer called the meeting to order and announced that Troy mayor John McClain had proposed a general meeting of citizens be called together at a later time, but before the flood ended. The committee meeting was then immediately adjourned.

The meeting to organize the relief committee was held in Mayor John McClain's office on Friday, March 28. McClain briefly addressed the crowd and announced he had chosen Walter Bowyer (pictured) and Horace Allen for the committee on organization. Bowyer made a motion to form the relief committee, with Judge E.W. Maier as general chairman, John H. Drury as secretary and treasurer, and J.S. Combs, Horace Allen, and Dr. B.W. Combs as members of the executive committee.

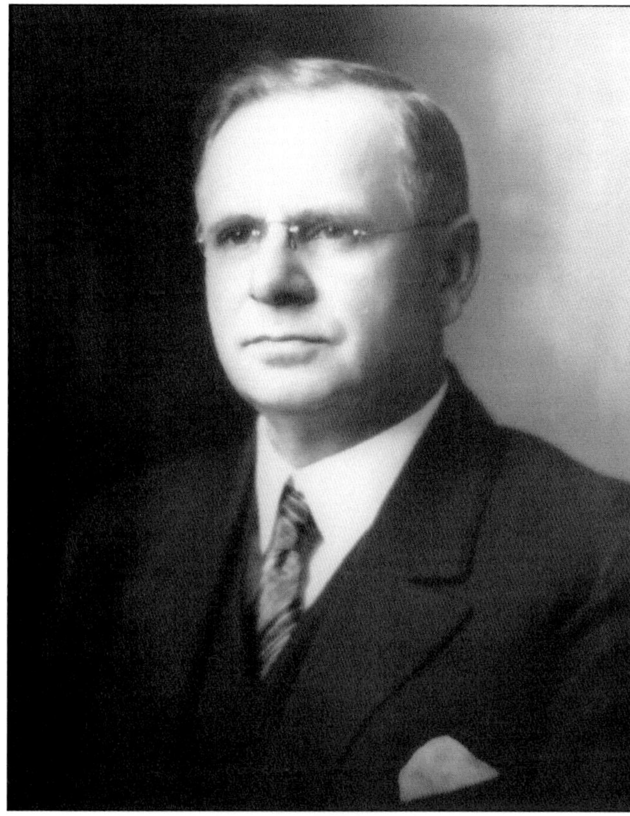

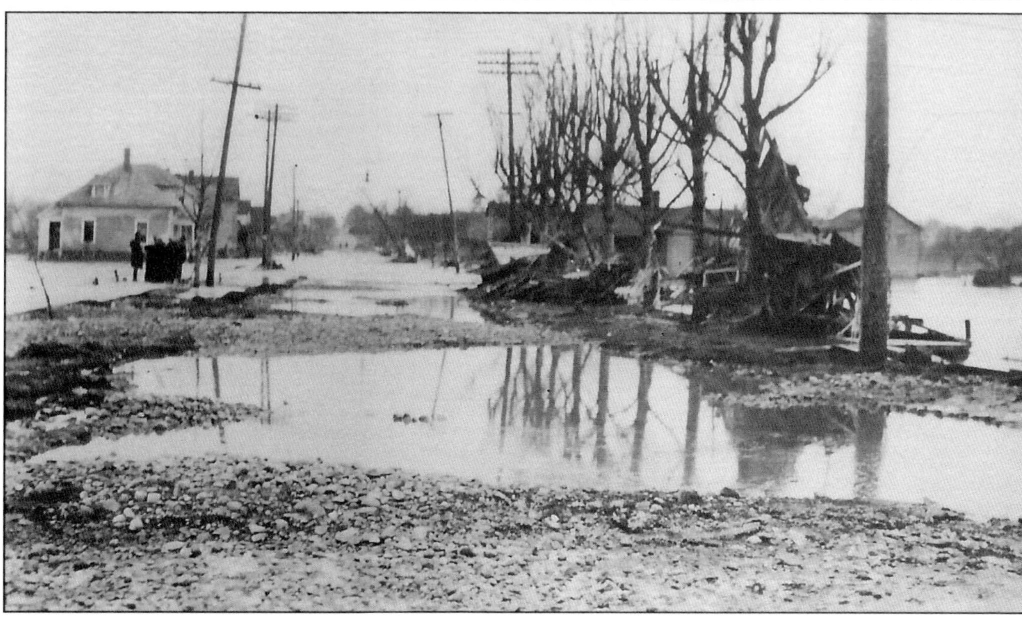

This controversial slogan was adopted at the Friday meeting: "Troy and vicinity will take care of her own suffering." The slogan is reported in the *Miami Union* on March 27. The April 1 *Troy Record* ridicules the statement for being "as wide of the truth as heaven is from hell." The newspaper felt that it would harm Troy's chances of receiving outside funding and goods.

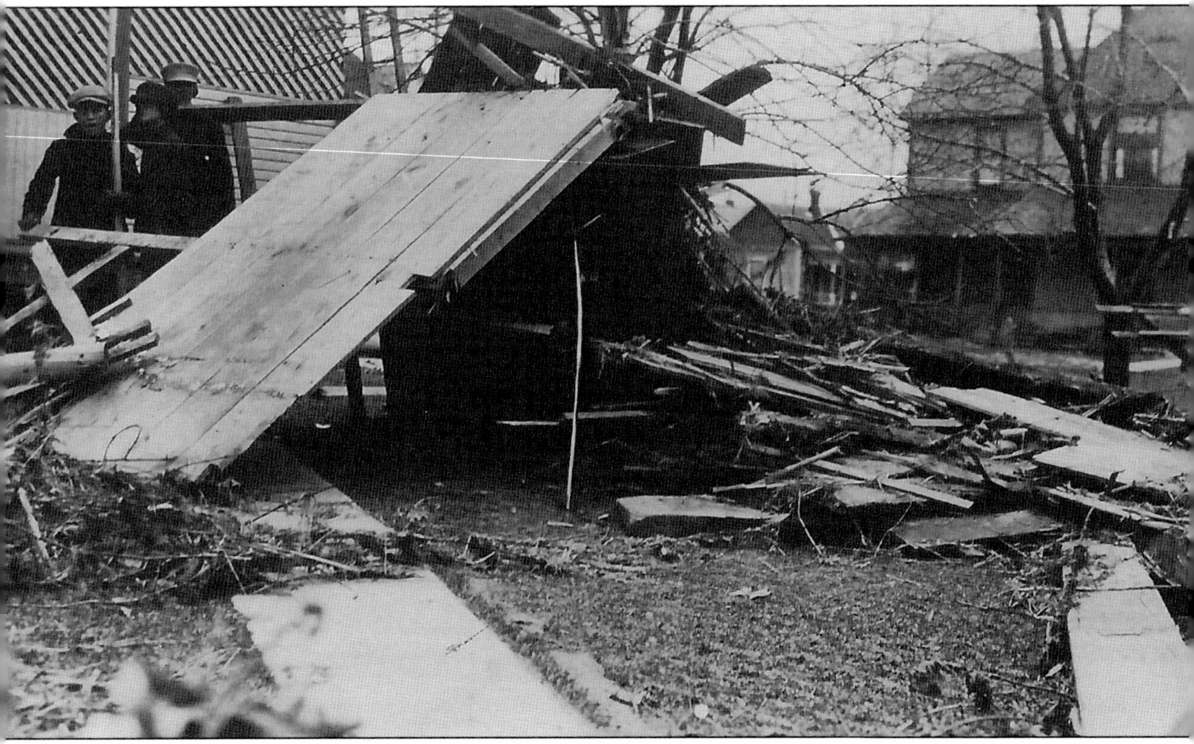

Robert Smallenbarger remembers, "When the water had gone down it was easier to see where it had covered. For it left, aside from mud, the marks of its height and the power of its destruction. The fence rows of fields on the south side were cluttered with debris of all kinds. Just anything that would float, every article of furniture conceivable, plus buildings in every degree of disintegration. And of course the current had been so strong that it rolled heavy materials, even good sized rocks were spread in layers here and there. I saw pianos and organs lodge in fence rows along with animals of various kinds. Some bodies of drowning victims were later retrieved from this area immediately south of Troy."

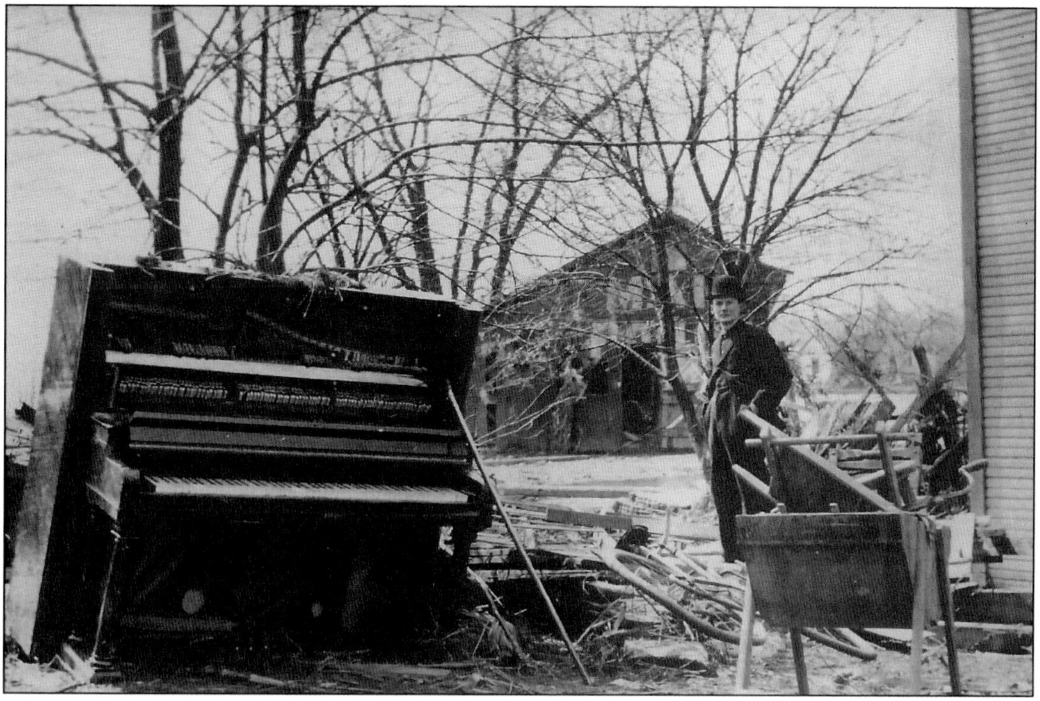

This piano came to rest in the yard of Henry Beck on Garfield Avenue. The April 3, 1913, *Miami Union* reports that it "lodged against a tree as neatly as if it had been carried and set there by human hands." It is believed that the piano floated to Troy all the way from Piqua. It was known among flood survivors as the "famous piano that came from Piqua."

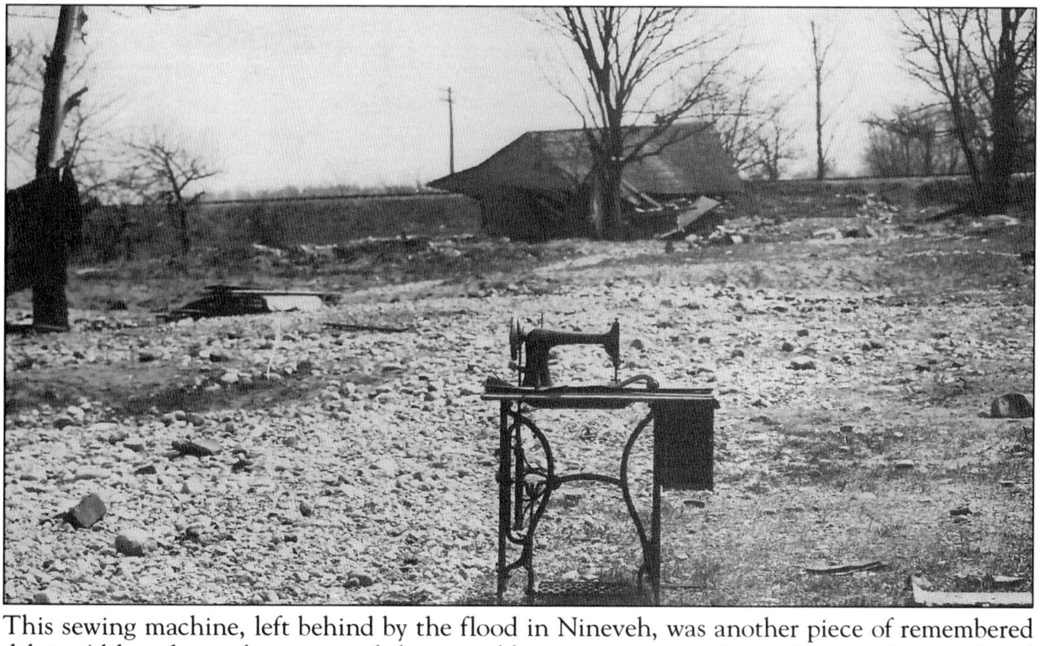

This sewing machine, left behind by the flood in Nineveh, was another piece of remembered debris. Although people were mostly honest, old newspaper stories do say that guards were placed at some flood-ravaged properties to keep vandals away. No one knows where the sewing machine came from, and there are no records of what happened to it.

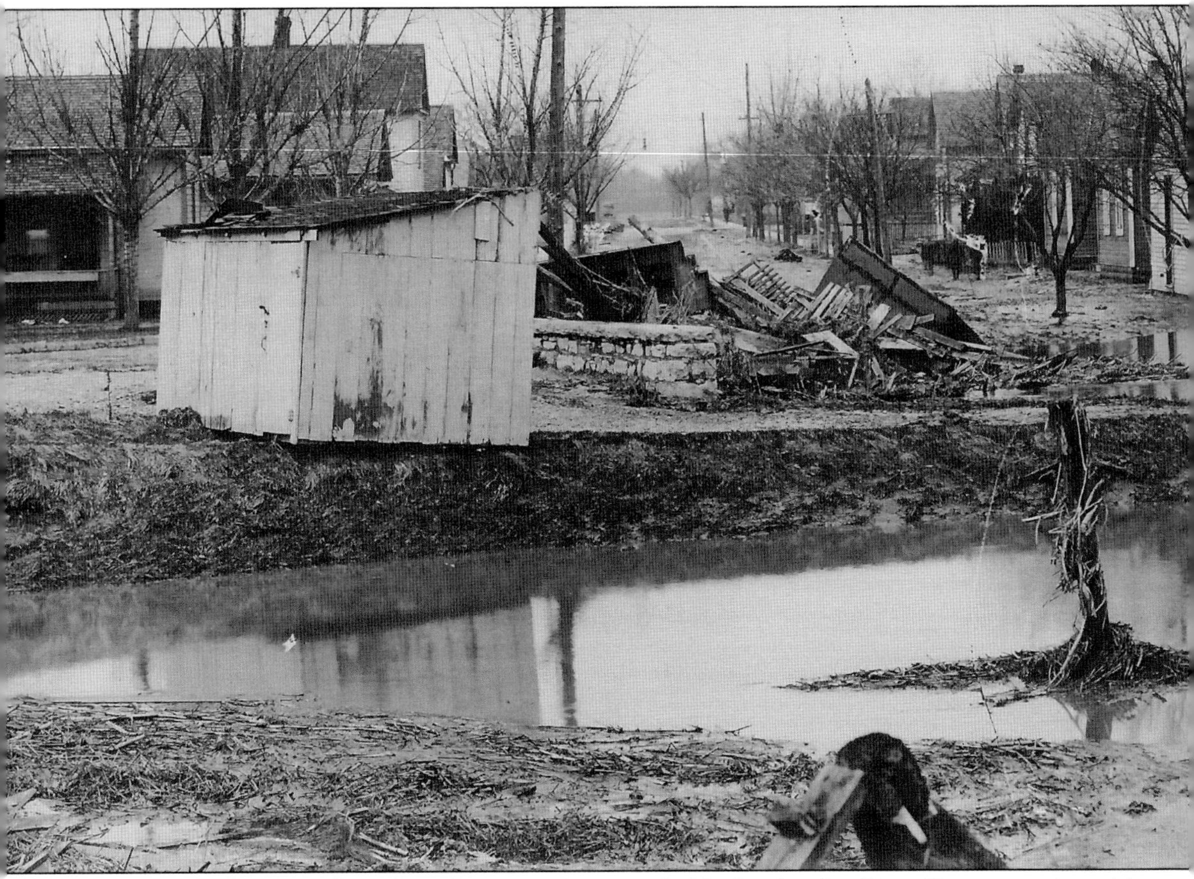

Lottie Swisher Tweed was from Casstown, but attended high school in Troy. She was staying with her aunt and uncle, Mr. and Mrs. J.F. Norris, in Troy during the flood. In an audiotaped 1975 interview, she remembers, "[The cleanup] was a terrific thing. My mother had a sister living on South Garfield. She had a one story house and the water was up to the ceiling. Of course, the furniture was ruined; the carpets were bad. Although she did take them out, and they washed and scrubbed . . . It just took weeks to clean up. That mud was unbelievable. This is a sad story all the way through. Everybody had the same experience." The relief committee reminded residents to do everything possible to save their furniture, as the committee's funds for furniture replacement were limited. This photograph shows West Franklin Street from Monroe Street.

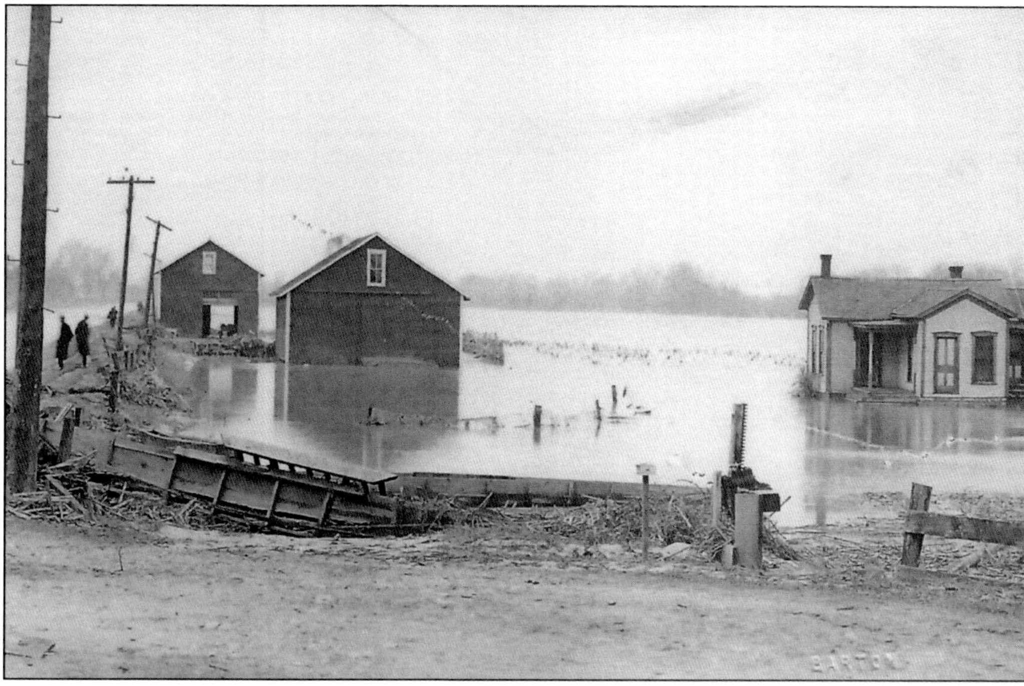

In a 1976 audiotaped interview, Ned English remembers cleaning his father's farmland near Dye Mill Road. He said, "After the flood we had to clean off our bottom fields of lumber shingles, boards, and everything." His family needed to get the debris off in time to plant the fields. As he was cleaning the field, English found a paperweight with a scene of the East River Bridge in New York City and kept it as a souvenir. Debris at Nineveh is shown here.

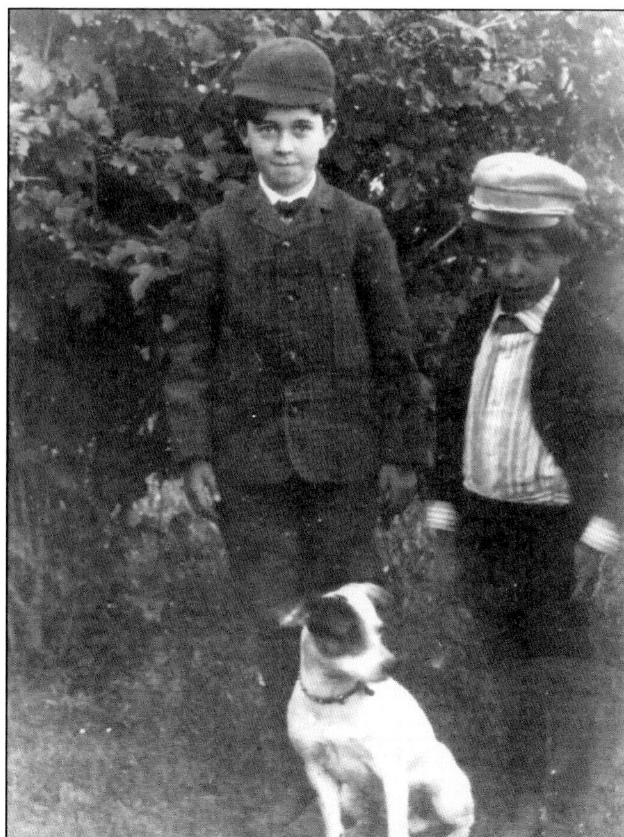

Dead animals were everywhere in Troy after the flood, putting a terrible smell in the air and posing a health threat. Newspaper accounts say that the animals were collected by the Hennessy brothers and given to James Rowe, who owned a fertilizer plant. Rowe put the animals in the canal and floated them to his plant. The fate of this dog and his unidentified owners is unknown.

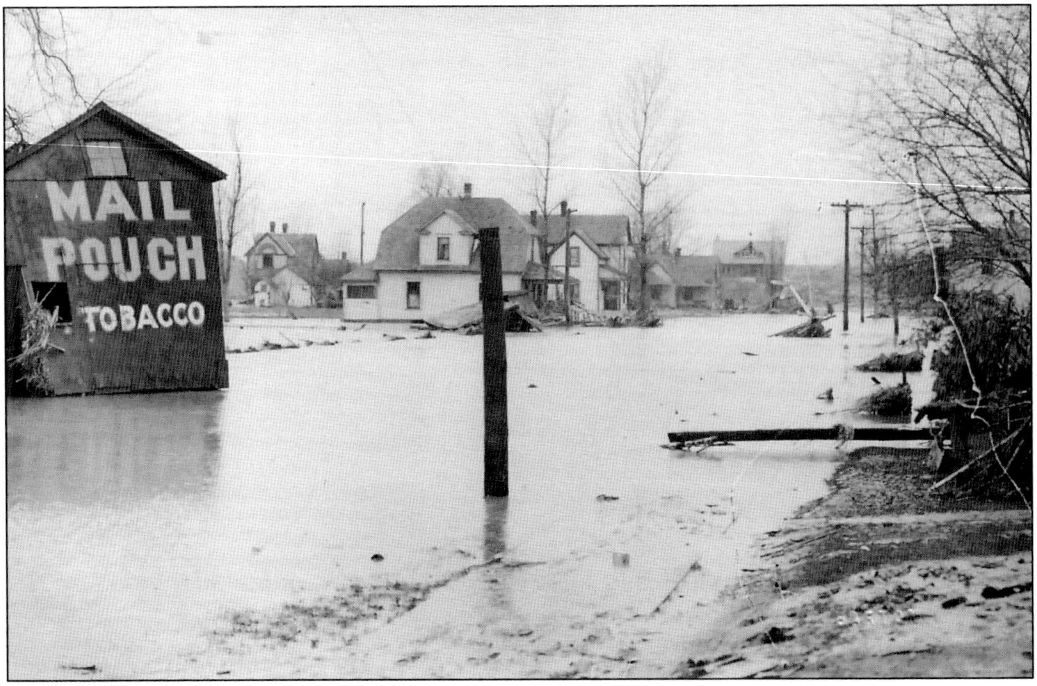

Several buildings in Troy were dangerously unstable because the water had knocked them off their foundations. There was a concern that a building might collapse on someone. The barn at left in this photograph has been washed onto Race Street. In addition to being disconnected from their foundations, most buildings were caked with mud.

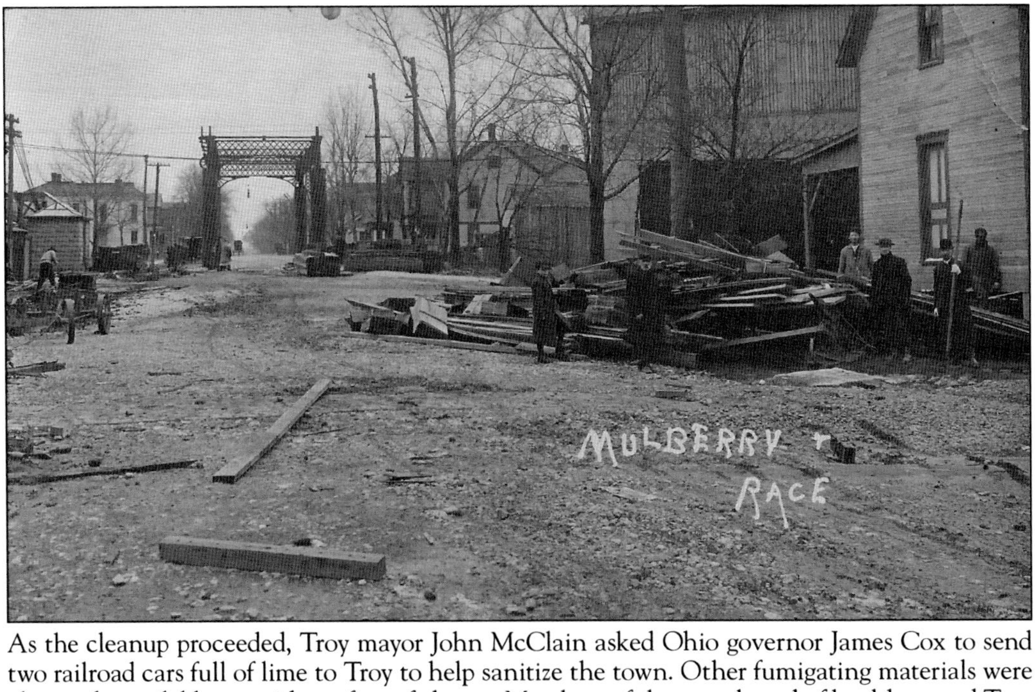

As the cleanup proceeded, Troy mayor John McClain asked Ohio governor James Cox to send two railroad cars full of lime to Troy to help sanitize the town. Other fumigating materials were also made available to residents free of charge. Members of the state board of health toured Troy on Friday, March 28.

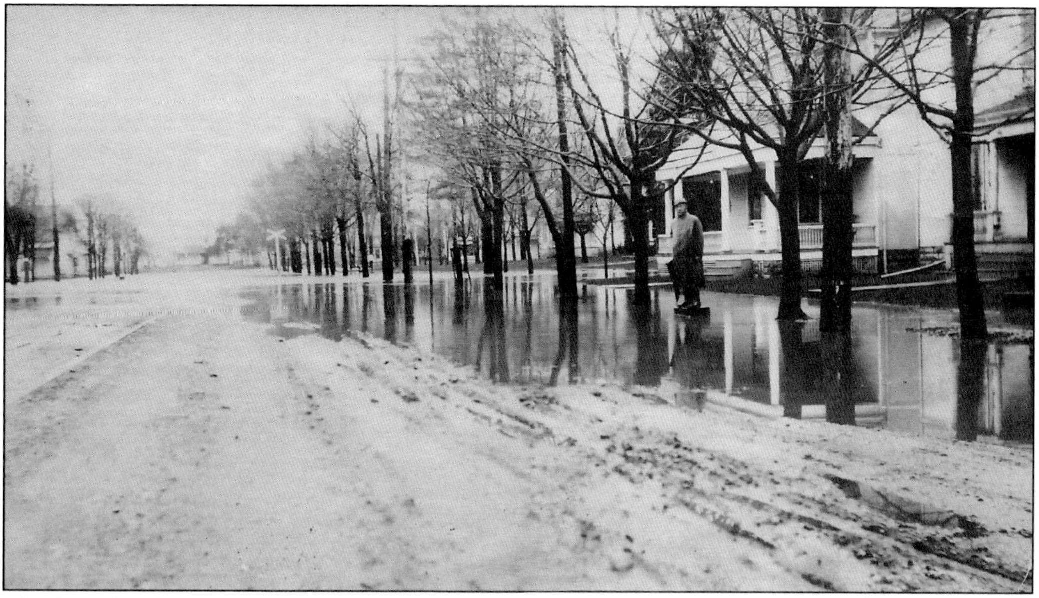

The board of health issued a warning that it was dangerous for people to go back to their homes before water had been removed from their cellars, as contaminated water could bring disease. It also advised that wet paper should be removed from properties, specifically wallpaper; walls and floors should be washed down with slacked lime to kill mold and mildew; and homes should be fumigated.

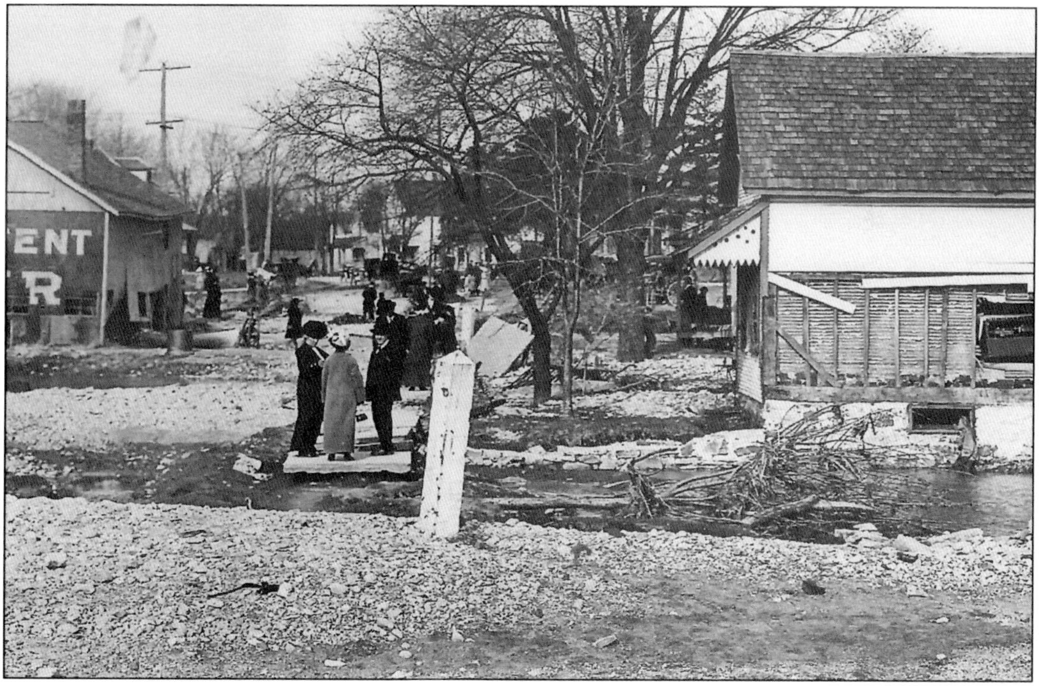

By week's end, other representatives came to give assistance. Ohio state senator Dr. I.C. Kiser toured the town and announced that the State of Ohio had appropriated $250,000 for flooded towns. A representative of the Red Cross also came to survey Troy's needs. Posters soliciting contributions for flood relief were placed around town.

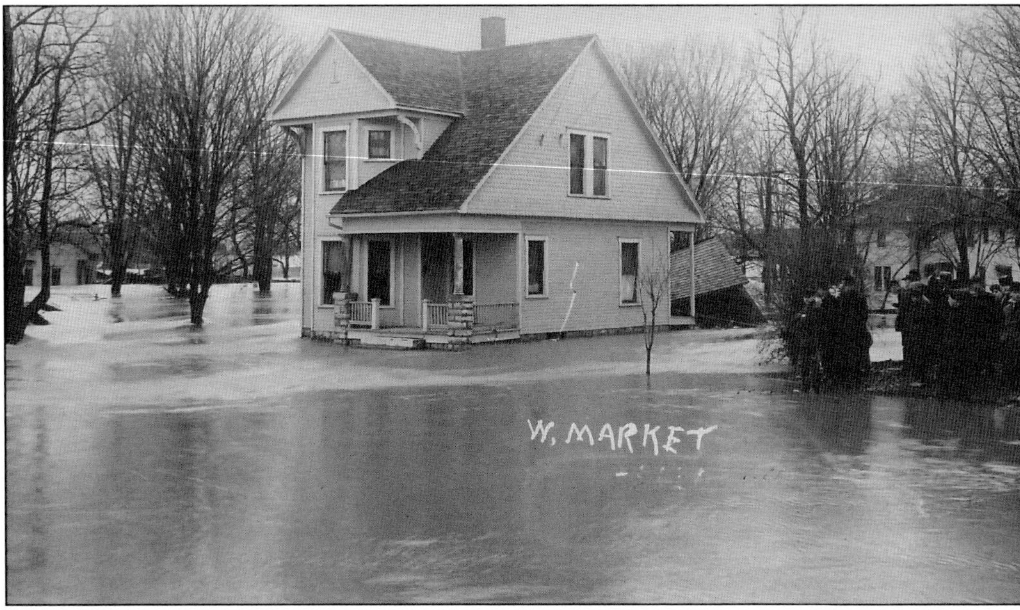

In a long-ago interview, flood survivor Olive Gillis recalled, "It was wonderful how people shared and shared everything they have. And people that had money gave to those who didn't have money." Newspapers published lists of contributors and their contributions, which were referred to as subscriptions.

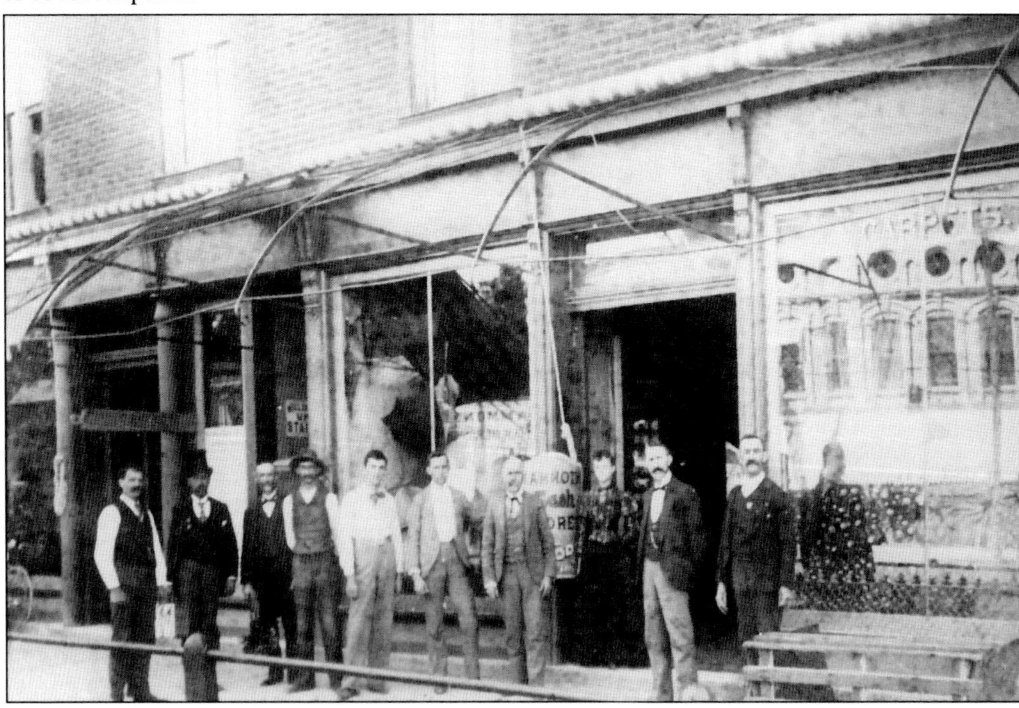

Troy companies, organizations, and individuals donated to flood relief. Large subscribers included the Hobart Electric Manufacturing Company ($500), the Troy Carriage and Sun Shade Company ($500), Troy Wagon Works ($500), the Troy Lodge Benevolent and Protective Order of the Elks ($200), and well-known families such as the Allens, Bowyers, Edgars, and Stouders.

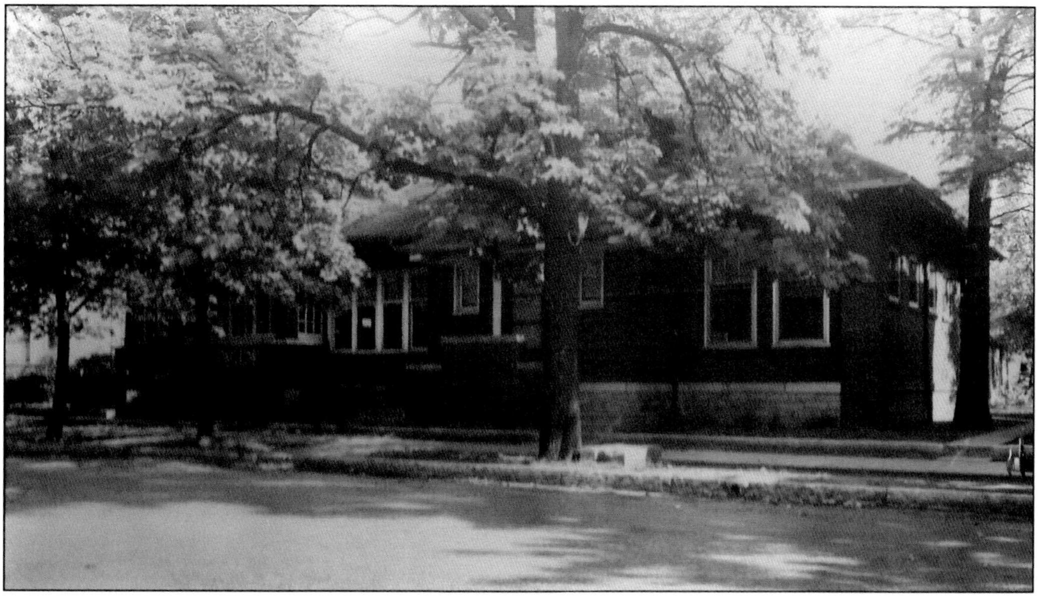

Some groups raised funds for flood relief through projects. The Altrurian Club, whose clubhouse is pictured here, presented two fundraising "entertainments" at the Edwards School Auditorium: *The Flower of Yeddo* and *The Return of Deborah*. Churches also participated in "Tag Day," where ministers and church members gave tags printed with a flood-relief slogan to those donating to the cause. Sunday church collections also went to flood relief.

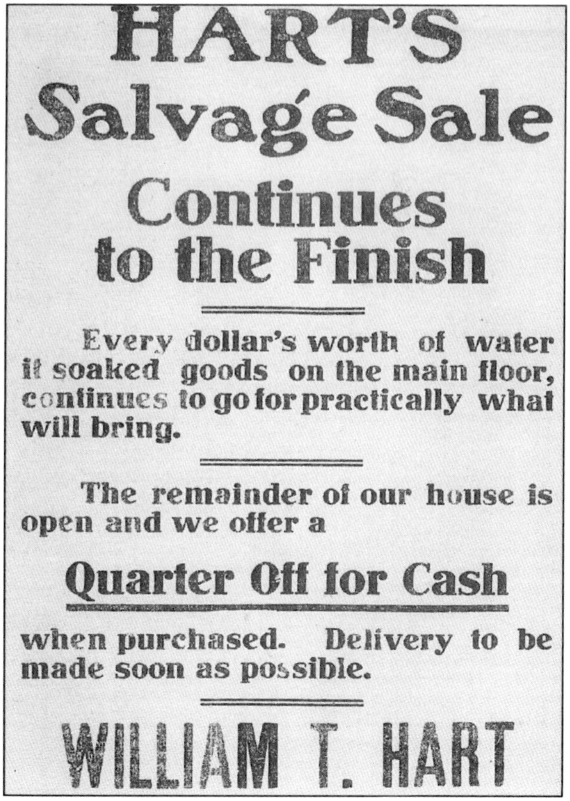

Local businesses tried to recoup their losses by selling damaged inventories at reduced prices. Many stores had "flood" sales. H.A. Cosley, who owned a hardware store in the Masonic Building on West Main Street, had a special flower sale in mid-April. Starting on April 12, 1913, he sold peach trees at 10¢ each, cherry trees at 15¢, and grape vines at three for 25¢.

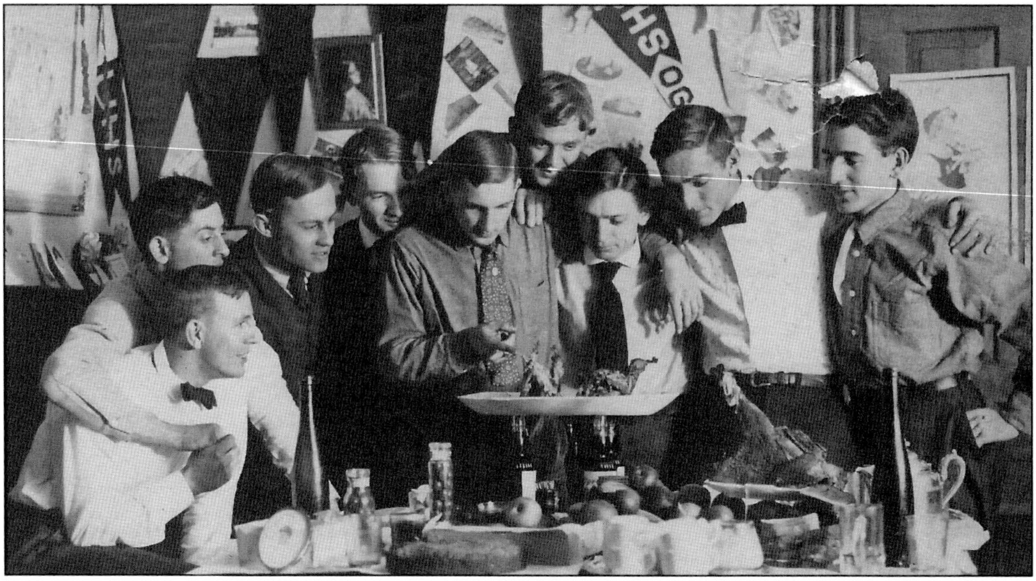

After the flood, Troy residents paid special attention to what they ate; people had to be careful about their food sources. This image shows several young men looking carefully over food. This photograph was actually made prior to the flood.

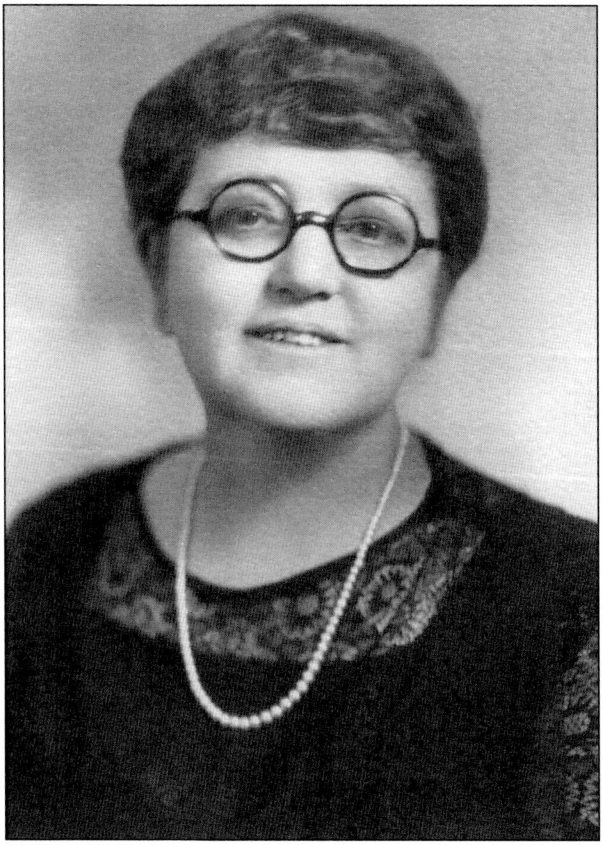

An epidemic of typhoid fever hit Troy after the flood. Anna Counts Snook, the newly elected president of the Altrurian Club, died of typhoid, reportedly after drinking infected milk. Eventually, laws were put in place forcing milk dealers to pasteurize and test their milk. Mrs. C.W. Cookson, the club president prior to Snook, is seen here.

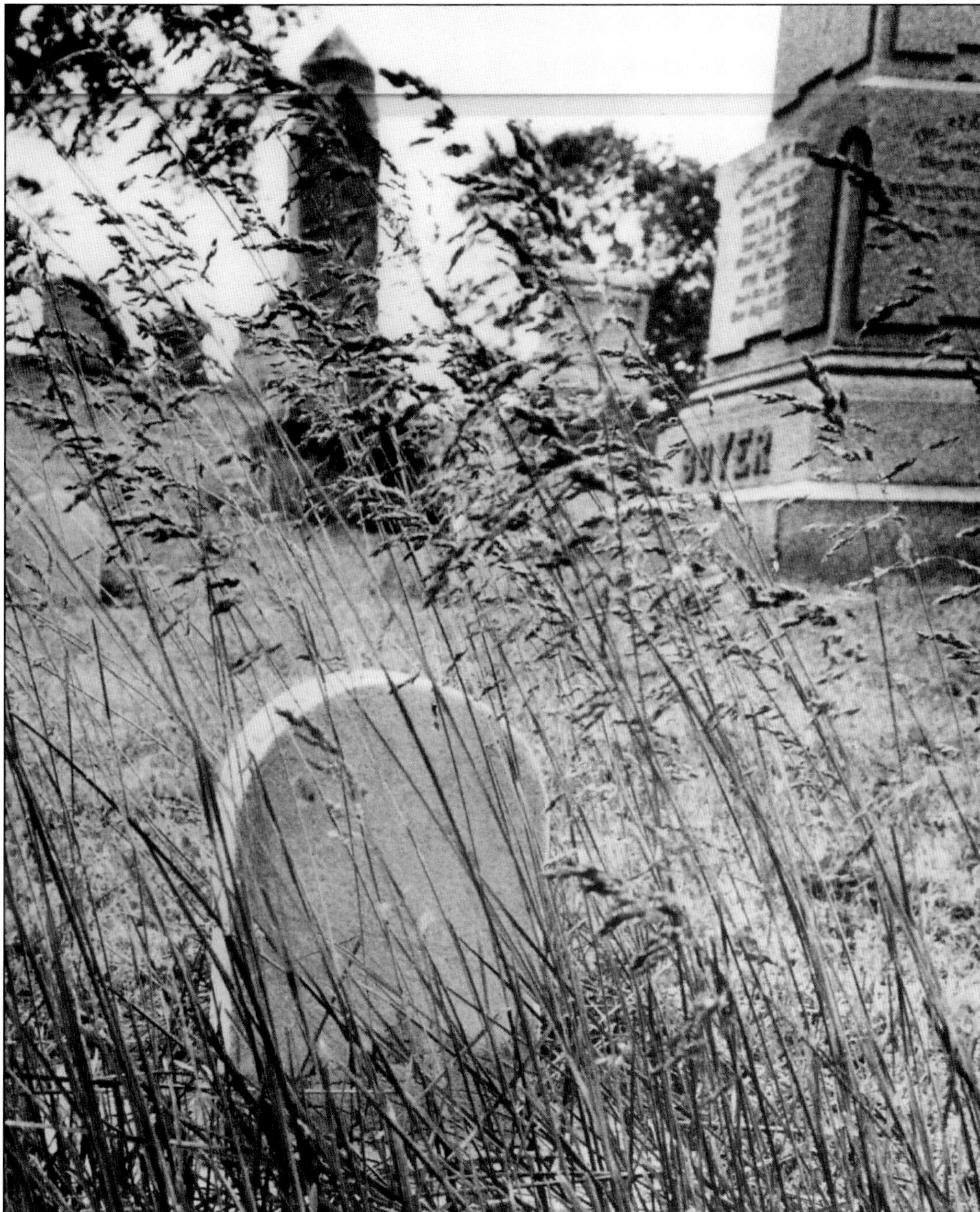

In a 1975 interview, Hortense Cairns Mumford discussed the typhoid epidemic that took the lives of her parents, Edwin and Carrie Cairns. According to Mumford, the epidemic was caused by contaminated water wells. Her mother remained at home after becoming ill because there was not a community hospital in Troy. Carrie was in a weakened condition because she had recently given birth to a son, contracted typhoid in July 1913, and died in August. Her husband, Edwin, had suffered physically while going through the illness and death of his wife. When he too developed typhoid fever, according to Mumford, "His physical condition was such that he gave up and died in October." The Cairns left three children as orphans. Rosehill Cemetery, where Troy residents are buried, is shown here.

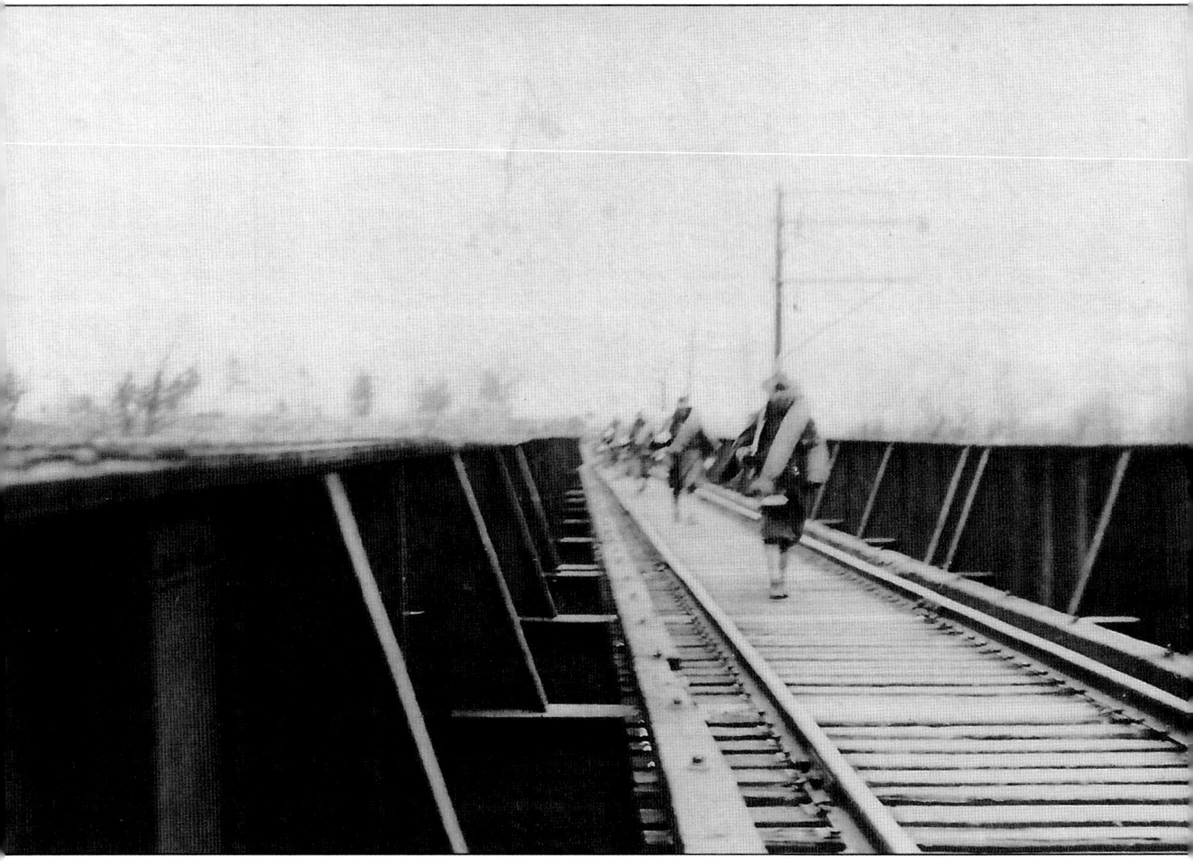

Company L of the 8th Ohio National Guard came through Troy on its way to Dayton. The regiment was headquartered in Bucyrus, Ohio, and Company L was based in Sidney. Guardsmen could not get to Dayton from Sidney by train, so they walked part of the way on foot. They are seen here coming into Troy over the Cincinnati, Hamilton & Dayton Railroad Bridge.

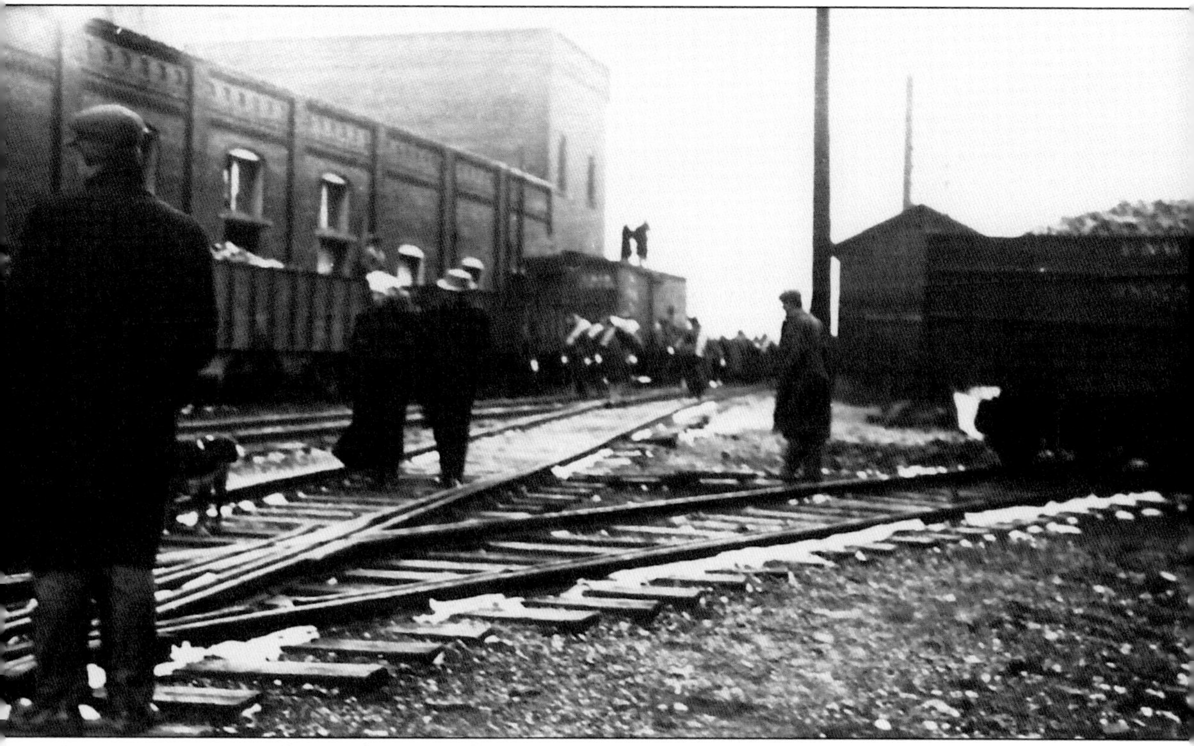

Company L National Guardsmen walk the railroad tracks in Troy. One former resident and soldier, a Lieutenant Sturdevant, also returned to Troy to offer assistance. Sturdevant was based at Fort Thomas, Kentucky, and came to Troy with a Sergeant Cripps and a Corporal Byers to offer assistance from the US government. Through Sturdevant's efforts, supplies and provisions were forwarded to both Troy and Piqua.

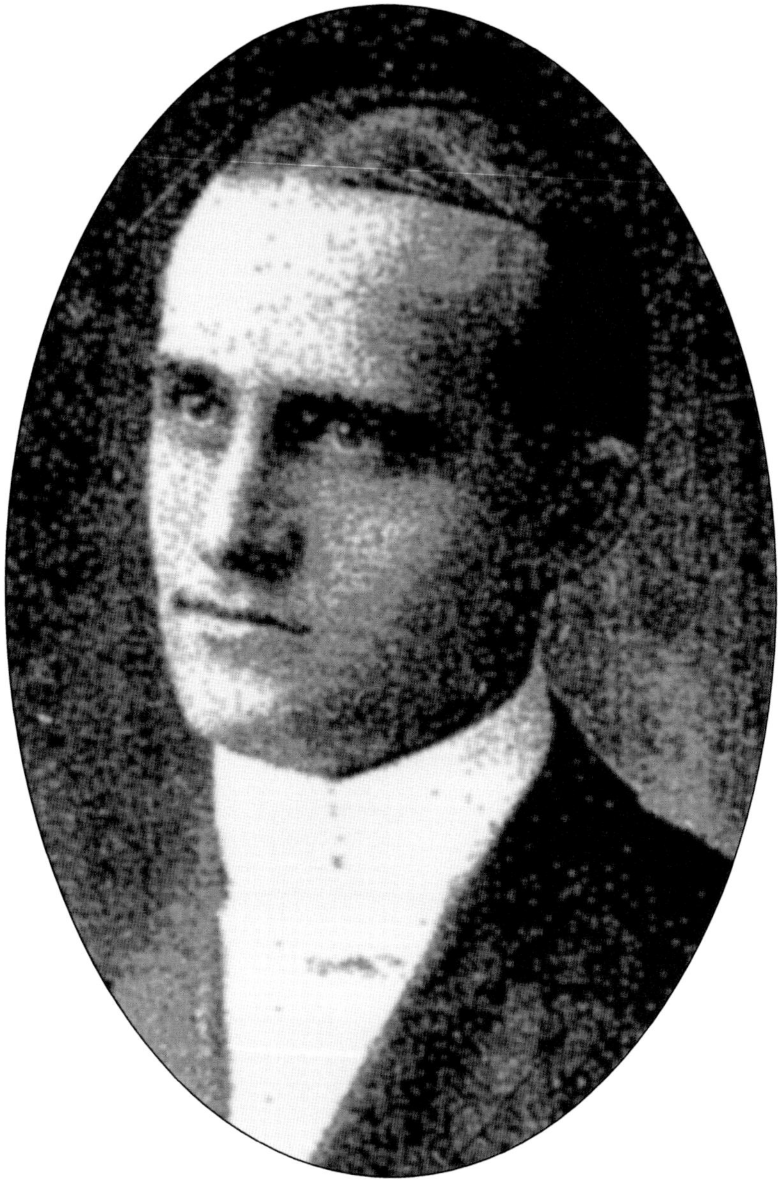

At the end of the flood, Rev. J.E. Etter, the pastor of First Christian Church of Troy (now First United Church of Christ) from 1909 to 1918, wrote an article titled "The Flood at Troy, Ohio" that was published in the 1914 *Christian Annual*. Some memorable lines from the work are as follows: "Here in our city we were all taught how dependent we were on each other. Our desires that separate us are mostly artificial. While our real needs that unite us in one brotherhood are few and fundamental. We were taught how to expect good from unexpected sources and to appreciate kindly deeds, acts of heroism, and sacrifice on the part of those in ordinary life." (Courtesy of the First United Church of Christ.)

Nine

Troy Will Never Flood Again

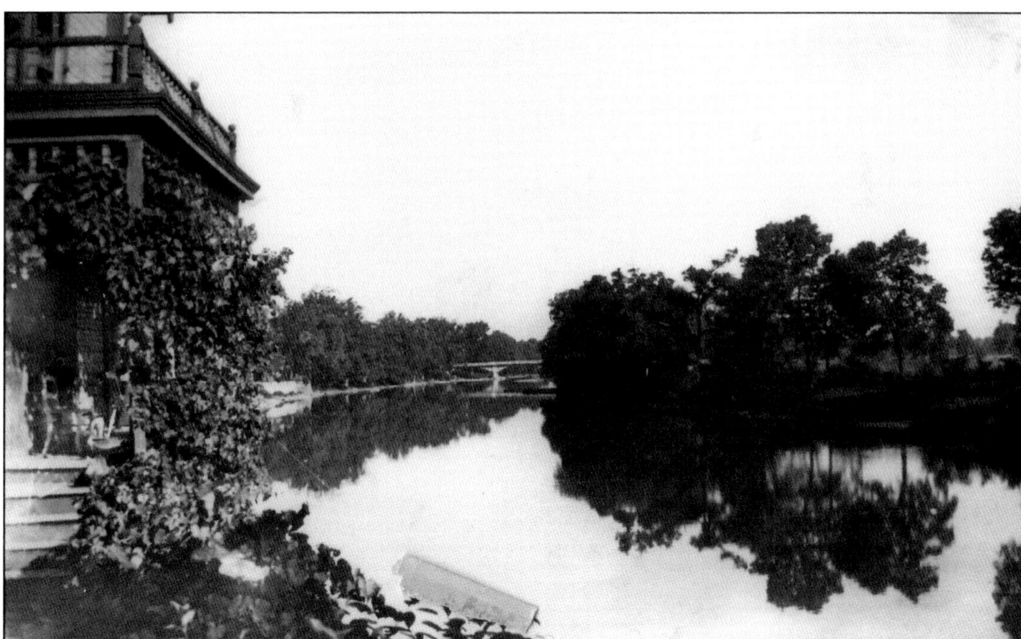

Many changes came to Troy after the Great Flood of 1913, most of them along the banks of the Great Miami River. This 1915 photograph shows a bend in the river that was removed after the flood and the Adams Street Bridge beyond it. The house on the left, 114 North Market Street, belonged to Dr. Van S. Deaton.

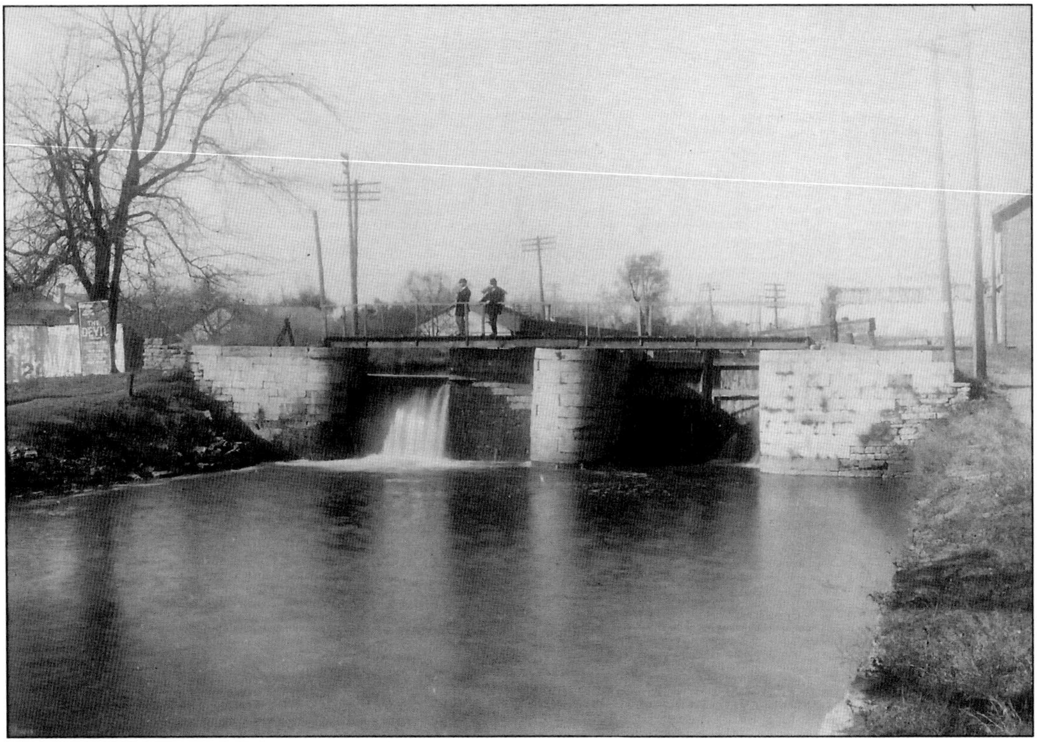

At the time of the flood, the Miami and Erie Canal was in deplorable condition; in fact, there was discussion at the time about what to do with the canal. It was referred to as dilapidated, unsightly, unhealthy, and useless. Articles in the *Miami Union* on February 27, 1913, and March 13, 1913, outline ideas for preservation and restoration or abandonment. Eventually, it was abandoned.

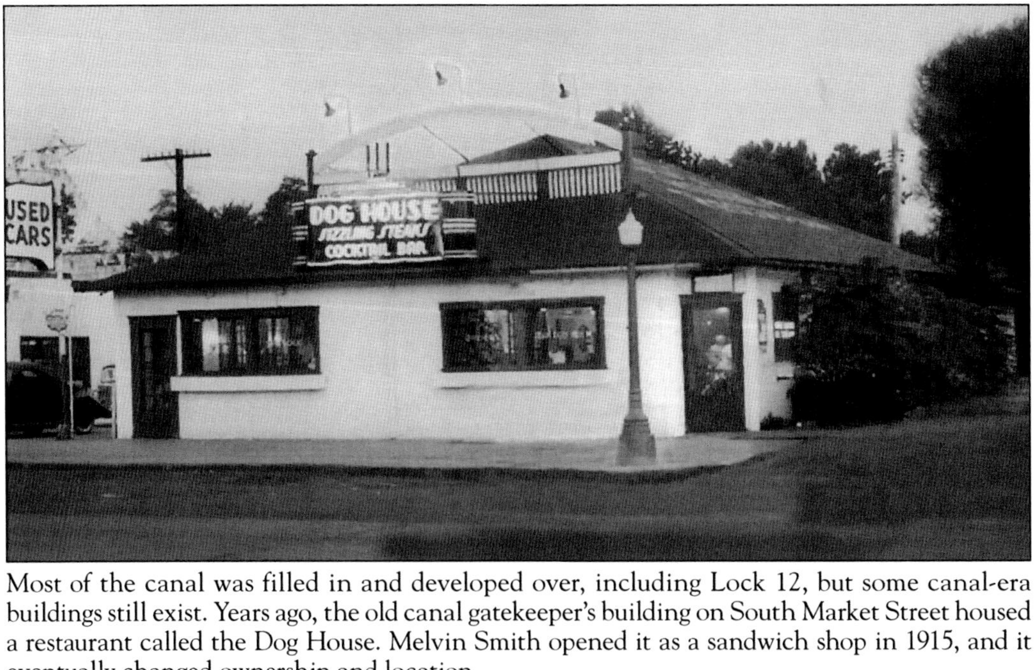

Most of the canal was filled in and developed over, including Lock 12, but some canal-era buildings still exist. Years ago, the old canal gatekeeper's building on South Market Street housed a restaurant called the Dog House. Melvin Smith opened it as a sandwich shop in 1915, and it eventually changed ownership and location.

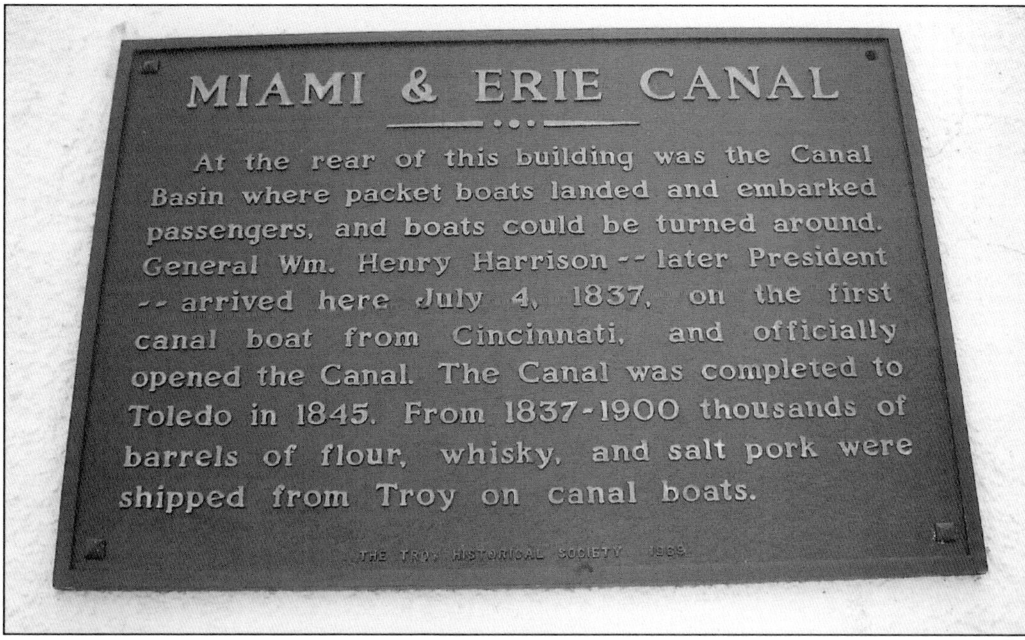

In the late 1960s, the Troy Historical Society placed a historical marker on the front wall of the Schnell Building on East Canal Street in remembrance of the Miami and Erie Canal in Troy. The marker tells the story of what was once an important feature of the town. The Troy Historical Society restored the marker in 2012. Scott Trostel, a Miami County historian and craftsman, did the restoration work. (Courtesy of Judy Deeter.)

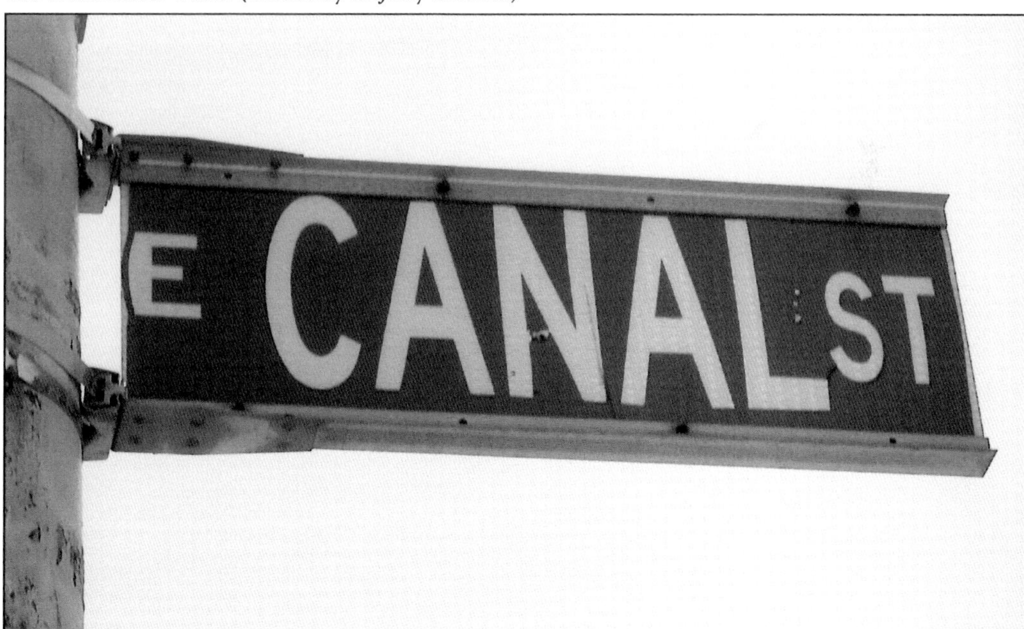

Canal and Race Streets in Troy are among the few reminders that the canal, which once flowed beside them, existed in Troy. Both run east-west through the south end of Troy and are geographical reminders of where the canal was located. In some places along the streets, remnants of the canal walls are visible. (Courtesy of Judy Deeter.)

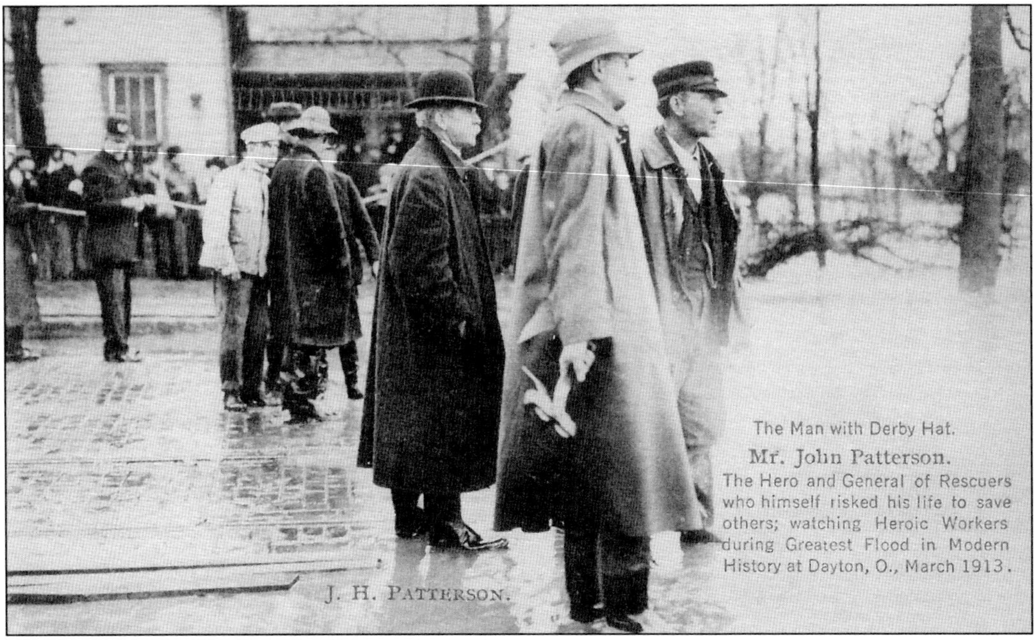

On April 21, 1913, a meeting was held to find ways to prevent future floods in Troy. The committee selected to research flood prevention plans included Henry M. Allen, Charles A. Geiger, and Augustus Stouder. On April 22, the committee wrote to John Patterson, a leader of the Dayton flood prevention committee. (Courtesy of Judy Deeter.)

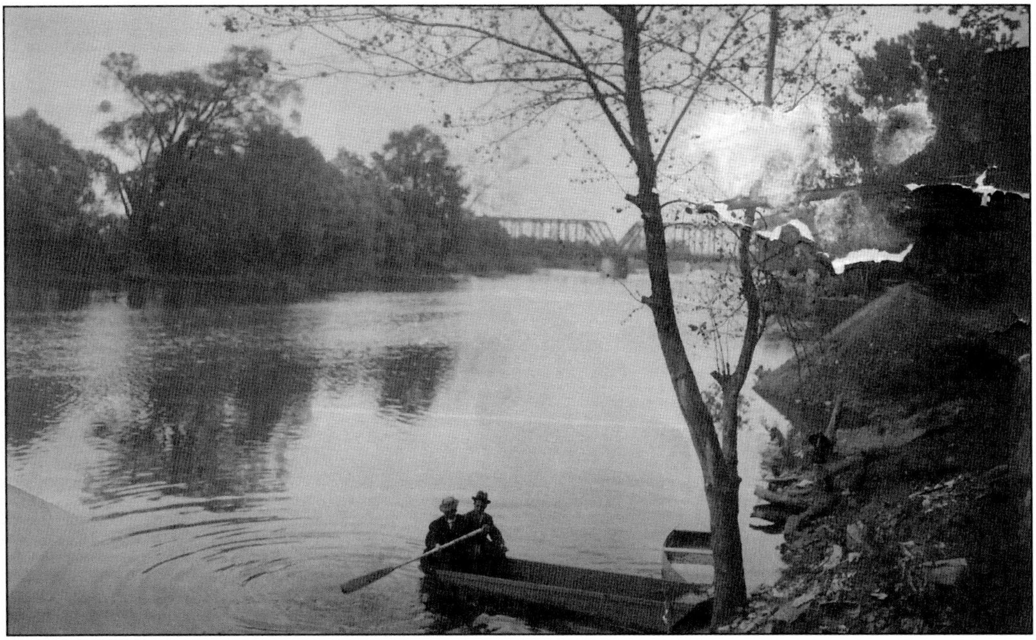

The Troy flood prevention committee worked with the Dayton committee. Edward Deeds and Walter Kidder were appointed to find an engineer to devise a flood prevention plan. On May 3, 1913, Kidder contacted engineer Arthur Morgan, of Memphis, to work on the project. He came to Dayton and was hired for the project. Miami Valley residents raised $2 million for flood control and prevention. Many residents opposed the plans.

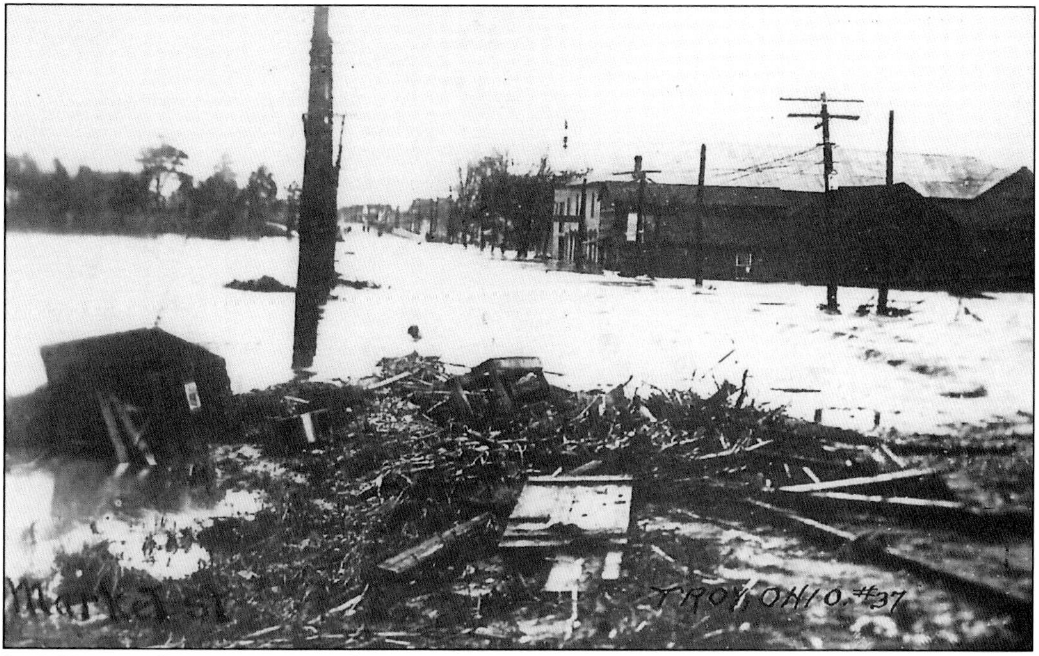

In *A History of Miami County, Ohio, 1807–1953*, one author writes, "It was many weeks before the city was able to clear away all reminders of the catastrophe. The fear of similar future disasters lay heavy on the minds of those who had lived through it until the efforts of the Miami Conservancy District officials began to bear fruit in measures calculated to prevent future floods."

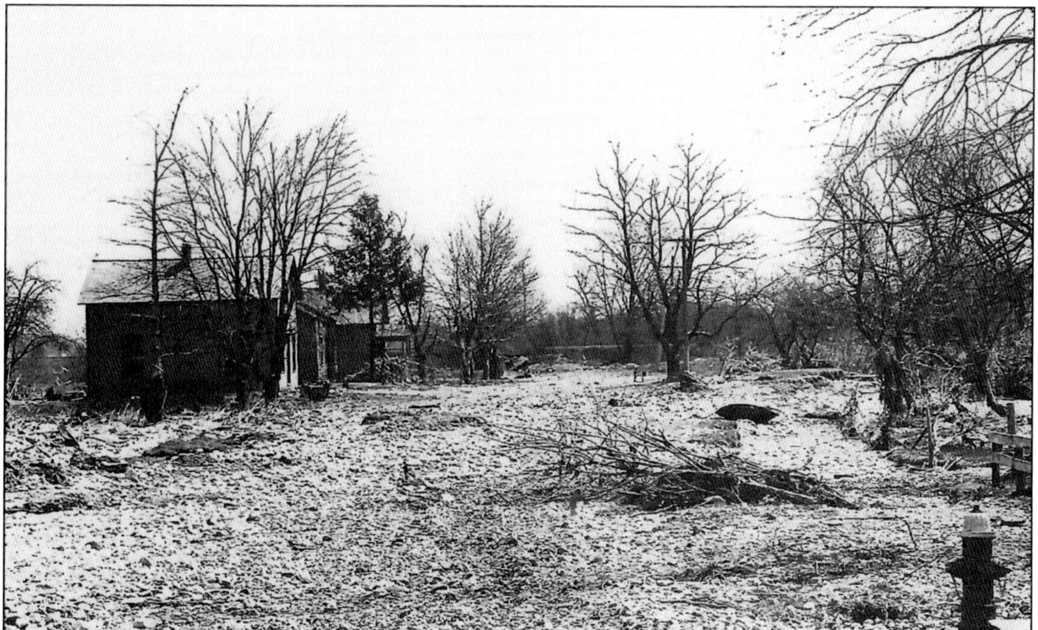

The Miami Conservancy District took over the floodplain of the Great Miami River along the river's northeast bank to Staunton Road. The floodplain included the ravaged African American community of Nineveh, seen here after the 1913 flood. Prior to the flood, Nineveh had homes and businesses, including a livery stable and a pool hall.

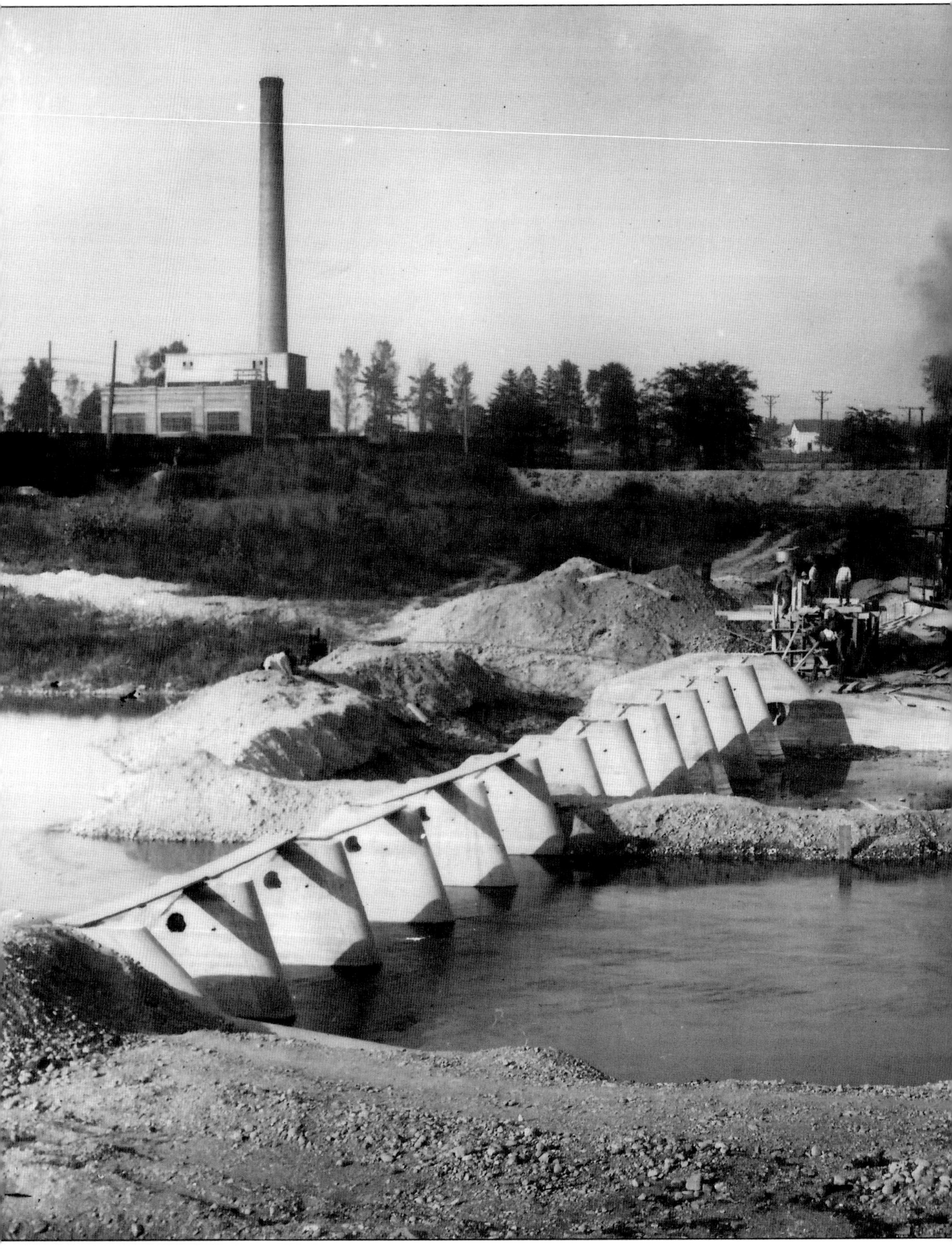

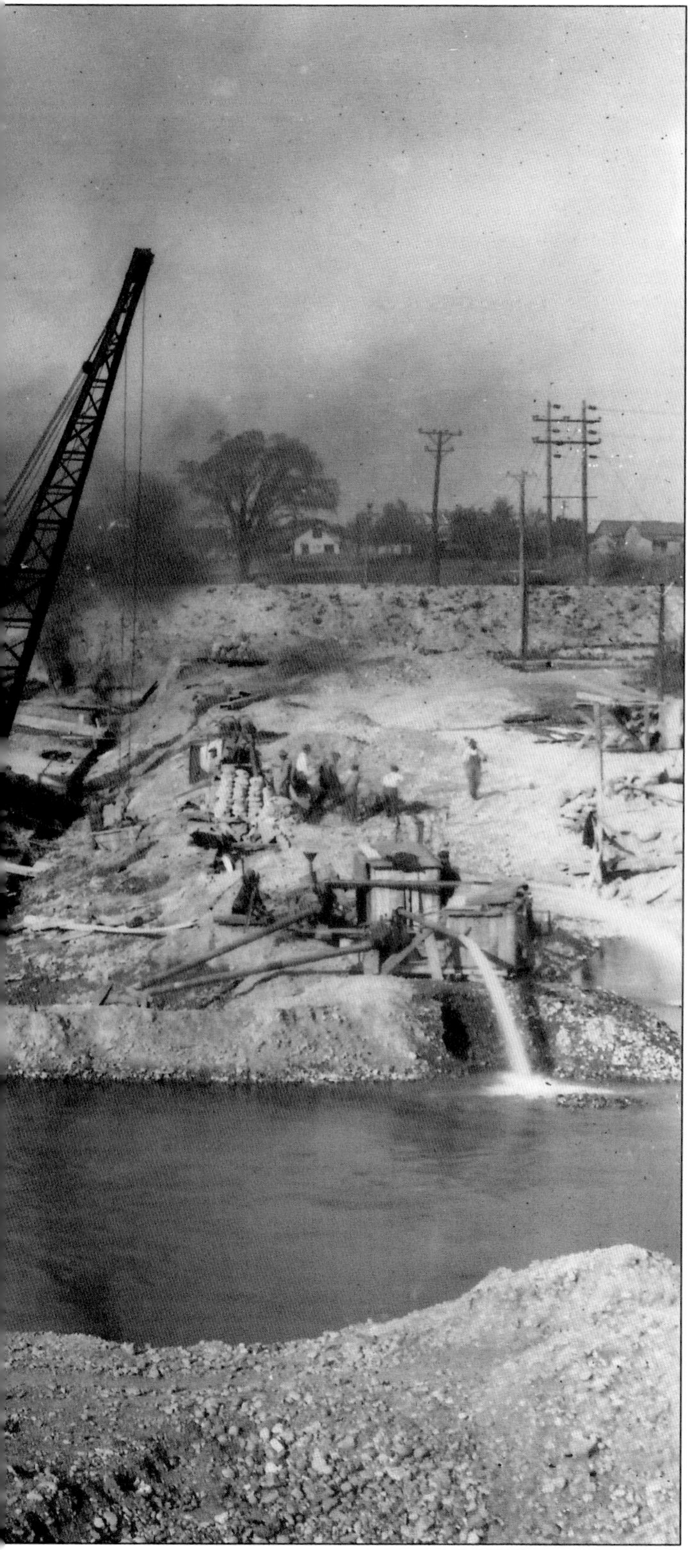

The home of Dr. Harry Shilling was on North Market Street near the south bank of the Great Miami River. The Shilling family witnessed the Miami Conservancy District reshape the river. In fact, the conservancy made a cut in the earth through the Shilling's yard. In an article in the April 4, 1988, edition of the *Troy Daily News*, Dr. Shilling's daughter, Lois Shilling Davies, describes the conservancy's work thusly: "In three noisy and exciting years, we saw houses moved, trees disappear, levees built, bridges raised and new spans added. By 1923, my memories of the flood were practically wiped out. The Miami Conservancy had not only changed the course of the river, but the course of events for years to come."

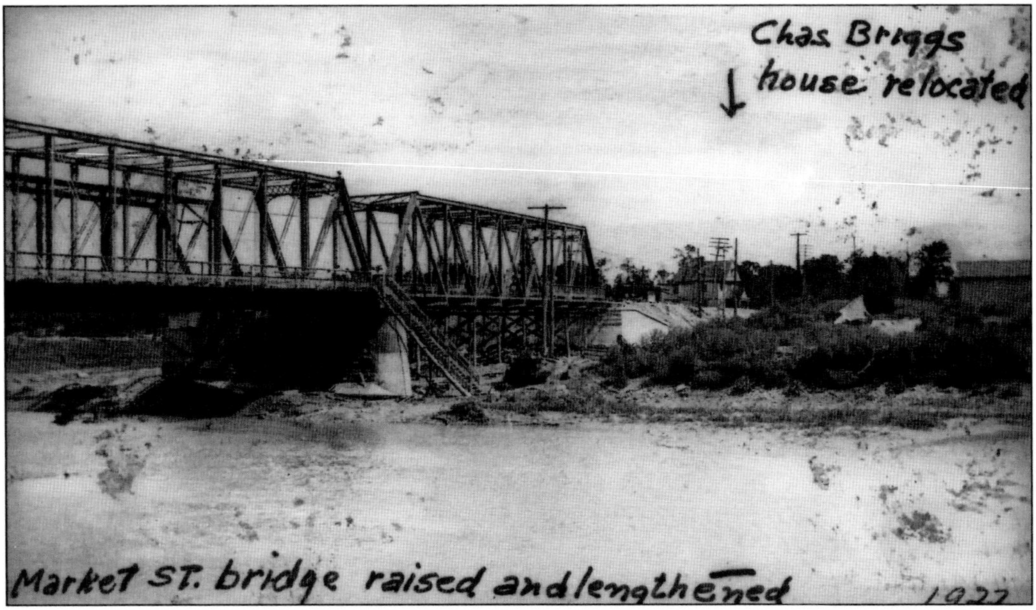

The Miami Conservancy District took possession of the Charles Briggs home on the floodplain and moved it to a high area on the west side of North Market Street. During construction along the Great Miami River, the family of division engineer A.F. Griffin lived in the house. Later, Troy City Service directors lived there and it was used as a senior citizens center. It was demolished in the 1960s.

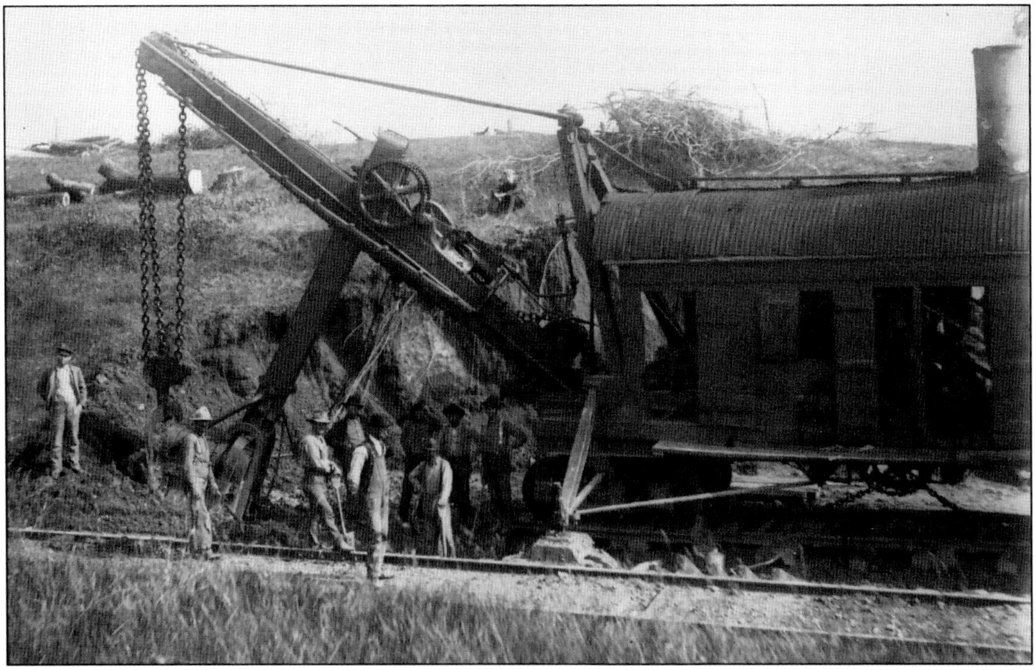

As a child in the 1920s, Lois Shilling Davies was fascinated as she watched the world she knew forever change. She writes, "Across the river they cut down all the pretty trees at the water's edge, blasted out the stumps, leveled off a field, and scooped up enough dirt to make a great big levee."

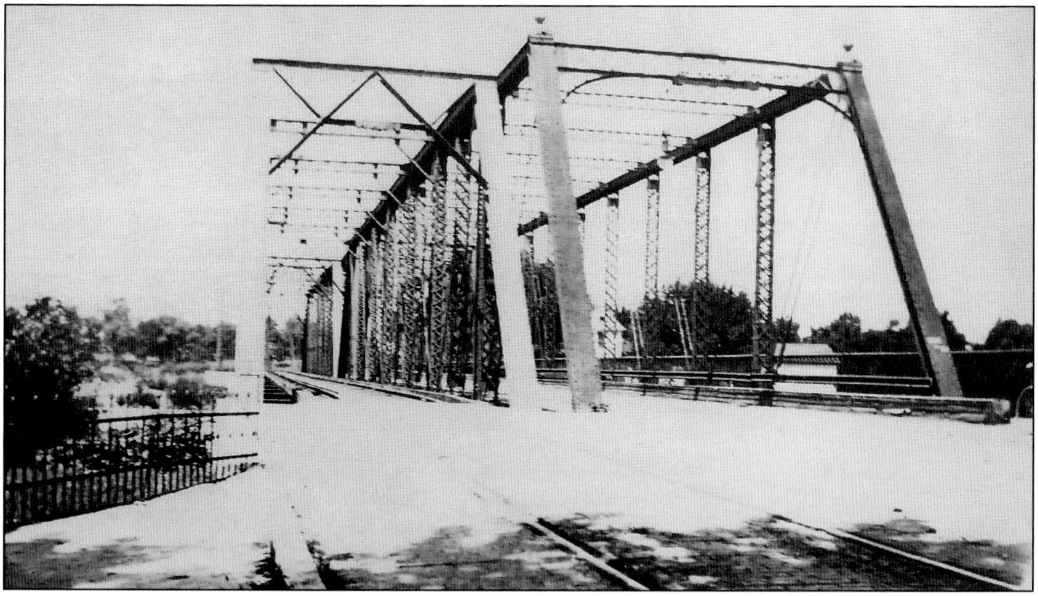

The Market Street Bridge and the Adams Street Bridge survived the flood, but both were inaccessible on their north ends because of water on the floodplain. Lois Shilling Davies writes, "To leave the bridges at that level and length would have condemned the flood plain area to serve no purpose except as a catch basin for occasional floods. This reasoning inspired the Conservancy planners with local input to conceive of bisecting the flood plain by a huge levee, raising the two-span iron Market Street bridge by three feet and lengthening it by another span to meet the top of the levee." The Market Street Bridge is seen above from the north side looking south. During the 1913 flood, water reached the bridge roadway, pictured below.

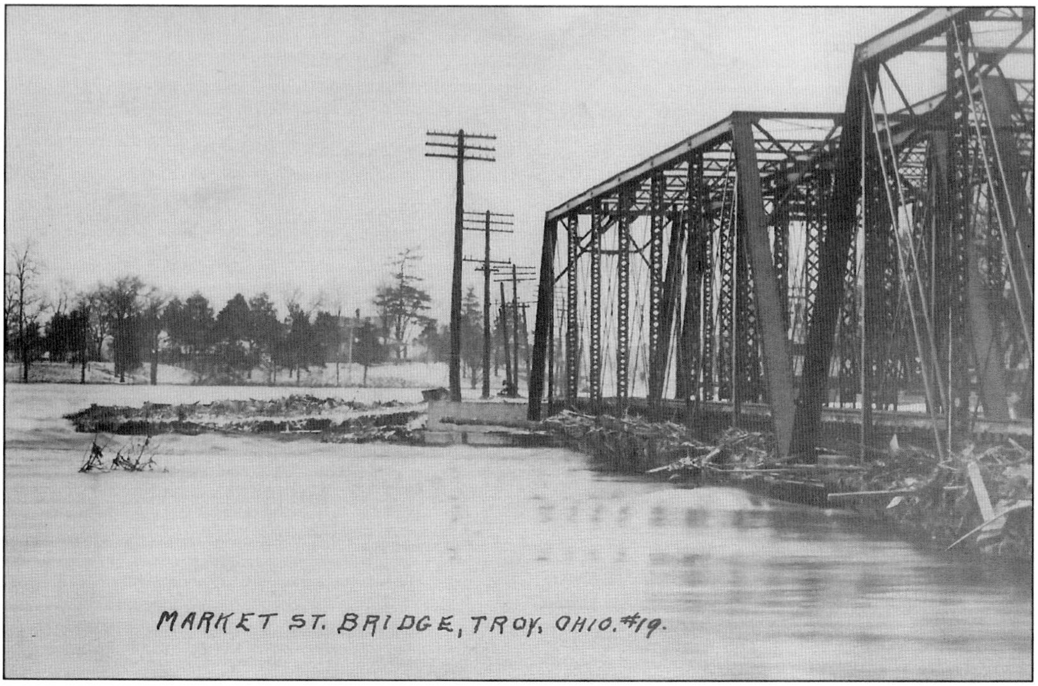

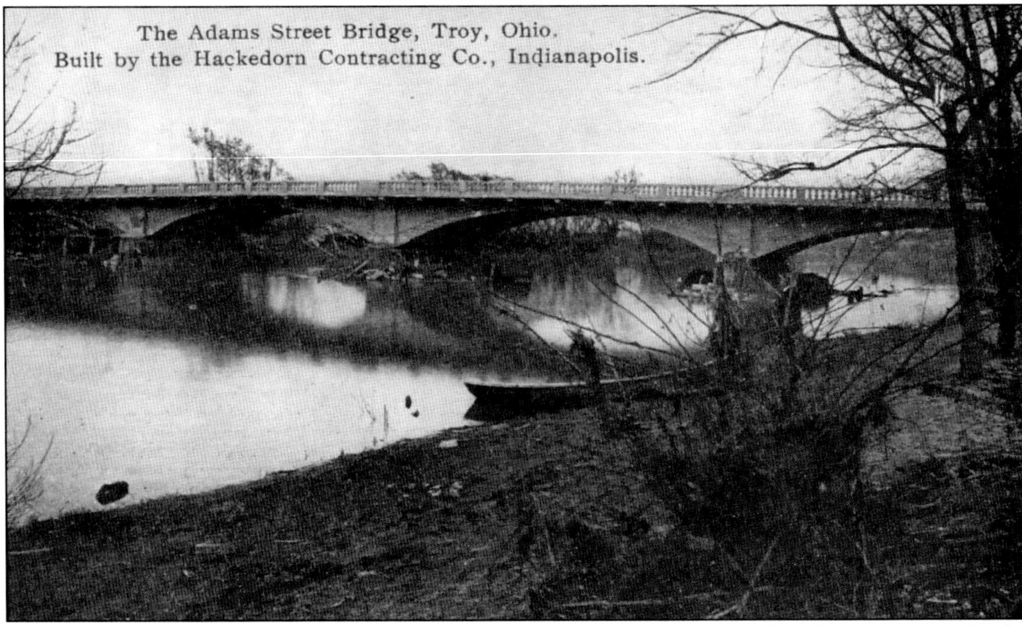

In the months prior to the flood, the old iron Adams Street Bridge was replaced by a concrete bridge by the Hackendorn Construction Company of Indianapolis. From an engineering perspective, changing the length of the bridge spans and raising the bridge height was more difficult with a concrete bridge than it would have been with an iron bridge. At the time of the flood, the Adams Street Bridge had four arches. Afterward, three smaller arches were added to the four existing arches. The tops of the arches in place were used as forms for new, higher arches. The bridge's three piers—supports for the spans—were made larger, and their footings were made deeper. This construction method had never been used before, and it was considered an engineering feat. These photographs show the Adams Street Bridge right after it was completed (above) and during the flood (below).

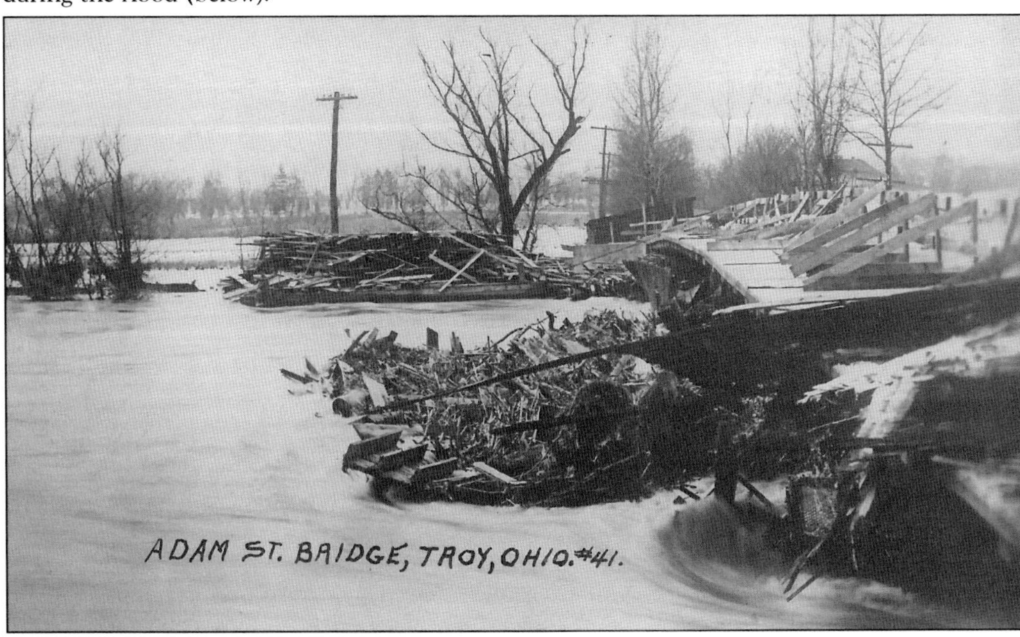

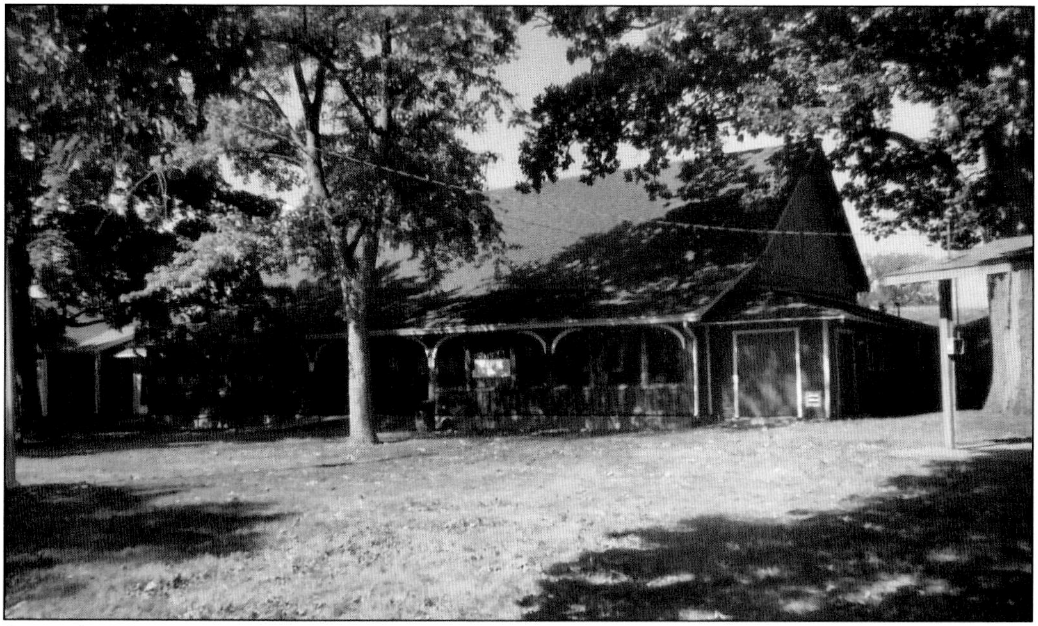

Once the Miami Conservancy District completed its work at Troy, it returned the land along the river to the City of Troy. A wooded area north of the Adams Street Bridge became a municipal park named Troy Community Park. Eventually, a nearby barn was moved into the park. In the early years of the park, the barn was used as a shelter house and dance hall. It is now home to the Troy Civic Theater.

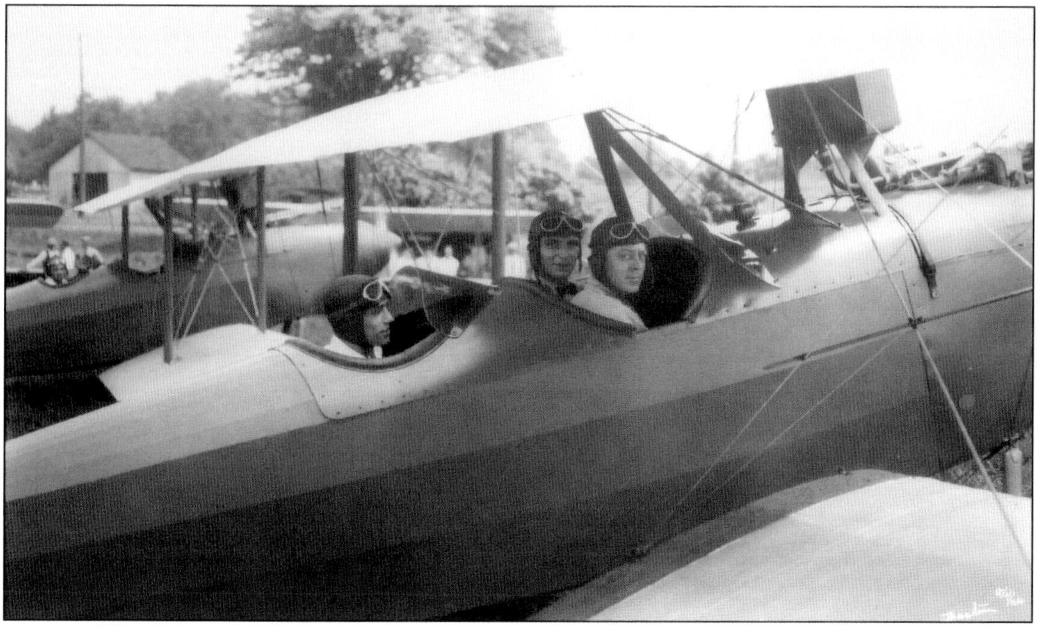

The land along the north bank of the Great Miami River between Adams Street and Market Street has an interesting history. Troy residents once knew the property as "Judd Boak's hayfield," where the City of Troy had arranged for Boak to grow and store hay. In the 1920s, the barn in what is now Troy Community Park was used by the Weaver Aircraft Company (WACO) as its final assembly plant for biplanes.

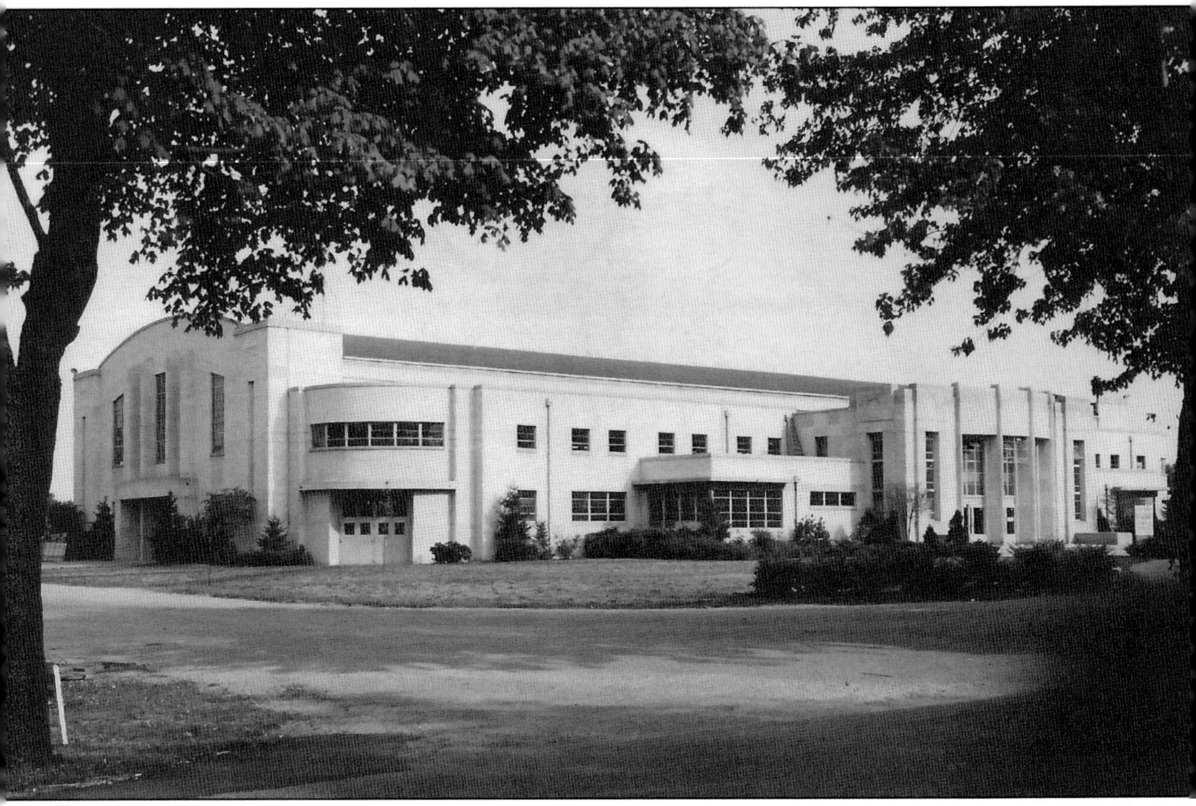

In the late 1800s, C.C. Hobart founded the Hobart Electric Manufacturing Company, which he sold to an investment group in 1904, as well as the American Fixture and Manufacturing Company and Hobart Brothers Company. In 1942, his sons, William H. and Edward A. Hobart, established the Hobart Foundation to honor their father. In 1946, along with several clubs and organizations, the foundation developed a plan for recreational use of the land along the north bank of the Great Miami River between the Adams Street Bridge and the Market Street Bridge. The plan included a 5,000-seat sports arena that housed a basketball court, a rink where residents could ice-skate all year long, and space for a variety of public events to be held. The Hobart Foundation donated $300,000 to the project with the stipulation that the city raise money to build a 10,000-seat football stadium next to the arena on land that was a municipal golf course at the time. Hobart Arena was dedicated and opened for public use on September 7, 1950, and has been an integral part of Troy life through the decades.

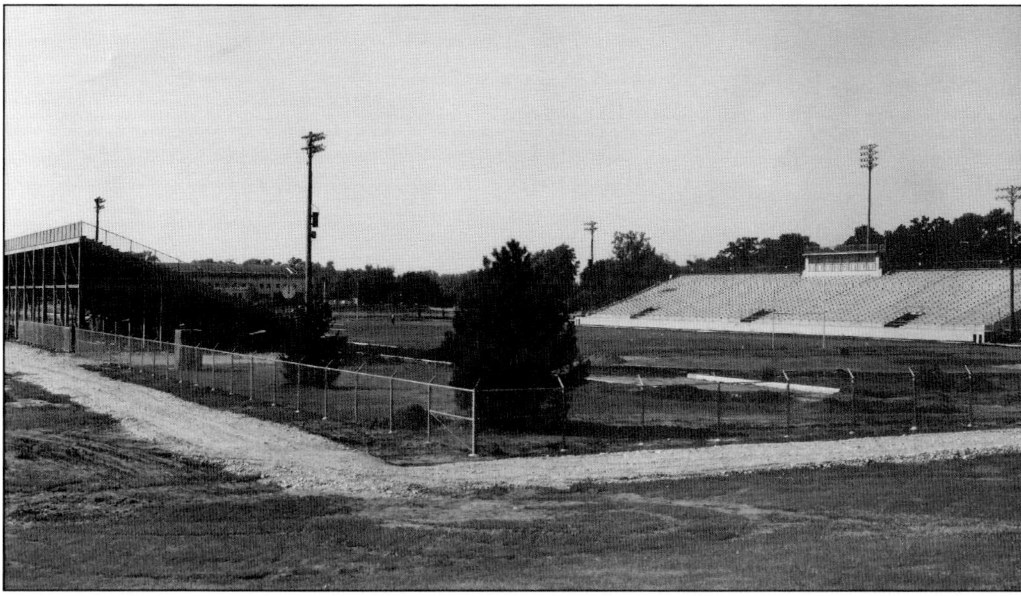

The city did raise money for the stadium, and the golf course was relocated. Ground was broken for the structure in October 1948, and it opened with a "preview" game on September 9, 1949. A total of 10,000 people came to the game, which featured players from Greenville, Piqua, Sidney, and Troy. The stadium was named Troy Memorial Stadium. At a ceremony held on September 22, 1949, it was dedicated as a "living memorial" to those who fought in World War II.

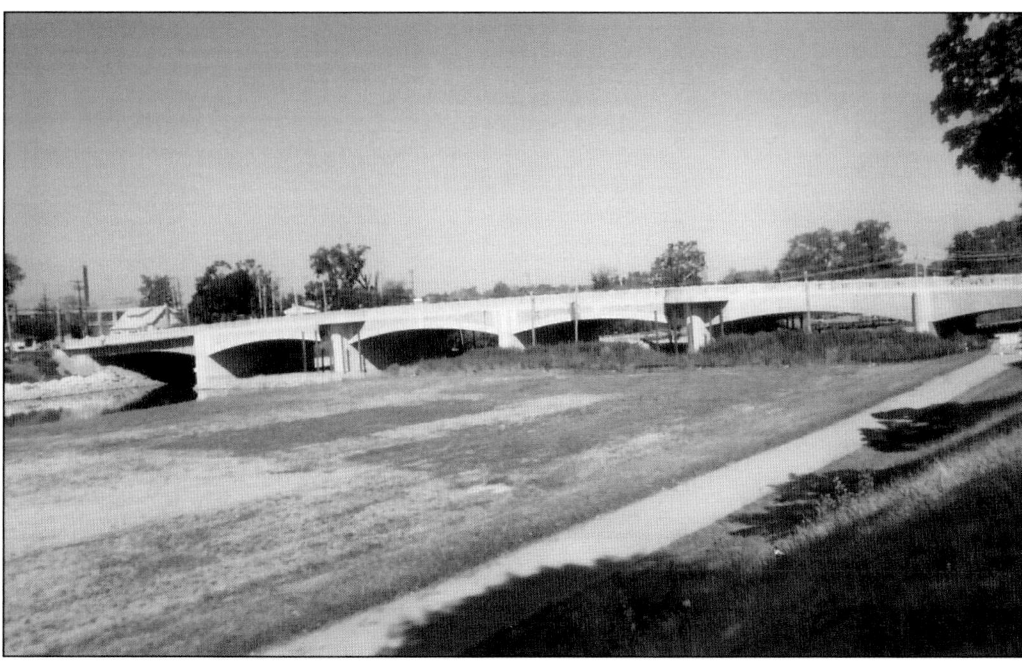

The Adams Street Bridge is seen here in the summer of 2012. A new bridge is under construction to replace the current structure. Planners with community input have kept the look of the bridge as it was nearly a century ago, with beautiful, wide spans. (Courtesy of Judy Deeter.)

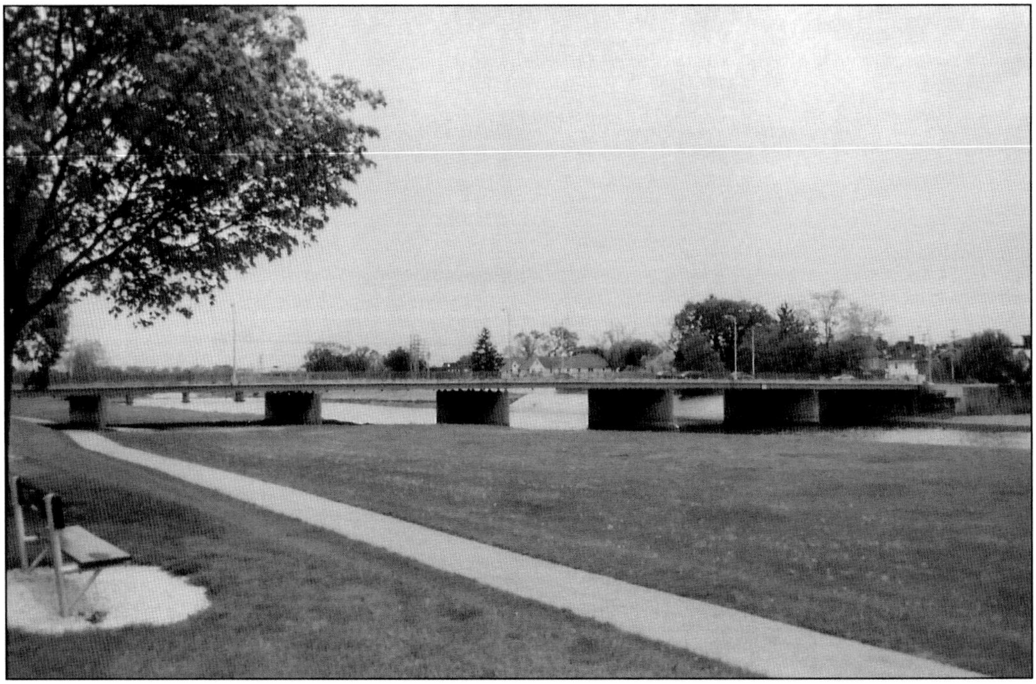

This is the beautiful area along the north bank of the Great Miami River, between the river, Hobart Arena, and Troy Memorial Stadium. Visitors can leisurely walk or bicycle along the river, and the site has been used for festivals such as the Troy Strawberry Festival and the Festival of Nations. (Courtesy of Judy Deeter.)

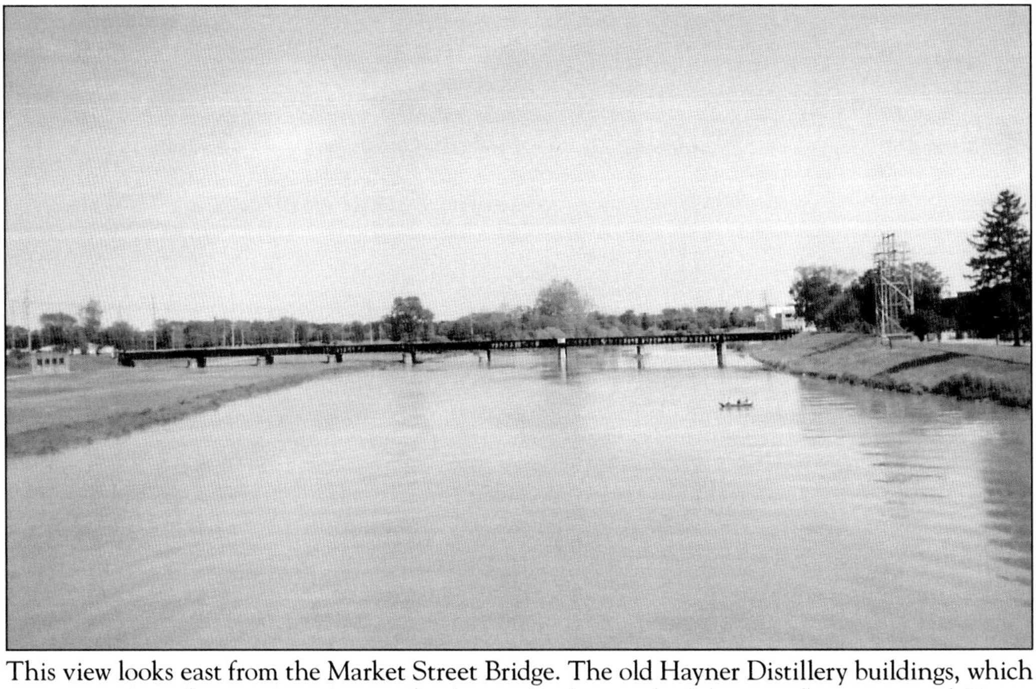

This view looks east from the Market Street Bridge. The old Hayner Distillery buildings, which were once along the river here, have either been torn down or had their top floors removed. Trains still travel across the railroad bridge as they did a century ago. (Courtesy of Judy Deeter.)

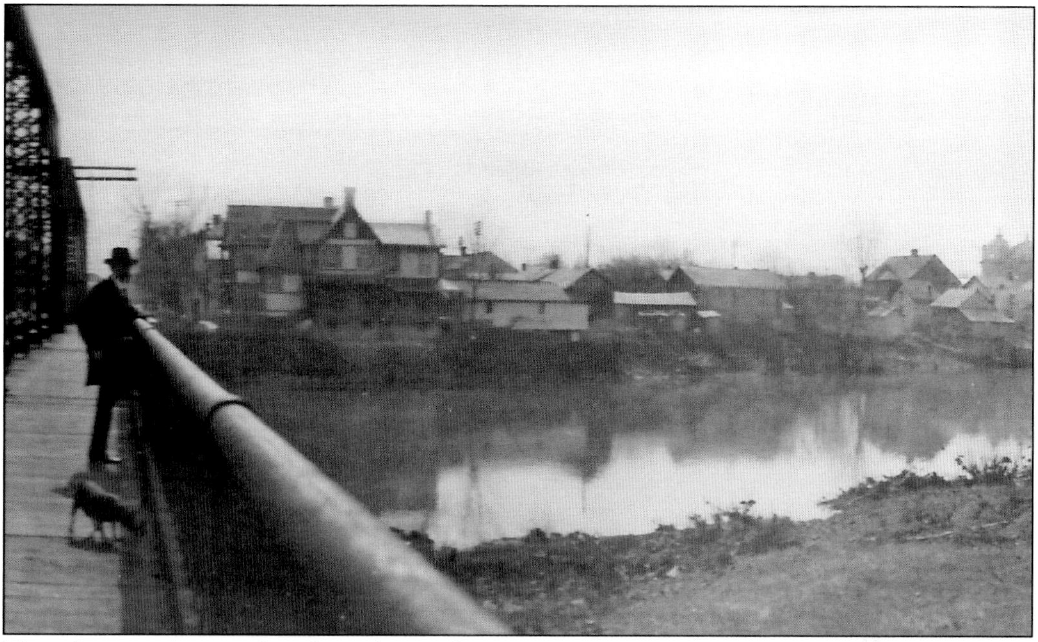

This photograph was taken from the Market Street Bridge around 1906. Here, the riverbank is mostly made up of dirt and weeds. The photograph was made from the west side of the bridge, where the Springfield, Troy & Piqua Electric Railway tracks crossed the river.

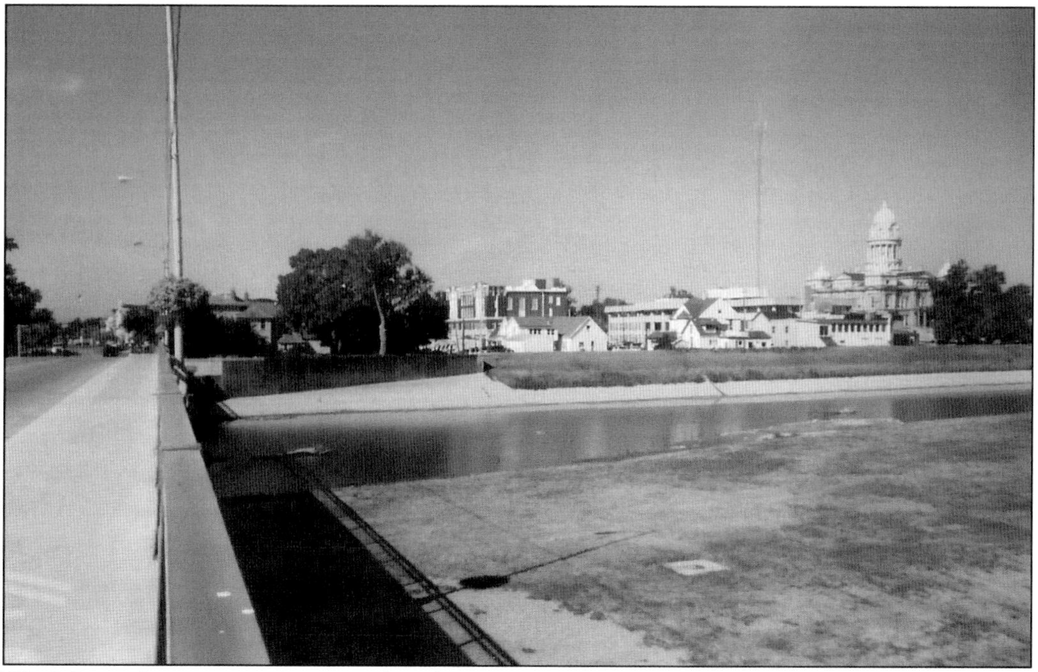

The Miami Conservancy District placed concrete retaining walls along the riverbank to control flooding on the south side. A floodplain was created on the north side of the river along with a high earthen embankment between the Adams Street Bridge and the Market Street Bridge and between the river and Troy Memorial Stadium and Hobart Arena. These changes provide protection to the structures on the north riverbank. (Courtesy of Judy Deeter.)

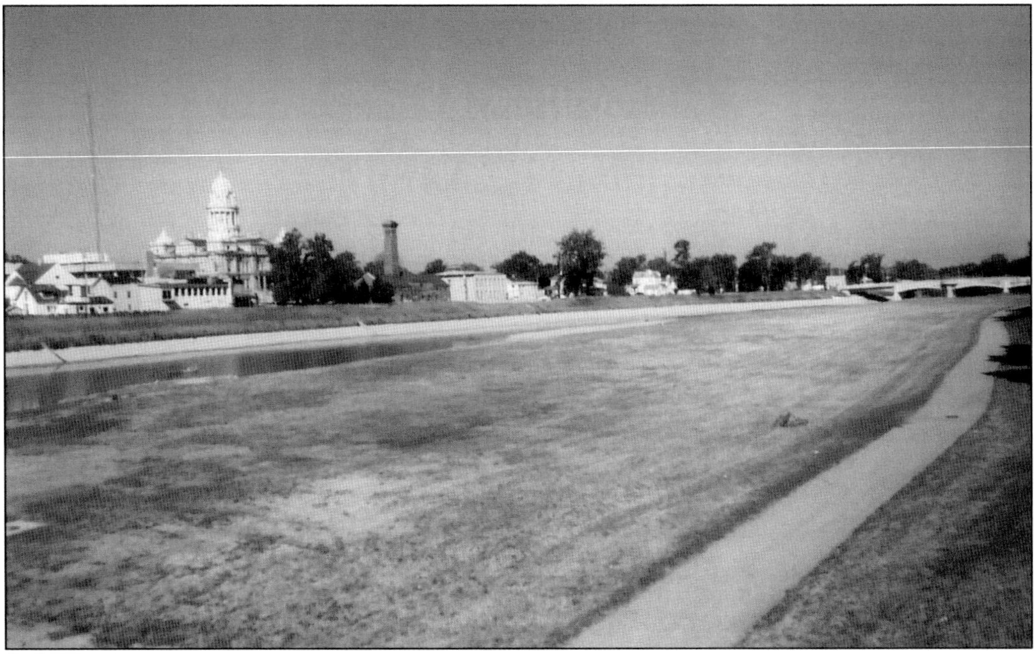

The Miami Conservancy District made the Great Miami River very straight between the Adams Street Bridge and the Market Street Bridge. On the other sides of the bridges, however, the river flows in much the same way it did more than 100 years ago, with bends, and plants growing naturally along its banks. (Courtesy of Judy Deeter.)

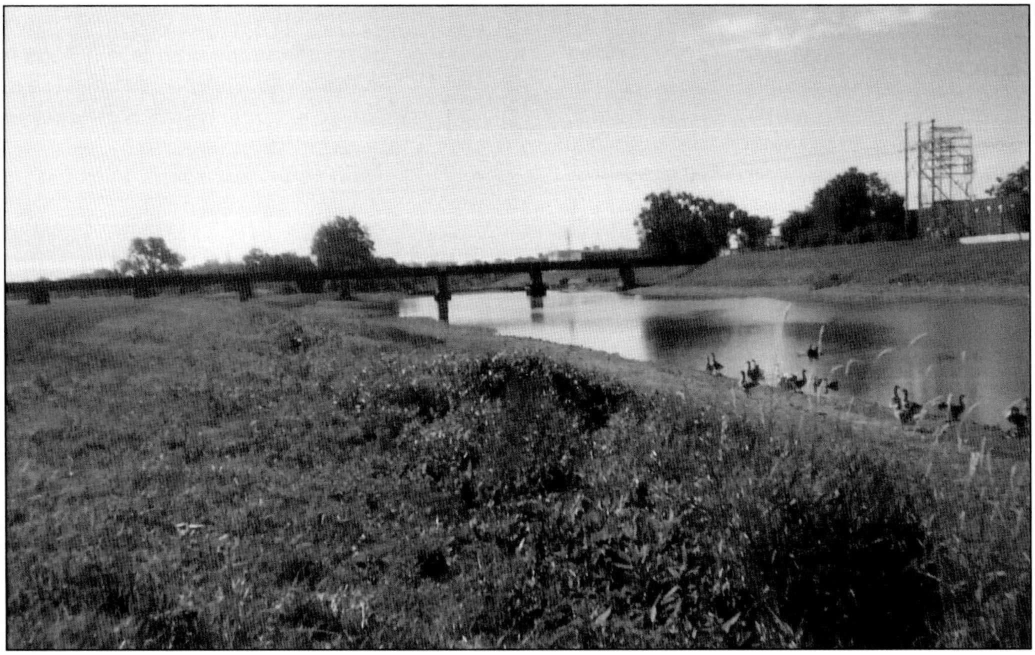

Birds still gather to play at the water's edge, as seen in this photograph taken between the Market Street Bridge and the railroad bridge. The community of Nineveh was just north of this area. In 1913, people cried out to be rescued as helpless crowds watched from the Market Street Bridge. (Courtesy of Judy Deeter.)

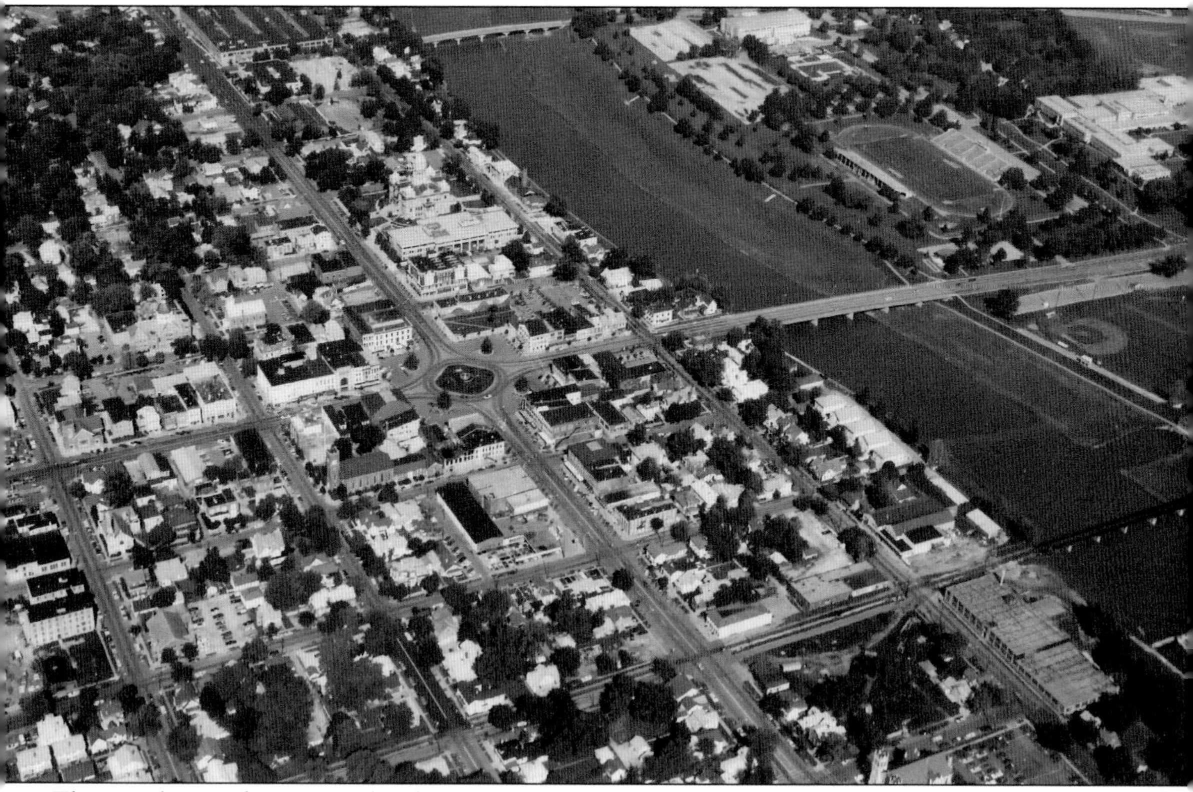

This aerial view of Troy was taken by Hoover Studios of Tipp City, Ohio, in 1999. The photograph shows the three bridges over the Great Miami River: the Adams Street Bridge (top), the Market Street Bridge (middle), and the railroad bridge (bottom). The river levee is between the Adams Street Bridge and the Market Street Bridge on the right side of the photograph. Troy High School's stadium is near the Market Street Bridge, Hobart Arena is near the Adams Street Bridge, and the Troy Aquatic Center swimming pool is between the two sites. On the other side of the Great Miami River, in the left center of the photograph, the Public Square appears as a circle. Market Streets runs north-south across the river (from right to left in photograph), and Main Street is an east-west roadway (from top to bottom in the photograph). The Hoover family donated this photograph to the Troy Historical Society.

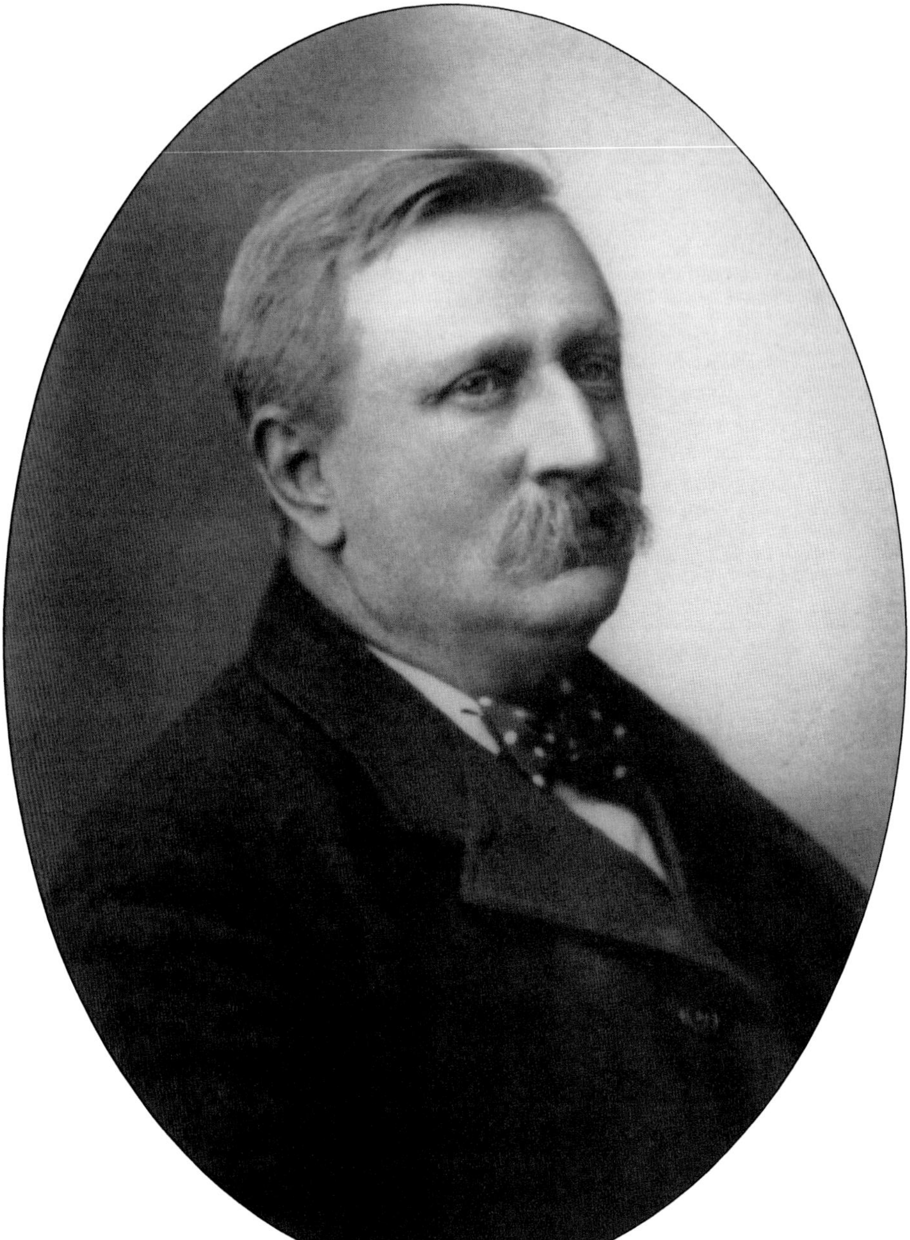

The poem "The Flood" was written by internationally known Miami County writer and poet Thomas Chalmers Harbaugh (1849–1924) and published in the *Miami Union* on April 10, 1913. Harbaugh was born in Maryland, but lived most of his life in Casstown, northeast of Troy. He wrote numerous articles for both the *Miami Union* and the *Troy Daily News*. His work includes a political column titled Tarcomed—the word *Democrat* spelled backwards. He also wrote more than 100 dime and nickel novels published by Beadle and Adams of New York. Some historians believe he wrote the first paperback books for boys. Miami County historical researchers also remember him as the author of the 1909 history book *A Centennial History: Troy, Piqua, and Miami County, Ohio*.

"The Flood"
by T.C. Harbaugh

It came in the pitiless darkness
It was armed with a demon's pow'r,
The landscape fair that spread afar
Was a waste in a fleeting hour;
The unchained flood in its ruthlessness
Swept on with its horrid boom,
And those who'd smiled but an hour before
Went swiftly down to doom.

Vain the pray'r and the heartening cry,
They were lost in the ceaseless roar,
The prattle of babes and the childish laugh
Alas! will be heard no more;
The homes where sweet contentment reigned
And love was a daily song,
Were crushed against the cruel piers,
Merciless, cold and strong.

On, on it dashed, that mighty tide,
On, on thro' the bitter night,
Leaving behind in its awful wake
Nothing but wreck and blight;
And where the fair Miami swept
Over its widening bed,
Angels wept as they looked upon
The scores of the drifting dead.

Never a moment the torrent stayed,
Nor breathed in its doomful course,
Southward still it sped away
With the ire of a maddened horse;
In vain did Man attempt to chain
The onward rushing lake;
Its heart was a mad whirlpool of death,
Its strength no hand could break.

Night turned to day and day to night,
But still the fiend rushed on,
The flood crest ever grim and cold,
Shone murky at the dawn;
From north to south, from east to west
As far as the eye could see,
The horrid pall of death was spread
O'er root and field and tree.

God pity those who felt its clutch,
And may we never know
Again the terror of that night
Nor see again such foe;
And in the many years to come
Unto our Valley wide,
May He hold back with loving hand
The demon of the tide.

Index

BIBLIOGRAPHY

Brown, Margaret Zeigenfelder. "The Memoirs of Margaret Zeigenfelder." Unpublished manuscript. Troy Historical Society–Troy-Miami County Public Library Local History Collection. Local History Library, Troy, Ohio

Davies, Lois. "Conservancy Project Changed Course of Troy Events," As I See It, *Troy Daily News*, April 4, 1988.

Dilworth, Sharon. "Remembering the Years of the Interurban," *Miami Valley Sunday News*, October 6, 1983.

English, Ned, interviewed by Lois Shilling Davies, of the Troy Historical Society, February 26, 1976. Troy Historical Society Oral History Collection. Local History Library, Troy, Ohio.

Francis, Dale. "Terror in Troy as Great 1913 Flood Roars Through City," *Troy Daily News*, March 25, 1963.

Gamblee, Joanne Duke. *The Dam Battle*. Wooster, OH: Wooster Book Company, 2008.

Great Miami River Corridor Committee of Miami and Shelby Counties, Inc. *The Great Miami River: Troy's Link with History*. Troy, OH: Great Miami River Corridor Committee of Miami and Shelby Counties, Inc., May 1983.

Harbaugh, T.C. "The Flood," *Miami Union*, April 10, 1913.

Heilig, Gabe. "Troy Dealt Stinging Blow by Famous 1913 Flood," *Troy Daily News*, September 15, 1964.

Hill, Leonard U. et al. *A History of Miami County, Ohio, 1807–1953*. Piqua, OH: Miami County, Ohio, Sesquicentennial Committee, 1953.

Hover, John C., Joseph D. Barnes, Walter D. Jones, Charlotte Reeve Conover, Willard J. Wright, Clayton A. Leiter, John Ewing Bradford, and W.C. Culkins, eds. *Memoirs of the Miami Valley*. Chicago: Robert O. Law Company, 1920.

Miami Union, April 1, 1913, April 3, 1913, April 10, 1913.

Morgan, Arthur Ernest. *The Miami Conservancy District*. New York: McGraw-Hill, 1951.

———. *The Miami Valley and the 1913 Flood: Technical Reports, Part I*. Dayton, OH: The Miami Conservancy District, 1917.

Piqua Daily Call, March 31, 1913 and April 1, 1913.

"Review of Highlights of Destructive 1913 Flood." *Troy Daily News*, March 24, 1947.

Smallenbarger, Robert. Untitled and undated manuscript. Troy Historical Society–Troy-Miami County Public Library Local History Collection. Local History Library, Troy, Ohio.

Trostel, Scott D. *The Lima Route*. Fletcher, OH: Cam-Tech Publishing.

Troy Historical Society Oral History Committee Audiotape Interviews, 1975–1976.

Troy Record, March 29, 1913 and April 1, 1913.

"Troy Will Take Care of Her Own," *Miami Union*, March 27, 1913.

Tweed, Lottie Swisher, interviewed by Olive Ryan, of the Troy Historical Society, June 10, 1975. Troy Historical Society Oral History Collection. Local History Library, Troy, Ohio.

Vandiver, Kermit. "The Great Flood." *Troy Daily News*, April 27, 1988.

Wheeler, Thomas B. "Early Area Flood Left Mud, Death." *Troy Daily News*, April 4, 1971.

———. *Troy: The Nineteenth Century*. Troy, OH: Troy Historical Society, 1970. Troy Historical Society–Troy-Miami County Public Library Local History Collection. Local History Library, Troy, Ohio.

———. *20th Century Notes*. Unpublished manuscript. Troy Historical Society–Troy-Miami County Public Library Local History Collection. Local History Library, Troy, Ohio.